# THE
# PREACHER'S PAPERBACK
# LIBRARY

The Preacher's Paperback Library
Edmund A. Steimle, Consulting Editor

# The

# Preaching of

# John Henry Newman

Edited and with an Introduction by
W. D. WHITE

FORTRESS PRESS • PHILADELPHIA

# ABOUT THE
# PREACHER'S PAPERBACK LIBRARY

The renewal of the church in our time has touched many aspects of parish life: liturgy and sacraments, biblical and theological concern, the place of the laity, work with small groups. But little has been said or done with regard to the renewal of the church in the pulpit.

The Preacher's Paperback Library is offered in the hope that it will contribute to the renewal of the preaching ministry. It will not stoop to providing "sermon starters" or other homiletical gimmicks. It will, rather, attempt to hold in balance the emphasis which contemporary theologians and biblical scholars lay upon the centrality of proclamation and the very practical concerns of theological students and parish pastors who are engaged in the demanding task of preparing sermons of biblical and theological depth which also speak to the contemporary world.

To that end, the series will provide reprints of fundamental homiletical studies not presently available and contemporary studies in areas of immediate concern to the preacher. Moreover, because the study of sermons themselves can be of invaluable help in every aspect of the preparation of the sermon, volumes of sermons with introductory notes will appear from time to time. The sermons will include reprints of outstanding preachers in the past as well as sermons by contemporary preachers who have given evidence both of depth and of imaginative gifts in communication. It is our hope that each volume in The Preacher's Paperback Library, prepared with the specific task of sermon preparation in mind, will contribute to the renewal of the preaching ministry.

The publication of a selection of John Henry Newman's sermons at this time is appropriate for two reasons. First, because Newman himself exemplified the new ecumenicity which crested in Vatican II. As W. D. White points out in his perceptive introduction, Newman was a "Protestant critic and Catholic ecumenist." Protestants and Catholics alike can gain much from a restudy of this man and his preaching, and in the process learn to know each other better.

A second reason, as Professor White also suggests, is more directly related to the task of preaching in our day. Because preaching is in deep trouble these days, there is an almost frenetic urge to make it "relevant": timely, contemporary, topical; the homiletical reflection of the activism characteristic of American church life. But this often frantic lust for contemporaneity is too frequently achieved at the expense of depth, both biblical and theological. Recalling that Newman too lived in a revolutionary period, the age of the industrial revolution, of Darwin and Karl Marx, a thoughtful consideration of the biblical and theological depth of these sermons delivered in a period of enormous change, should be a salutary exercise for the preacher today.

It may be objected that Newman's sermons sacrificed contemporaneity for a kind of timeless quality. And that is true. But we need not follow the masters of the past in every detail. What we *can* learn from these sermons is the recovery of depth without necessarily sacrificing our own proper desire for contemporaneity. For without the dimension of biblical and theological depth, preaching is indeed a *causa finita*.

EDMUND A. STEIMLE

*Union Theological Seminary*
*New York, New York*
*Ash Wednesday, 1969*

# ACKNOWLEDGMENTS

I wish to express my sincere appreciation to the several people and institutions who have assisted me in the preparation of this volume: (1) to the Cooperative Program in the Humanities, Duke University and the University of North Carolina, for an appointment as a Fellow during the academic year 1967/68, freeing me to do Newman research; (2) to the Yale University Library for permission to use their microfilm of the Newman papers, and particularly to Professor A. Dwight Culler of Yale, who identified for me the reels and batches of film containing sermonic materials; (3) to Donn Michael Farris of the Duke Divinity Library for putting at my disposal the rich resources of the library; (4) to Father Charles Stephen Dessain of the Birmingham Oratory for permission to quote unpublished Newman materials; (5) to the editors of the *South Atlantic Quarterly*, the *Southern Humanities Review*, and the *Journal of the American Academy of Religion* for permission to use materials of mine published previously by them; (6) to Harold Ober Associates, of New York, for permission to quote from Muriel Spark's "Foreword" to *Cardinal Newman's Best Plain Sermons*, edited by Vincent F. Blehl (1964); (7) to Professor Charles Johnson of St. Andrews College for help in translating passages from Newman's quoting of the fathers; (8) to Professor Horton Davies of Princeton University, who first inspired my interest in Newman, and to Professor Edmund Steimle for his encouraging this venture. To each of these I offer my continuing gratitude and thanks.

W. D. WHITE

*St. Andrews Presbyterian College*
*Laurinburg, North Carolina*
*All Saints Day, 1968*

# CONTENTS

## INTRODUCTION *by W. D. White*

1. John Henry Newman: Protestant Critic and Catholic
   Ecumenist                                                        1

2. Newman's Critique of Popular Abuses of Preaching        10

3. Newman on the Art and Vocation of Preaching             24

4. Newman's Continuing Significance for Preaching          46

5. A Note on the Present Edition                           61

## PAROCHIAL AND PLAIN SERMONS
### *Newman's Selection of His Best*

1. FREEDOM IN BONDAGE TO CHRIST
   "The Strictness of the Law of Christ"
                (PPS, IV, Sermon 1, July 9, 1837)        67

2. HOLLOW OBEDIENCE
   "Obedience Without Love"
                (PPS, IV, Sermon 2, April 2, 1837)       80

3. THE CENTRALITY OF CHARITY
   "Love, the One Thing Needful"
                (PPS, V, Sermon 23, February 10, 1839)   95

4. THE JOY OF CHRISTIAN RISK
   "The Ventures of Faith"
                (PPS, IV, Sermon 20, February 21, 1836)  106

5. STRENGTH PERFECT IN WEAKNESS
   "The Weapons of Saints"
        (PPS, VI, Sermon 22, October 29, 1837)   116

6. TOWARD CHRISTIAN HONESTY
   "Unreal Words"
        (PPS, V, Sermon 3, June 2, 1839)   127

7. THANKFULNESS AS REMEMBRANCE
   "Remembrance of Past Mercies"
        (PPS, V, Sermon 6, September 22, 1838)   141

8. GOD HIDDEN AND REVEALED
   "Christ Hidden from the World"
        (PPS, IV, Sermon 16, December 25, 1837)   152

9. THE TRUE HUMANISM
   "The Greatness and Littleness of Human Life"
        (PPS, IV, Sermon 14, October 23, 1836)   163

10. THE CHRISTIAN CHARACTER OF WAITING
    "Waiting for Christ"
         (PPS, VI, Sermon 17, December 6, 1840)   173

11. CHRISTIAN EXPECTATION
    "Subjection of the Reason and Feelings to the
    Revealed Word"
         (PPS, VI, Sermon 18, December 13, 1840)   189

12. TOWARD CHRISTIAN MATURITY
    "Equanimity"
         (PPS, V, Sermon 5, December 22, 1839)   201

13. THE CHRISTIAN CHARACTER OF JOY
    "Peace in Believing"
         (PPS, VI, Sermon 25, May 26, 1839)   212

Indexes   221

*To*
*Nancy and Brenda*
*and*
*Jonathan Paul*

# Introduction

## 1. John Henry Newman:
### Protestant Critic and Catholic Ecumenist

EVERYONE RECOGNIZES THAT
John Henry Newman had a wealth of splendid powers. To speak of his manysidedness has become almost a truism. The list of important offices held by him is itself indicative of his broad genius. He was a fellow and tutor of the most intellectually distinguished college in the Oxford of his day, and was looked upon as one of the leading personalities in Oriel. As vicar of St. Mary-the-Virgin, the University Church in Oxford, he was for some fifteen years in a position peculiarly suited to the highest expression of his powers as a preacher, as instructor and counselor, and as inspirer of young men. From this focal point of the most intellectual and influential pulpit in the most significant center of learning and authority in England, Newman extended his influence to include virtually every significant group in England. Here he also became the charismatic leader in a great upheaval of religious thought and sensibility, and found himself at the center of a splendid concentration of religious passion and intellectual vigor and moral earnestness. From the outset he was held up and revered, particularly by younger intellectuals, as an example of austere selflessness and of learning joined with piety.

During his long and eventful career, Newman was from time to time the editor of magazines, learned and semipopular. He was the translator and popularizer of saints and fathers of earlier eras of the church. He enjoyed great renown as a preacher and considerable success as a compelling and

1

even popular lecturer. He organized and ran for years a school for boys, many of whom were underprivileged; he was a dutiful parish priest, raising funds, building buildings, teaching music, saying prayers, visiting parishioners, and running Sunday schools; he was the organizer and builder of an oratory, and the head of a new and courageous university. He eventually became a cardinal.[1]

In the midst of this remarkable diversity of important public activity, Newman at the same time produced a prodigious amount of literature. Even his private correspondence, in which he extended his pastoral and intellectual ministry immeasurably, would be a monumental achievement if judged solely by its bulk. But his public writings are yet more impressive, no less for their diversity than for their many excellences. By his own classification, Newman wrote poems, tracts, essays, controversial polemics, dialogues, histories, open letters, biographies, lectures, treatises, autobiographies, sermons, editorial commentaries and prefaces, and even novels of a sort.

During his lifetime and since his death, Newman has been a controversial figure. There were, and are, divergent responses to his personality and ideas. There are a variety of views about his overall significance. As a religious leader and as a person, he inspired markedly contradictory responses—and he still does. But there is no disagreement about his crucial role in his own time. No one questions that Newman was a luminous genius in an era of great men: a supreme religious genius, and a supremely literary genius.

Newman's continuing claim to greatness doubtless lies primarily in his religious genius. For Newman's entire life finds a unity of purpose and expression in the service of what

[1] There have been many studies of Newman's life and work. The most judicious and informed recent biography of Newman, covering his entire career, is that of Charles Stephen Dessain, *John Henry Newman* (London: Thomas Nelson & Sons, 1966). Meriol Trevor has written a two-volume study: *Newman, The Pillar of the Cloud* (Garden City, N.Y.: Doubleday & Co., 1962); and *Newman, Light in Winter* (Garden City, N.Y.: Doubleday & Co., 1963).

he himself called "revealed religion"; all of Newman's powers concentrate themselves around this supreme commitment. As Coleridge once observed concerning George Herbert, so with Newman: "Religion is the element in which he lives, and the region in which he moves."

Yet, despite his great stature in the period 1828–1845, it is only recently that Newman's contributions to religious thought and sensibility have begun to find full fruition. While aiming in his Anglican years at providing the eroding Church of England with a coherent doctrinal base and freeing it from the Erastianism and worldliness which characterized it, he was constantly engaged in divisive controversy that finally issued in the forming of a sharply delineated party. At the height of his influence in the late 1830's, he was something of an Athanasius against the whole world: he was severely critical of the old high-and-dry establishment with its Erastian privileges and prejudices; he was polemical against the abuses of the Evangelicals both within and without the establishment, particularly of their emphasis upon religious experience and feeling; he was appalled by the worldly nominal Christianity of the average Englishman; he was antagonistic toward the "spirit of the age" with its pragmatic, utilitarian orientation. Though he sometimes looked longingly toward Rome, he was still deeply imbued with that Protestant and distinctly Anglo-Saxon notion that the Pope was the Antichrist and the head of a godless system. In effect, he was at home only with that relatively small band of intellectual and highly gifted spiritual leaders which made up the Oxford Movement.[2]

---

[2] Still the best history of the Oxford Movement is Richard W. Church, *The Oxford Movement: Twelve Years 1833–1845* (London: Macmillan Co., 1891). For a good selection of primary sources, see Eugene R. Fairweather (ed.), *The Oxford Movement* (New York: Oxford University Press, 1964); and also Owen Chadwick (ed.), *The Mind of the Oxford Movement* (Stanford: Stanford University Press, 1961). For a succinct and judicious appraisal of the movement, see Horton Davies, *Worship and Theology in England: From Watts and Wesley to Maurice, 1690–1850* (Princeton: Princeton University Press, 1961), pp. 243–82.

Newman's accession to Rome in 1845 came as a wrenching shock to this group, and indeed to the religious consciousness of all England. No more traumatic breach in religious allegiances and sensibilities could have been imagined in England in that day. Nothing in our time short of the conversion of the Archbishop of Canterbury to a militant communism would be comparable. But even at Rome Newman did not find an adequate audience. Held suspect by the old Catholics, and much too English in his restrained devotion to please the new converts and other ultramontanes, Newman spent most of his Catholic life in the relative obscurity of the oratory at Birmingham. Even the belated attempt by Leo XIII to right these wrongs through the bestowing of the Red Hat on Newman in his old age did not remove the suspicions that Newman was secretly a "modernist" or a "Protestant in Roman clothing." In short, despite his prominence, in his own time Newman's actual impact was considerably less than his potential. One of the half-dozen ablest men of his generation, and one who invested enormous intellectual and spiritual energy in his cause, Newman nevertheless failed to do for theology what Darwin did for science and Marx did for politics in their time.

But this is to be explained not because Newman proposed the spirit of a former age over against that of his own—as has been popularly thought since this charge was leveled against him by his one-time protégé, later turned critic, F. D. Maurice. Rather, Newman was at least a full century ahead of his time. Like Augustine, he was essentially a *seminal* thinker; and his insights and sensibilities are only now beginning to take their proper form in Western Christian consciousness. Considered in his own day the narrowest of party controversialists and a symbol of the divisions within Christendom, he has become in our time a powerful force toward unity.

The current renaissance of Newman studies was given impetus in 1933 and in 1945 by the centenary celebrations of the beginning of the Oxford Movement and of Newman's conversion to Rome. But perhaps the greatest activation of

4

Newman interest has come out of Vatican II, which has been aptly referred to as "Newman's Council." Indeed, Bishop Butler, Catholic Auxiliary Bishop of Westminster, speaks of the Second Vatican Council as the "first, immensely important, step . . . towards the vindication of all the main theological, religious, and cultural positions of the former Fellow of Oriel." [3] Newman is now coming into his own as a Protestant critic and Catholic ecumenist.

As a Protestant critic Newman rejected the easy morality and lazy worldliness of an Erastian establishment, the subjectivity and enslavement to activism and feeling characteristic of Evangelicals, and the theological fuzziness and antidogmatic stance of the so-called Broad Church, which was in fact a radical accomodation of the faith to the new developments in social and natural and historical sciences. He held that "Bible Christianity" and the so-called Protestant principle ultimately lead to reliance on private judgment, a decisive opening for skepticism. As one might say that Luther aimed to un-Romanize the church without Protestantizing it, so Newman intended to un-Protestantize the church without Romanizing it.

As a Catholic ecumenist he insisted upon a free and open church which would exercise its authority in truth and love, and respect the ultimate human freedom rooted in conscience; he contended that the laity as well as the clergy and the bishops must be actively consulted in the definition of dogma, that all are first-class citizens in the Body of Christ; he fought for significant attention to the Bible in the devotion and theology of the church; he resisted the ossification of dogma, working out a dynamic theory of doctrinal development as an organic growth from the original deposit of faith; he insisted upon free and liberal education for churchmen, for both clergy and laity alike, and contended that this was requisite to the life of the church in the modern world; he opposed

---

[3] B. C. Butler, "Newman and the Second Vatican Council," in John Coulson and A. M. Allchin (eds.), *The Rediscovery of Newman: An Oxford Symposium* (London: Sheed & Ward and S.P.C.K., 1967), p. 245.

the declaration of papal infallibility, thinking it unnecessary and certainly inopportune, and insisting that the authority of the church rests ultimately in the collegiality of the bishops; he developed a new and creatively modern religious epistemology which makes a distinction between intellectual certainty and religious certitude, denying the possibility of the former and asserting the necessity of the latter. Newman succeeded, both as an Anglican and as a Catholic, in making a decisive bid for the personal, existential character of faith while also insisting upon the normative value of the historical, and the particularity of truth.

From the perspective of history it is now clear that Newman's life as an Anglican and as a Roman Catholic exhibits an essential and dynamic unity. If the English church "sold its brother into Egypt," God sent him there "to preserve life"! Modern Protestants therefore have to take his entire work seriously, as do indeed Roman Catholics as well. In the changed situation of the contemporary church, Newman is no longer a cause of division, but a force for reconciliation.[4]

And it is instructive that this new "ecumenical" interest in Newman has centered largely in his parochial preaching, in sermons which Newman first gave and published as an Anglican and which he then reissued as a Catholic, with no substantial changes, under the editorship of his old friend and onetime curate, W. J. Copeland, himself still an Anglican.[5] It is not surprising that modern interest centers on Newman's preaching. For as the Wesleyan movement and the evangelical revival associated with it constitute the most important religious development in eighteenth-century England, so the Oxford Movement is the most significant factor in the deepen-

[4] See John Coulson and others, *Newman: A Portrait Restored* (New York: Sheed & Ward, 1965).

[5] Newman originally published his parochial sermons in eight volumes, appearing between 1834 and 1843 under the title *Parochial and Plain Sermons*. The republication of these Anglican sermons began in 1868, twenty-three years after Newman's conversion, in the uniform Longmans edition, edited by Copeland.

ing of religious awareness in England in the nineteenth century. And Newman is at the heart of the Oxford Movement, indispensable to it and of supreme importance; indeed, representing in his own person its fundamental qualities. It was primarily through his preaching that Newman gained and exercised this position of prominence and influence. This was the consensus of informed opinion in Newman's own day, and contemporary scholarship has without notable exception tended to confirm this judgment.[6] One of the outstanding things about Newman's career is the consistent preaching that he did week by week for almost two decades after his ordination. From his first parish appointment at St. Clement's (1824) to his farewell sermon to his parish and friends at Littlemore, Oxford (1843), Newman preached over one thousand sermons.[7]

Newman's new role as Protestant critic and Catholic ecumenist is subtly suggested in the current renewal of interest in his preaching.[8] For one of the ironies of his career is that in virtually all of his public utterances on the subject, Newman sought to mitigate the widespread enthusiasm attached to popular preaching—while he himself was carrying a large segment of the English church along with him primarily through the power of his own preaching at St. Mary's. Insisting upon a balanced ministry of word and sacrament, Newman was vigorously opposed to the elevation of preaching to a position of primacy in the church. In the modern situation, both Catholic and Protestant traditions are reasserting the

[6] See Church, pp. 129–30; and also Dessain, pp. 43–46.

[7] Werner Becker, "Anmerkungen zu einer Liste der Predigten Newmans," in Heinrich Fries (ed.), *Newman Studien* (Nürnberg: Glock und Lutz, 1954), II, 309.

[8] Recent publications of Newman's sermons include the following: Lawrence F. Barmann (ed.), *Newman at St. Mary's: A Selection of the Parochial and Plain Sermons* (Westminster, Md.: The Newman Press, 1962); Vincent F. Blehl (ed.), *Cardinal Newman's Best Plain Sermons* (New York: Herder and Herder, 1964); and selections from the parochial sermons edited by Armel J. Coupet, *A Newman Companion to the Gospels* (London: Burns & Oates, 1966).

wisdom of Newman's insight. Preaching, which in the past has tended to take a secondary place in the Catholic mass, is now being stressed as essential to full-scale worship. There is a new recognition of the importance of the word in generating and deepening faith. This new accent on preaching was spurred by the Second Vatican Council, which ordered a stop to the casual omission of sermons, and called for their inclusion as a prime means of spreading the gospel. In its decree on the ministry, the council insists that the preaching of the word is needed "for the very administration of the sacraments," for the sacraments are sacraments of the faith and "faith is born of the word and nourished by it." [9] Pope Paul, in his *Ecclesiam Suam* encyclical, also stressed the extreme importance of preaching—indeed, calling it "the primary apostolate." While this emphasis upon a reaffirmation of the cruciality of preaching is occurring amongst Catholics, Protestants are moving toward restoring the sacraments to a more significant role along with preaching. These developments amongst both Catholics and Protestants represent a healthy renewal of a proper balance of the two elements, a balance for which Newman himself stoutly contended all his life.

Since the First World War, Newman has enjoyed growing prominence amongst a circle of continental scholars and churchmen. This interest has issued in three international symposia of Newman scholars, and the publication of a noteworthy series of Newman studies.[10] While English and American scholars have participated to some degree in these ventures, only as late as 1966 has Newman really "come home" in the fullest sense. The first Oxford Newman Symposium was convened at Oriel College in late March, 1966, attended (as Newman would have had it) by Protestant and

[9] "The Ministry of Priests," in Walter M. Abbott (ed.), *The Documents of Vatican II*, trans. Joseph Gallagher (New York: The American Press, 1966), p. 540.

[10] Heinrich Fries and Werner Becker (eds.), *Newman Studien* (6 vols.; Nürnberg: Glock und Lutz, 1948–1962).

Catholic churchmen and scholars from throughout the world. This meeting was in many ways a celebration. A report of this symposium, and the text of the papers read there, has been published; this constitutes the best introduction to Newman and his religious significance that is available.[11]

Now that English scholarship has caught up with the Continent and finally brought Newman home again, it remains to be asked whether Newman will in force ever cross the Atlantic to America. To be sure, we know something about Newman: his name graces many university organizations of Roman Catholic students, and a number of parochial schools are named for him; most undergraduates read snippets of his "sinuous prose" in the sophomore anthologies that pass for literary textbooks, and get some notion of his "definition of a gentleman"; no liberal educator would ever discuss educational theory without at least an allusion to Newman's *Idea of a University*—despite its foreign ring in an educational system dominated by utilitarian and democratic commitments; seminarians are at least aware that Newman once played a role in trying to revitalize a moribund religious establishment. But the real force of Newman has yet to strike American awareness. Perhaps one reason for this is the implicit criticism in Newman of so much of what might be considered typically American.

At the second session of Vatican II, Pope Paul beatified the man who received Newman into the Roman Catholic Church—the Passionist Father Dominic Barberi. In his allocution, the Pope spoke of "those two holy figures, blessed Dominic and Cardinal John Henry Newman." Then he continued to speak, in English, of Newman as one who, "guided solely by love of truth and fidelity to Christ, traced an itinerary, the most toilsome, but also the greatest, the most meaningful, the most conclusive, that human thought ever travelled

11 John Coulson and A. M. Allchin (eds.), *The Rediscovery of Newman: An Oxford Symposium* (London: Sheed & Ward and S.P.C.K., 1967).

9

during the last century, indeed one might say during the modern era, to arrive at the fullness of wisdom and peace." [12] It is to be hoped that the church in America will find time to give attention to any man concerning whom such a tribute might honestly be made.

## 2. *Newman's Critique of Popular Abuses of Preaching*

During the eventful years of 1828 to 1843 Newman's fame and influence in the Church of England rested primarily upon the unmatched splendor of his preaching in the so-called University Church, St. Mary-the-Virgin, Oxford. While exercising in a superb manner what can only be called his "charisma" as a preacher, Newman nevertheless was singularly free from the temptation to exalt preaching for its own sake or to luxuriate in his own powers. He did, indeed, exalt the office and calling of a minister, but this exaltation of the office was the basis for his deep sense of awe and reverence before his own vocation. The zeal with which Newman discharged his responsibilities and embraced new opportunities is concrete witness to the sincerity of his response to the vows taken in ordination, and is evidence of his high sense of calling as a minister of Christ.

During Advent of his first year as a minister, Newman preached a sermon at St. Clement's entitled "On Ministers of Christ," using as a text I Corinthians 4:1, "This is how one should regard us, as servants of Christ and stewards of the mysteries of God." [1] In this sermon Newman sets forth clearly his high view of the office of minister, and the inclu-

---

[12] Quoted by Christopher Hollis, *Newman and the Modern World* (Garden City, N.Y.: Doubleday & Co., 1968), p. 215, citing *Herder Correspondence,* January, 1964.

[1] Preached December 12, 1824. Like many other manuscripts, a copy of this sermon has been preserved at the Oratory, Birmingham, England. Microfilm copies of the Newman Archives are held in the Yale, Fordham, and Notre Dame libraries in this country. This sermon is in reel 23, batch 119 of the Yale microfilm.

sive functions and concerns of this office. He develops a sharp contrast between "the world" and "ministers of Christ," showing that ministers of the church are in fact first ministers of Christ who hold a general office in the services of the church, and that they in effect continue in themselves the ministry of Christ which he has entrusted to them in his church. The emphasis here is on the *service* of the church, which is seen as Christ's continuing service, through his ministers, to those who are his. Furthermore, this service is performed through faithfulness as "stewards of the mysteries of God" and through the ministry of preaching. Ministers of the church, who are not merely servants of the people or functionaries of the social order or state, are sharply set apart as "servants of Christ" who are given the unique and awful role of "stewards of the mysteries of God." Newman makes a special point to emphasize the importance of the minister as preacher; he comments on the dignity, the difficulty, and the responsibility of the task of preaching. Three things must be said about this early sermon: (1) It displays with great force Newman's high sense of calling, and the reverence and sense of duty that he brings to his office as minister. In this it simply brings together in a structured way the recurring intimations disclosed by Newman's early private journals. (2) There is a clear attempt to see the ministry in an inclusive sense, with a balanced treatment of word and sacrament. (3) But this attempt is not entirely successful. The profound influence of Evangelicalism upon the young Newman seems evident in that he does in fact tend to give preaching a place of disproportionate importance. The most impressive thing about this sermon is the honor and importance Newman gives to the preaching office. This is not surprising, however, in view of what Newman himself characterizes as the "evangelical tone" of this period.[2]

---

[2] John Henry Newman, *Autobiographical Writings,* ed. Henry Tristram (New York: Sheed & Ward, 1957), p. 149.

One of the fascinating aspects of the Newman story is his relationship to the evangelical emphases and traditions in the church. Having himself come early in his youth under such influences, he always respected the profound contributions which the Evangelicals had made to the life of the church in England, and indeed to his own personal life. Writing about himself in the third person in his "Autobiographical Memoir," he pays tribute to the evangelical tradition: "That teaching had been a great blessing for England; it had brought home to the hearts of thousands the cardinal and vital truths of revelation, and to himself among others. The divine truths about our Lord and his person and offices, his grace, the regeneration of our nature in him, the supreme duty of living, not only morally, but in this faith, fear and love, together with the study of Scripture in which these truths lay, had sheltered and protected him in his most dangerous years, had been his comfort and stay when he was forlorn, and had brought him on in habits of devotion till the time came when he was to dedicate himself to the Christian ministry, and he ever felt grateful to the good clergyman who introduced them to him." [3]

Yet it is not surprising that as the Oxford Movement developed, Newman found himself becoming more and more critical of evangelical emphases and traditions. In his judicious and balanced analysis of the Evangelicals of Newman's day, Dean Church says that they "presented all the characteristics of an exhausted teaching and a spent enthusiasm." [4] Although they accomplished great things in humane and philanthropic crusades, overthrowing the slave trade, attacking the brutalities

[3] *Ibid.*, p. 79. For a study of the relationship between the Oxford Movement and Evangelicalism, see Yngve Brilioth, *Three Lectures on Evangelicalism and the Oxford Movement* (London: Oxford University Press, 1934). For an analysis of the common elements and differences amongst Tractarians and Evangelicals, see Davies, pp. 243–52. For a succinct description and fair appraisal of the state of religious parties in England in the early nineteenth century, see Church, pp. 9–20.

[4] Church, p. 15.

in prisons, creating mission societies, renewing a deep sense of the call to holiness and austerity of life and a zeal for true religion in the church, the Evangelicals, upon becoming respectable and even popular amongst men of position and weight, tended to "be on very easy terms with the world." [5]

At this point, quite ironically, they were not fundamentally different from the old "high-and-dry orthodox" whom they denounced as "unspiritual, formal, unevangelical, self-righteous; teachers of mere morality at their best, allies and servants of the world at their worst." [6] In many ways Newman combined the better parts of these two groups, with amazing freedom from their peculiar faults. With the Evangelicals he exhibited a zeal for pure religion, an undoubted and serious piety, a brave and (in his case) consistent protest against "the world," and above all, an urgent quest for personal holiness. But from the position of Anglican orthodoxy he was critical of the popular preaching from fashionable chapels which tended to recommend Evangelicalism through "gifts of flowing words or high-pitched rhetoric" to those tempers "which required to be excited by novelty." [7] Newman was critical of the contracted circle of themes dwelt on by this school in the church, and of its increasingly poor and thin and unreal language. Dean Church describes these limitations succinctly: "What it failed in was the education and development of character. . . . It shrank, in its fear of mere moralising, in its horror of the idea of merit or of the value of good works, from coming into contact with the manifold realities of the spirit of man: it never seemed to get beyond the 'first beginnings' of Christian teaching, the call to repent, the assurance of forgiveness: it had nothing to say to the long and

[5] *Ibid.*
[6] *Ibid.*, p. 12.
[7] *Ibid.*, p. 14. For an interesting commentary upon the popularity of the Victorian pulpit, see Amy Cruse, *The Victorians and Their Books* (New York: Houghton Mifflin Co., 1935), pp. 107–20. See also Horton Davies, *Worship and Theology in England: From Newman to Martineau* (Princeton: Princeton University Press, 1962), pp. 282–348.

varied process of building up the new life of truth and goodness: it was nervously afraid of departing from the conse-
crated phrases of its school, and in the perpetual iteration of
them it lost hold of the meaning they may once have had. It
too often found its guarantee for faithfulness in jealous suspicions, and in fierce bigotries, and at length it presented all the
characteristics of an exhausted teaching and a spent
enthusiasm." [8]

It is no surprise that as the special religious genius of the
earlier Evangelicals declined in their second- and third-
generation offspring, concerted attempts were made, whether
consciously or not, to recapture the dynamic of former days.
One of the attempts that proved in time to be abortive, and
which from the outset drew the criticism of Newman and the
other Oxford leaders, was the exaltation of preaching to a
position of primacy. From the perspective of the Oxford
leaders, the whole complex of errors represented by the Evangelicals and the dissenters alike was symbolized by this one
thing, the undue exaltation of preaching. This is seen as *the
characteristic* that distinguished the majority of dissenters and
those, though nominally within the church, whose doctrines
and sympathies were essentially on the side of dissent.
Around this central symbol of popular preaching gathered a
multitude of distortions and errors: (1) the insistence upon a
particular method of understanding, and in every situation
proclaiming the doctrine of the atonement as the central tenet
of the faith; (2) the loss of the sense of common prayer and
participation in the sacraments as central to the Christian life;
(3) the encouragement of a critical spirit toward the minister,
and an argumentative stance with reference to doctrine; (4)
the dependence upon the personality of the preacher, and his
rhetorical ability and eloquence; (5) the notion that service
to God consisted largely, or even primarily, in "hearing
sermons"—the more the better; (6) the breakdown of the

[8] Church, p. 15.

discipline and control of preachers under the commission and authority of the church; (7) the emphasis upon "experience" as a test of faith, a centering of attention not upon the reality of Christ and his work, but upon human response to that reality; (8) the degrading of the long-range, day-by-day process of indirect, imperceptible Christian nurture through the services of worship and the pastoral work of the minister. Newman and other Oxford leaders were convinced that when preaching assumes a disproportionate place of primacy it is perforce attended by a host of such distortions or active evils. While it might also aim at building men up in the faith, and at teaching them to show forth fruits of the Spirit in sanctification, it would always be in danger of merely stirring up certain subjective feelings and engendering a devotion not to the church but to the personality of the preacher. Above all, the Tractarians felt that such popular preaching was in danger of substituting human means of propagating the gospel for the means commissioned by God, and that such a substitution inevitably moved the emphasis from the objective given reality of God's self-revelation in Jesus Christ and the church to a subjective receiving or hearing or experiencing of this revelation.

Throughout his Anglican career, Newman shared in this increasing criticism of evangelical practices. And the center of his critique was precisely his opposition to the Evangelicals' narrowing of the Christian tradition, and their exalting of preaching to a position of primacy. It was these points of peculiarity and the evangelical teaching "considered as a system" [9] that drew Newman's polemical response. At the core of Newman's criticism of enthusiasm and the emphases of the Evangelicals was his high sense of the vocation of the Christian ministry, understood in an inclusive and rich sense.

Newman was particularly uncomfortable with the *lack of reserve* characteristic of many of the so-called "gospel preachers." He shrank from the "rudeness, irreverence, and

[9] See *Autobiographical Writings*, p. 149.

almost profaneness" which is "necessarily involved in pulpit addresses, which speak of the adorable works and sufferings of Christ, with the familiarity and absence of awe with which we speak about our friends." [10] This note is found repeatedly in Newman, often oblique and implied, but frequently quite deliberate and direct. In a sermon preached at Littlemore on October 23, 1836, Newman openly attacks this lack of reserve. "Many people," he contends, "like loud preachers. They are taken by them—by their loudness of voice and striking manner, moving about the body; and some perhaps, end making a great effect all at once with limbs, voice, look and language too. This seems like great earnestness—and leads hearers to say . . . 'This man . . . does me good . . . and I will trust him and follow him.' " [11]

The *result* of all this, Newman continues, is disastrous. For it often happens that "unwary, thoughtless Christians . . . without any other thought than that such a person does them good, as they call it, will follow him . . . just as if he were the Lord Jesus Christ himself. They leave the guides of their youth, and all that is quiet and sober, orderly and devout in religion, they leave the silent and unvaried worship of the church, as something dull and unimpressive, to pursue what they consider so striking." [12]

Newman admits that the temptation to such a response is quite understandable, for there is indeed a pleasure, an attraction, a striking manner in such preachers. They do in fact, as their followers claim, warm them at the heart as a cordial might! "I do not doubt these feelings," Newman admits. "But

[10] See David Newsome, "Justification and Sanctification: Newman and the Evangelicals," *The Journal of Theological Studies*, XV (April, 1964), 49, citing the draft of a Newman letter preserved in the Birmingham Oratory. Newman deplored equally the Tillotsonian school, "the chilly, meagre, timid, secular divinity . . . in fashion during the last century" (*ibid.*).

[11] From an unpublished Newman manuscript in the Birmingham Oratory. This quotation is taken from a sermon numbered 427 that appears in the Yale microfilm in reel 23, batch 119.

[12] *Ibid.*

what I *do* doubt, is whether all this warmth and pleasant feeling is good for them. They say it does them good—I say it does not—they say it makes them warm and alive—so it may, but still I say it does them harm not good." [13] Newman contends that followers of such preachers secretly know it is not right, for they *protest too much*.

Over against such lack of reserve, such blatant handling of sacred matters, Newman proposes the way of the church through the ages. "We worship God silently," he says, "and in our hearts more than by much talking. . . . The holy church, of which we are members, has ever preached silently (I may even say)—that is, by sign and token, much more than by violent and strong words. . . . God comes to the quiet, humble, gentle, silent souls who seek him—and he speaks by a still, small voice, not by the mouth of loud speakers." [14]

In this critique, Newman is echoing the thesis of Tract 87, written by his poet friend Isaac Williams, entitled "On Reserve in Communicating Religious Knowledge," the first of the tracts to generate hot controversy upon its appearance.[15] Williams contends that reserve is *intrinsic* to the life of the church—that the church is by definition deeply opposed to what he calls "the restless systems of the world." He concludes Tract 87 with these moving words: "If we wish to do good to the world we must not look to it, but unto God; our strength must be in secret where God is; the bad instruments of the world . . . must not be ours; the platform is not our strength, nay, even the pulpit is not our chief strength; in these we must yield to others if they wish it. But our chief strength must be the altar; it must be in sacraments and prayers, and a good life to give efficacy to them; and in secret alms to the poor. . . . Our strength must be in secret where God is." [16]

13 *Ibid.*
14 *Ibid.*
15 For the text, see Isaac Williams, Tract 87, *Tracts for the Times* (Oxford: J. H. Parker, 1840), V.
16 *Ibid.*, p. 125.

That Newman and Williams were thinking very much alike during the late 1830's, and particularly in their criticism of Evangelicals, is further seen in Newman's *Lectures on Justification* (1838). Like Williams' essay on reserve, this volume is one of the key documents, frequently neglected, but necessary for an understanding of the Oxford Movement. Newman intends in these lectures to expose the distortions of solifidianism while also indicating the opposite errors of Pelagianism. He tries here, as always, to find the middle ground of Anglican doctrine which avoids the exaggerations of both Rome and Wittenberg. Rejecting the conflicting formulae of imputed righteousness and inherent righteousness for his own doctrine of *imparted* righteousness, he declares: "Whether we say we are justified by faith or by works or by sacraments, all these but mean this one doctrine, that we are justified by grace, given through sacraments, impetrated by faith, manifested in works." [17] Newman's ultimate aim in this work is essentially irenical and ecumenical. He wishes to show that the teaching of Catholic theologians on God's gift of grace to men, and that of Protestants in the mainstream, can be reconciled by presenting revealed truth in fullness and balance.

Having developed the main body of his thesis, Newman then almost as an afterthought gives a final lecture to the subject "On Preaching the Gospel." This statement is a rousing critique of the evangelical theory and practice of preaching. It summarizes the Tractarian attitudes toward the Evangelicals: it attacks their emphasis upon feeling, their insistence upon "internal" versus "external" religion, their unnatural and strained idiom, their elevation of preaching to primacy over baptism and other sacraments, their innate tendency to dissent, their substituting of faith in faith for faith in Christ—in short, their allegiance to what Newman would see

[17] John Henry Newman, *Lectures on the Doctrine of Justification* (London: Longmans, Green & Co., 1892), p. 348. For a modern edition of the heart of this text, see Fairweather (ed.), pp. 219–59.

as a human system replacing the system ordained by God for the propagation of the gospel.

Newman centers his polemic around the charge that Evangelicals put more emphasis upon the *state* of a believer than on the nature, attributes, and work of Christ; that is, Newman charges that the Evangelicals have shifted the center of gravity from an ontological to a psychological level. He sums it up in this way: "A system of doctrine has risen up during the last three centuries, in which faith or spiritual-mindedness is contemplated and rested on as the end of religion instead of Christ. I do not mean to say that Christ is not mentioned as the author of all good, but that stress is laid rather on the believing than on the object of belief, on the comfort and persuasiveness of the doctrine rather than on the doctrine itself. And in this way religion is made to consist in contemplating ourselves instead of Christ; not simply in looking to Christ, but in *seeing* that we look to Christ; not in his divinity and atonement, but in conversion and our faith in them." [18] Such "over-earnest dwelling upon the state of our minds" quite naturally leads to a false notion of faith, to a centering of attention upon faith itself which destroys the possibility of true faith.

Hence it is no surprise that such Christians insist upon "true holiness seated in the heart" as over against "mere external works." For when self-contemplation has replaced true faith, men become "their own historians and panegyrists"; they reject the ordained ways of God and substitute human schemes. Hence the emphasis upon feeling, and preaching to arouse feeling. "For where the thought of self obscures the thought of God," Newman declares, "prayer and praise languish and preaching flourishes. Divine worship is simply contemplating our Maker, Redeemer, Sanctifier, and Judge; preaching, conversing, making speeches, arguing, read-

[18] *Lectures on the Doctrine of Justification,* p. 369.

ing, and writing about religion, tend to make us forget him in ourselves." [19]

Over against this semi-idolatry of the self, Newman proposes the ancient and normative way of the church. "When men are to be exhorted to newness of life," he contends, "the true object to be put before them is Jesus Christ. . . . The true gospel preaching is to enlarge, as they can bear it, on the person, natures, attributes, offices, and work of him who once regenerated them, and is now ready to pardon; to dwell upon his recorded words and deeds on earth; to declare reverently and adoringly his mysterious greatness as the Only-begotten Son, one with the Father, yet distinct from him. . . . The true preaching of the Gospel is to preach Christ." [20]

But, Newman argues, the fashion of the day is quite otherwise. The fashion has been "to attempt to convert by insisting on conversion; to exhort men to be converted; to tell them to take care they look on Christ, instead of simply holding up Christ; to tell them to have faith, rather than to supply its object; to lead them to work up their minds, instead of impressing on them the thought of him who can savingly work in them; to bid them be sure that their faith is justifying, that it is not dead, formal, self-righteous, or merely moral, instead of glorifying him, whose image fully delineated, destroys deadness, formality, and self-righteousness; to rely on words, vehemence, eloquence, and the like, rather than to aim at conveying the one great idea in words or not. And thus faith and (what is called) spiritual-mindedness are dwelt on as *ends* and obstruct the view of Christ." [21]

But Newman insists that we do not influence men by *telling* them to weep or laugh; we cannot bring about conversion by insisting upon it. We cannot effectively protect men from the dangers of formality and self-righteousness by warning them of these; in a sense, all this merely intensifies the

[19] *Ibid.*, p. 383.
[20] *Ibid.*, p. 369.
[21] *Ibid.*, p. 371.

threat. For "the more you fasten men's thoughts on themselves, the more you lead them to unconscious show, pretence, and duplicity," with the final result that "convulsions become in their view the only real manifestation of spiritual life and strength." [22]

In a scathing and satiric passage Newman turns his analysis upon the evangelical idiom, its emphasis upon subjectivism, upon *my* faith (not Christ's love and grace), on *receiving* (not on Christ's giving), on *renouncing* (not on Christ's overcoming), on *knowing* fellowship (not on having it), on *my* devotion, my *own* worship, my *personal* sense of wants, my *desire* and *expectation*. At the end he explodes: "Poor miserable captives, to whom such doctrine is preached as the gospel! What! Is *this* the liberty wherewith Christ has made us free, and wherein we stand, the home of our own thoughts, the prison of our own sensations, the province of self, a monotonous confession of what we are by nature, not what Christ is in us, and resting at best not on his love towards us, but in our faith towards him!" [23]

All of these misconceptions, Newman contends, are the result of adopting human for divine means of propagating the gospel: particularly the human decision that substitutes for baptism as a "cause of regeneration," the theory that preaching, which is not *formal* and *unchanging* like baptism, is the cause. Such an argument against the sacraments in favor of preaching falsifies the proper use of each. To Newman, this is a distortion of both baptism and preaching. And the irony of rejecting the use of one form because of its abuse is precisely that in the very nature of things another form will take its place. "It may be fairly questioned," Newman argues, "whether religion does not necessarily imply the belief in such sensible tokens of God's favour as the sacraments are accounted by the church. . . . Our nature requires something

[22] *Ibid.*, p. 373.
[23] *Ibid.*, p. 375. This is perhaps the most polemical passage Newman ever wrote as an Anglican against the Evangelicals.

special; and if we refuse what has been given, we shall be sure to adopt what has not been. . . . This we see fulfilled before our eyes in many ways; those who will not receive baptism as the token of God's election, have recourse to certain supposed experiences of it in their hearts." [24]

Here Newman puts his finger succinctly on a crucial problem for "twice-born" or "Bible" Christians; they falsely assume, as a kind of first principle, that the Christian religion can be free from incipient formality and abuse. This assumption itself is specious; it rests upon a form of docetic Christology—or at least on an implicit anthropological or cosmic dualism that, in effect, turns religion into an abstraction, an abstraction that can express itself only in what Newman would have called "unreal words." All this is a very subtle form of self-idolatry masked as "true" and "interior" Christian faith. Over against this, Newman contends for a concrete, historical church, commissioning and perpetuating an apostolic ministry, sustained by a balanced emphasis on word and sacrament, depending utterly upon God's gift of his own life through the Incarnation. In such a notion "personal experience" and "private judgment" never rise to primacy; and preaching is always subordinated to the more inclusive ministry of the church.

Finally, Newman admonishes, if Christians are to be freed from the idolatry of self-contemplation, from being taken up with their own feelings, let them follow the example of the "Holy Catholic Church in her best ages." He continues: "The ancients worshipped; they went out of their own minds into the infinite temple which was around them. They saw Christ in the Gospels, in the creed, in the sacraments and other rites; in the visible structure and ornaments of his house, in the altar, and in the cross; and, not content with giving the service of their eyes, they gave him their voices, their bodies, and their time." [25]

[24] *Ibid.*, pp. 367–68.
[25] *Ibid.*, pp. 383–84.

The service of these Christians was not something extraordinary, addressed to the throne of grace once a week, or some one day, "painfully, as if ambitiously and lavishly given." Rather, it was the routine business of every day, and "every day and every portion of the day" was begun and sanctified with devotion. In a grand climax, Newman concludes: "Consider those seven services of the Holy Church Catholic . . . which, without encroaching upon her children's duties towards this world, secured them in their duties to the world unseen. Unwavering, unflagging, not urged by fits and starts, not heralding forth their feelings, but resolutely, simply, perseveringly, day after day, Sunday and week-day, fast-day and festival, week by week, season by season, year by year, in youth and in age, through a life, thirty years, forty years, fifty years, in prelude of the everlasting chant before the throne— so they went on, 'continuing instant in prayer,' after the pattern of psalmists and apostles, in the day with David, in the night with Paul and Silas, winter and summer, in heat and in cold, in peace and in danger, in a prison or in a cathedral, in the dark, in the day-break, at sun-rising, in the fore-noon, at noon, in the afternoon, at eventide, and on going to rest, still they had Christ before them; his thought in their mind, his emblems in their eye, his name in their mouth, his service in their posture, magnifying him, and calling on all that lives to magnify him, joining with angels in heaven and saints in paradise to bless and praise him for ever and ever. O great and noble system, . . . not of those Christians who are taken up with their own feelings, and who describe what they should exhibit." [26]

Such a passage as this, of which there are many in Newman, makes clear that his essentially historical orientation saw a much greater threat to the church in England from the Evangelicals within and without the church than from the Catholic tradition. And the symbol of evangelical error seemed to be fixed in a special way in popular preaching.

[26] *Ibid.*, pp. 384–85.

23

Around this center gathered a host of accompanying errors, particularly the errors of subjectivism and the exaltation of religious experience. In short, to Newman, all this smacked of a new and human system essentially of the same stripe as other systems of the day built upon pragmatic and utilitarian principles. Such human systems might be very good indeed for dealing with sewage problems, for extending the empire, and for building railroads; but they are anathema for the church. For, as Isaac Williams had put it, "If we wish to do good to the world we must not look to it, but unto God; our strength must be in secret where God is." [27]

## 3. Newman on the Art and Vocation of Preaching

Although Newman's own achievement in preaching makes it clear that he had thought long and deep on the vocation and art of preaching, only after he became a Roman Catholic did he commit his insights on this subject to a systematic statement. One of his great ambitions as founder and rector of the new Catholic university in Dublin was to employ the pulpit of the University Church as a place from which he and other distinguished preachers could give religious direction to the academic community in its corporate life. It is said that to each guest preacher he addressed with his invitation a memorandum containing two brief stipulations, the exclusion of political topics, and a time limit of forty minutes—both salutary in mid-nineteenth-century Ireland! [1] At the request of a group of these ministers, Newman wrote for their guidance a brief treatise entitled "University Preaching." [2] Here we find

[27] Tract 87, *Tracts for the Times*, V, 125.

[1] Fergal McGrath, *Newman's University: Idea and Reality* (London: Longmans, Green & Co., 1951), p. 414.

[2] The text of this essay is found in John Henry Newman, *Lectures and Essays on University Subjects* (London: Longman, Brown, Green, Longmans, and Roberts, 1859), pp. 187–220. All references are to this edition.

Newman's best thought, distilled from his study and reading and his own rich experience and brilliant success as preacher at St. Mary's, succinctly articulated. It is at once Newman's best statement on the art of preaching and a fine commentary upon the style and substance of his sermons. Here he expresses theoretically the notions that find concrete embodiment in his own preaching.

The essay is informed by Newman's familiarity with Aristotle and the fathers. In asserting the principle that the *specific audience* determines to a large degree the "subject-matter or the method" of preaching, Newman suggests some specific ways to communicate effectively with university men. But the heart of the essay has to do with the essence of Christian preaching, which is "one and the same in all cases." [3] In view of this central concern, the essay represents Newman's normative statement on the vocation and art of parochial preaching.

A first principle that dominates Newman's thought concerning preaching—and indeed a characteristic of all his thought—is his insistence upon concreteness of aim and statement. Every sermon must have a clear and consistent intent, a definable aim or end. It must avoid at all costs the threat of generalizations, of abstractness, both in purpose and in statement. He puts it this way: "Definiteness is the life of preaching. A definite hearer, not the whole world; a definite topic, not the whole evangelical tradition; and, in like manner, a definite speaker. Nothing that is anonymous will preach; nothing that is dead and gone; nothing even which is of yesterday, however religious in itself and useful. Thought and word are one in the Eternal Logos, and must not be separate in those who are his shadows on earth. They must issue fresh and fresh, as from the preacher's mouth, so from his breast, if they are to be 'spirit and life' to the hearts of his hearers." [4]

[3] *Ibid.*, p. 188.
[4] *Ibid.*, p. 218.

But this rhetorical principle in itself must be understood in a Christian context, the conviction that the ultimate aim of all preaching is the salvation of the hearer. In a sermon of moving and classic beauty, preached early in his Catholic career at Birmingham, Newman raises the question of the motives of preachers. After a lengthy analysis of the motives of "the world," and hence the problem of showing clearly to the world the unworldly motives of the church, Newman then answers the question he has put: the *salvation of the hearer* is the motive of the preacher. "What is so powerful an incentive to preaching as the sure belief that it is the preaching of truth? What so constrains to the conversion of souls, as the consciousness that they are at present in guilt and peril? What so great a persuasive to bring men into the church, as the conviction that it is the special means by which God effects the salvation of those whom the world trains in sin and unbelief?" [5]

Such a zeal, Newman continues, has been the very life of the church, and the breath of her preachers and missionaries in all ages. Indeed, it was such a "sacred fire which brought our Lord from heaven, and which he desired, which he travailed, to communicate to all around him." This has been the secret of the propagation of the church from the beginning and will be to the end; this is "why the church, under the grace of God, to the surprise of the world, converts the nations." Let no one think that such charisma requires heroic personal qualities in the preacher; it is not merely a characteristic of saints and martyrs, but indeed is fundamental to all ministers. "It requires no great zeal in us, no great charity, to come to you . . . and entreat you to turn from the path of death. . . . It requires nothing great, nothing heroic, nothing saintlike; it does but require conviction . . . that the Christian religion is from God. . . ; it requires nothing more than faith,

[5] John Henry Newman, "The Salvation of the Hearer the Motive of the Preacher," *Discourses Addressed to Mixed Congregations* (Boston: Patrick Donahoe, 1853), p. 13.

a single purpose, and a distinct utterance." [6]

This "distinct utterance," whose aim is the salvation of the hearer, must be directed to particular men. In his insistence upon definiteness as the life of preaching, Newman shows his concern for the redemption of *individuals*. Though his thought is always qualified by his theological commitment to the notion of the corporate nature of the church, Newman's preaching is impregnated with the urgency of his concern for persons. Largely because of this dominating awareness of the awful responsibility which rests upon the preacher, the responsibility for the salvation of individual men, Newman never succumbed to the temptation to be a pulpit orator in the grand style of a Bossuet or a Lancelot Andrewes. In most of his own preaching, and in all of his stated theory, Newman extols a different emphasis in preaching. As distinguished from the large-scale aims and methods of classical pulpit oratory, Newman concentrates on the concrete, the definite, the individual. He is concerned with hitting upon a single aspect of Christian truth, and so developing it that it is set firmly and efficaciously in the interior self of the hearer. His aim is to move the individual one step forward toward the perfection demanded of and open to the Christian. This emphasis upon definiteness issues ultimately from Newman's conviction of the awful significance and uniqueness of the individual. An infinite concern for the individuality of every human self lies at the heart of each Newman sermon. Its classic expression is found in a sermon entitled "The Individuality of the Soul." [7] Here Newman's aim is to bring his auditors to an urgency for salvation, in the realization "that every soul of man which is or has been on earth, has a separate existence; and that, in eternity, not in time merely,—in the unseen world, not merely in this,—not only during its mortal life, but ever from the hour of its creation."

[6] *Ibid.*, p. 15.
[7] John Henry Newman, *Parochial and Plain Sermons* (London: Longmans, Green & Co., 1897), IV, 80–93.

But this awareness, Newman continues, is almost incomprehensible. "Nothing is more difficult than to realize that every man has a distinct soul, that every one of all the millions who live or have lived, is as whole and independent a being in himself, as if there were no one else in the whole world but he." In concrete ways again and again in the sermon Newman shows why it is so easy to forget this fundamental Christian assertion. Typical of this emphasis is this passage: "Survey some populous town: crowds pouring through the streets; some on foot, some in carriages; while the shops are full, and the houses too, could we see into them. Every part of it is full of life. Hence we gain a general idea of splendor, magnificence, opulence, and energy. But what is the truth? Why, that every being in that great concourse is his own centre, and all things about him are but shades, but a 'vain shadow,' in which he 'walketh and disquieteth himself in vain.' He has his own hopes and fears, desires, judgments, and aims; he is everything to himself, and no one else is really any thing. No one outside of him can really touch him, can touch his soul, his immortality; he must live with himself for ever. He has a depth within him unfathomable, an infinite abyss of existence; and the scene in which he bears part for the moment is but like a gleam of sunshine upon its surface." [8]

So with the great cities; so with the hordes of history; so with those faces we see vanishing in a moment. Implications of vast consequence are hidden even in a childhood glance. "We may recollect when children, perhaps, once seeing a certain person; and it is almost like a dream to us now, that we did. It seems like an accident which goes and is all over, like some creature of the moment, which has no existence beyond it. The rain falls, and the wind blows; and showers and storms have no existence beyond the time when we felt them; they are nothing in themselves. But if we have but once seen any child of Adam, we have seen an immortal soul. It has not passed away as a breeze or sunshine, but it lives; it lives at this moment in one of those many places, whether of bliss or misery, in which all souls are reserved until the end." [9] Such passionate concern for every individual human being is at the root of Newman's zeal for the salvation of the hearer, and it is the ground for his maxim that "definiteness is the life of preaching." It is also the basis for his conviction that earnestness is requisite to efficacious preaching.

While the ultimate aim of all preaching is the salvation of each particular hearer, this end can be achieved only when the preacher points toward a particular and defined immediate spiritual good. His subject must therefore be "a definite topic, not the whole evangelical tradition." In preaching, purity of heart is to will one thing! Single-minded commitment to a particular spiritual good is the "one thing necessary" for effective preaching; the preacher must sustain "an intense perception and appreciation of the end . . . to be the minister of some definite spiritual good to those who hear him." To insure such particularity, the preacher should "place a distinct categorical proposition before him, such as he can write down in a form of words." This would then be the canon for his study and preparation, to aim in all he says to bring out this one proposition and to fix it efficaciously in the depths of his hearers. This would require the unequivocal rejection of every remark, however original, and every sentence, however eloquent, which does not in some way tend to bring out and make concrete this one distinct proposition which the preacher has defined as his aim. "As a marksman aims at the target and its bull's-eye, and at nothing else, so the preacher must have a definite point before him, which he has to hit. So much is contained for his direction in this simple maxim, that duly to enter it and use it is half the battle; and if he mastered nothing else, still if he really mastered as much as this, he would know all that was imperative for the due discharge of

[9] *Ibid.*, pp. 85–86.

his office." [10]

Such a concentration frees a preacher to exert all his resources, however rich or poor, toward a simple and spontaneous immediacy. It answers, even before they are put,
such questions as the value of embellishments of style and
rhetorical devices. "We ask about diction, elocution, rhetorical power; but does the commander of a besieging force
dream of holiday displays, reviews, mock engagements, feats
of strength, or trials of skill, such as would be graceful and
suitable on a parade ground when a foreigner of rank was to
be received and *feted;* or does he aim at one thing and one
thing only, viz., to take the strong place? Display dissipates
the energy, which for the object in view needs to be concen-
trated and condensed." [11] Himself the most eloquent of
preachers, Newman repeatedly shows his disdain of "what the
world calls eloquence" in the pulpit; he repeatedly shows his
dislike of artificiality and decorativeness as an end in itself.
He speaks contemptuously of "flowers of rhetoric, which
bloom, smell sweet, and die," [12] and of the "rhetorical col-
ouring of the whole composition, so contrary to the sobriety
of truth." [13] Newman scoffs at the notion that one can effectively develop a "literary style," as if language were "the

[10] *Ibid.*, p. 189. Newman continues, somewhat humorously, "nothing
is so fatal to the effect of a sermon, as the habit of preaching on three
or four subjects at once" (*ibid.*, p. 197).

[11] *Ibid.*, p. 190. In this connection, Newman quotes St. Francis de
Sales to the effect that "the highest art will be to have no art at all.
Let the words be stimulating, not by means of loud shouting and excessive gesticulation, but by their intrinsic influence. Let them arise from
the heart rather than from the voice. Whatever we shall say with the
voice, let it be spoken soberly in the heart of hearts" (*ibid.*, p. 195,
trans. Charles Johnson).

[12] Cited by Sister Mariella Gable, *The Rhetoric of John Henry Newman's Parochial and Plain Sermons with Reference to Aristotle's Rhetoric*
(Doctoral dissertation, Cornell University, 1934), p. 136, quoting Newman, *Discussions and Arguments* (London: Longmans, Green & Co.,
1872), p. 263.

[13] *Ibid.*, quoting Newman, *Apollonius Tyanaeus,* in *Encyclopaedia
Metropolitana* (London, 1824), p. 354.

hired servant, the mere mistress of the reason, and not the lawful wife in her own house." Style cannot be *"an addition from without* to the matter treated of—a sort of ornament superinduced, or a luxury indulged in, by those who have time and inclination for such vanities, as if *one* man could do the thought, and *another* the style." [14]

Newman's contempt for such a view is based upon his philosophical conviction that "thought and speech are inseparable from each other. Matter and expression are parts of one: style is a thinking out into language." [15] This fact is suggested by the Greek notion of *Logos,* a word which "stands both for *reason* and for *speech,"* meaning both at once "because they really cannot be divided." [16] All this is not to deny the powers of rhetoric and grace of expression to the preacher. It is rather to assert the priority of the fundamental aim of the preacher to have clear conceptions and to be exact and intelligible in expressing them, toward the end of a particular spiritual good for a particular hearer. The least pardonable fault in a preacher is to fail in clarity of expression.

But elaboration of style, even lavishness of rhetoric, is proper when it faithfully reproduces and elicits the thought and feeling prompting it. A great preacher is master of the *Logos* of word and of thought, distinct, but inseparable each from the other; he has but one aim, and he follows it singlemindedly, to give forth one particular good that he has within him. This very earnestness and "incommunicable simplicity" make his style "the lucid mirror of his mind and life." Hence, his style will vary according to the particular occasion: "He writes passionately, because he feels keenly; forcibly, because he conceives vividly; he sees too clearly to be vague; he is too serious to be otiose; he can analyze his subject, and therefore he is rich; he embraces it as a whole and in its parts, and

14 John Henry Newman, "Literature," in *The Idea of a University* (London: Longmans, Green & Co., 1910), pp. 277, 279.
15 *Ibid.,* p. 276.
16 *Ibid.,* pp. 276–77.

therefore he is consistent; he has a firm hold of it, and therefore he is luminous. When his imagination wells up, it overflows in ornament; when his heart is touched, it thrills. . . . He always has the right word for the right idea, and never a word too much. If he is brief, it is because few words suffice; when he is lavish of them, still each word has its mark, and aids, not embarrasses, the vigorous march of his elocution." [17]

Likewise, Newman denies that learning and erudition for their own sakes have any place in preaching, even in university preaching. "Let no one suppose that anything recondite is essential to the idea of a university sermon. The most obvious truths are often the most profitable." [18] With considerable ironic satire—as well as learning—Newman comments on preachers whose erudition and sheer complexity of thought and style defeat their purpose of communicating persuasively with a congregation. "There are authors, who are as pointless as they are inexhaustible, in their literary resources. They measure knowledge by bulk, as it lies in the rude block, without symmetry, without design. How many commentators are there on Holy Scripture, from whom we rise up, wondering at the learning which has passed before us, and wondering why it passed! How many writers are there of ecclesiastical history who, breaking up their subject into details, destroy its life, and defraud us of the whole by their anxiety about the parts! The sermons, again, of Protestant divines in the seventeenth century, how often they are mere repertories of miscellaneous and officious learning! Take those of Jeremy Taylor, for instance, and what an array of quotations, anecdotes, similes, and good sayings, strung upon how weak a thread of thought! Turn, for example, to his 'House of Fasting'; which sets about proving nothing short of this, that 'plenty and pleasures of the world are not proper instruments of felicity,' and that 'intemperance is its enemy.' One might have thought it difficult

[17] *Ibid.*, p. 292.

[18] "University Preaching," in *Lectures and Essays on University Subjects*, p. 203.

either to dispute or to defend so plain a proposition; but Taylor contrives to expend upon it twenty closely printed pages, not of theology or metaphysics, but of practical exhortation." [19] Then Newman analyzes in detail the argument of the sermon, cataloging the names and authorities Taylor appeals to in trying to "do justice to the marvelous availableness of this writer's erudition for enforcing truisms and proving proverbs." He charges that Taylor uses for his purpose no common-sense principles or clear, broad rules, but he comes at his subject by way of a battery of authorities, after thirty-two closely printed pages "leaving the subject pretty much as he found it." "Such is learning," Newman concludes, "when used, not as a means, but as an end; less dignified even than . . . 'the cracking of thorns under a pot,' for they at least make the water boil, but nothing comes of pedantry." [20]

Erudition, authority, eloquence, rhetorical brilliance—all these and other human excellences contribute to great preaching only when they enter unobtrusively and, as it were, unself-consciously into the enterprise. Their legitimate function can only be to strengthen the sermon in its aim, not to divert it by attracting attention to themselves. Given such an order of priorities, however, Newman is quick to affirm these qualities as gifts of God. "I am far from forgetting that every one has his own talent, and that one has not what another has. Eloquence is a divine gift, which to a certain point supersedes rules, and is to be used, like other gifts, to the glory of the giver, and then only to be discountenanced, when it forgets its place, when it throws into the shade and embarrasses the essential function of the Christian preacher, and claims to be cultivated for its own sake, instead of being made subordinate and subservient to a higher work and to sacred objects. And how to make eloquence subservient to the evangelical office, is not more difficult, than how to use learning or intellect for

[19] John Henry Newman, *Discourses on the Scope and Nature of University Education* (Dublin: James Duffy, 1852), pp. 221–22.
[20] *Ibid.*, p. 223.

a supernatural end." [21] Again, the basic premise of the essay is that "preachers should neglect everything whatever besides devotion to their one object, and earnestness in enforcing it, till they in some good measure attain to these requisites." [22]

In keeping clearly before him such a disciplined aim, the preacher will quite unconsciously exhibit the earnestness which he brings to his task, and this in turn will elicit a sympathetic response and hearing from the congregation. Such earnestness on the part of the preacher and such an open hearing from the congregation are essential to efficacious preaching. To be sure, such earnestness comes only from an infinite concern for the salvation of the hearer; but given this, it follows naturally upon commitment to a fixed objective, and by sympathy it creates earnestness in others. The more a preacher loses himself in his subject, the more he communicates it to his brother. What is powerful enough to absorb and possess the preacher, on the face of it has some claim to the attention of his hearers. But for the preacher to *aim at earnestness* is to protest too much! This is fatal. With great insight Newman insists that "no one will become really earnest by aiming directly at earnestness." He satirizes excessive displays of mock earnestness: "We may of course work ourselves up into a pretence, nay into a paroxysm, of earnestness; as we may chafe our cold hands till they are warm. But when we cease chafing, we lose the warmth again; on the contrary, let the sun come out and strike us with his beams, and we need no artificial chafing to be warm. The hot words, then, and energetic gestures of a preacher, taken by themselves, are just as much signs of earnestness, as rubbing the hands or flapping the arms together are signs of warmth; though they are natural where earnestness already exists, and pleasing as being its spontaneous concomitants. To sit down to compose for the pulpit, with a resolution to be eloquent, is

21 "University Preaching," p. 219.
22 *Ibid.*, pp. 191–92.

one impediment to persuasion; but to be determined to be earnest is absolutely fatal to it." [23]

Authentic earnestness presupposes a certain measure of faith and love, and it presupposes also a vivid minute mental view of "the four last things." In point of fact, only such unpremeditated earnestness evokes a response of earnestness. "It is this earnestness, in the supernatural order, which is the eloquence of saints; and not of saints only, but of all Christian preachers. . . . As the case would be with one who has actually seen what he relates, the herald of tidings of the invisible world also will be, from the nature of the case, whether vehement or calm, sad or exulting, always simple, grave, emphatic, and peremptory; and all this, not because he has proposed to himself to be so, but because certain intellectual convictions involve certain external manifestations." [24]

Such a concentration on a particular end not only tends to project and elicit earnestness, but also fixes in the hearer the spiritual benefit intended. General and abstract sermons do not do this. Only the concrete can find its way home to the hearer. "As a distinct image before the mind makes the preacher earnest, so it will give him something which it is worth while to communicate to others. Mere sympathy, it is true, is able to transfer an emotion or sentiment from mind to mind, but it is not able to fix it there. He must aim at imprinting on the heart what will never leave it, and this he cannot do, unless he employs himself on some definite subject, which he has to handle and weigh, and then, as it were, to hand over from himself to others." [25]

Since the end of preaching is persuasion, the preacher must address the intellect and the affections; he must instruct and convince the intellect as well as move the affections and fix the will of his hearer. Hence the necessity to have

23 *Ibid.*, p. 193.
24 *Ibid.*, p. 194.
25 *Ibid.*, p. 196.

something specific to say if he wants to be heard. Newman summarizes this insistence in these words: *"Definiteness
of object* is in various ways the one virtue of the preacher;—
and this means, that he should set out with the intention of
conveying to others some spiritual benefit; that, with a view
to this, and as the only ordinary way to it, he should select
some distinct fact or scene, some passage in history, some
truth, simple or profound, some doctrine, some principle, or
some sentiment, and should study it well and thoroughly, and
first make it his own, or should have already dwelt on it and
mastered it. . . ; and that then he should employ himself, as
the one business of his discourse, to bring home to others,
and to leave deep within them, what he has, before he began
to speak to them, brought home to himself. . . . If then a
preacher's subject only be some portion of the divine message, however elementary it may be, however trite, it will have
a dignity such as to possess him, and a virtue to kindle him,
and an influence to subdue and convert those to whom it goes
forth from him." [26]

Newman is equally insistent upon the necessity of keeping
firmly in mind the particularity of the audience hearing
preaching. Since preaching aims to persuade, a particular person or group to be persuaded is implied. Hence, "such as is
the hearer will be preaching." Here is a distinction Newman
makes between rhetoric and logic. Whereas logic, intending to
prove a point, is the same all over the world, rhetoric intends
not to prove but to persuade, and this involves differences of
approach to different audiences. "Aristotle, in his celebrated
treatise on rhetoric, makes the very essence of the art lie in the
precise recognition of a hearer. It is a relative art, and in that
respect differs from logic. . . . As then the Christian preacher
aims at the divine glory, not in any vague and general way, but
definitely by the enunciation of some article or passage of the
revealed word, so, further, he enunciates it, not for the instruction of the whole world, but directly for the sake of those

[26] *Ibid.*, p. 199.

very persons who are before him. He is, when in the pulpit, instructing, enlightening, informing, advancing, sanctifying, not all nations nor all classes nor all callings, but those particular ranks, professions, states, ages, characters, which have gathered around him." [27] While it is true that all preaching in its essence is the same, and therefore exhibits a continuity from particular sermon to particular sermon, the subject matter and its method of treatment vary according to particular circumstances, one of which is the auditory. Each congregation has something of a character of its own, which when properly understood imparts to the sermon, both in its subject matter and the mode of treating it, "a peculiar color and expression."

Newman once spoke of the art of rhetoric as "the reduction of reasonings, in themselves sound, into the calculus of the tastes, opinions, passions, and aims of a particular audience." [28] This is the process of restating in a fresh language, a new idiom or medium, truths or sound reasonings that stated in the usual manner would either be truisms and hence not arresting, or mere assertions that would meet with active resistance from the hearer. The great problem is how to penetrate and employ for the preacher's own aims the peculiar "calculus" of the ethos of a particular audience. Hence the caution that Newman sounds to be certain that one has intimate and personal knowledge of his audience; otherwise let the preacher take the safe course of choosing a topic that would be suitable to any congregation under any circumstances. To direct a sermon toward a particular issue for a given congregation when no such issue is in fact alive there does more harm than good; the preacher must avoid such a misunderstanding of his audience at all costs. Hence also the value of *indirectly* approaching the particular needs of the hearers, of working "covertly, not showing on the surface of

27 *Ibid.*, pp. 201–2.
28 John Henry Newman, "Prospect of the Anglican Church," in *Essays Critical and Historical* (London: Longmans, Green & Co., 1910), I, 288–89.

his discourses what he is aiming at." [29] Too direct an approach is not merely a blunt weapon; too direct an approach above all lacks the necessary imaginative appeal and the essential power of the principles of indirection, suggestivity, or evocation.

Furthermore, it lacks the principle of reserve, to which Newman was deeply committed in theory and in practice, that reserve and indirection which touch the heart and conscience, or suggest trains of thought to the intellect, without overtly proclaiming the main reason why they have been chosen. These principles of sensitivity to the audience, of subtle refinement and indirection and reserve, are not merely rhetorical devices which are pragmatically sound. They are rooted in deep theological assumptions, indeed in the very principle of the economy of God in his incarnational self-revelation to man. Newman points out that St. Paul employed such an economy in his preaching to the heathens, as did also the fathers of the church in their dealings with pagans and heretics. In an earlier study of Arianism, Newman had made this same point: "There are instances in various ways of the economical method, that is, of accommodation to the feelings and prejudices of the hearer, in leading him to the reception of truth. It professes to be founded in the actual necessity of the case. . . . And it cannot be denied that those who attempt to speak at all times the naked truth, or rather the commonly-received expression of it, are certain, more than other men, to convey wrong impressions of their meaning to those who happen to be below them, or to differ widely from them, in intelligence and cast of mind. On the other hand, the abuse of the economy in the hands of unscrupulous reasoners, is obvious. Even the honest controversialist or teacher will find it very difficult to represent without misrepresenting, what it is yet his duty to present to his hearers with caution or reserve. Here the obvious rule to guide our practice is, to be careful

[29] "University Preaching," p. 206.

ever to maintain substantial truth in our use of the economical method." [30]

This understanding of the need for an intimate apprehension of the particularity of a congregation is but one other aspect of Newman's commitment to the concrete. And it is an indication of his fundamental epistemological assumptions, indeed of his understanding of what a man is and how a man comes to give his assent to any claim. "The whole man moves"; and hence preaching intends to persuade the whole man—to convince his intellect, to move his affections, to fix his will. Newman makes a distinction between "notional" and "real" assent,[31] and his preaching is based upon such an understanding. Men can be led to notional assent through arguments that appeal largely to the intellect, and that move almost entirely upon verbal distinctions and abstractions. Such notional assent, however, is always working in the realm of logical probability or mere intellectual certainty at best. It has to do primarily with, as one modern novelist has put it, "the forebrain that chatters." It is not the kind of assent that one would risk his person and his destiny upon; it is not the assent of authentic faith. Possessed himself of a fierce logic and a superb intellect, Newman was nevertheless very suspicious of too much dependence upon reason. In one of his later Anglican works he says, "Reason is slow and abstract, cold and speculative; but man is a being of feeling and action; he is not resolvable into a . . . series of hypotheticals, or a critical diatribe, or an algebraical equation." [32] This fundamental insight is still basic in his old age as a Catholic, when Newman writes in the *Grammar of Assent*: "Deductions have

[30] John Henry Newman, *The Arians of the Fourth Century* (London: Longmans, Green & Co., 1908), pp. 71–72.

[31] This distinction is developed at great length in Newman's *An Essay in Aid of a Grammar of Assent*, his major philosophical work, written out of a lifetime of thought and experience, first published in 1870.

[32] John Henry Newman, "Private Judgment," in *Essays Critical and Historical*, II, 353.

no power of persuasion. The heart is commonly reached, not through the reason, but through the imagination, by means of direct impressions, by the testimony of facts and events, by history, by description. Persons influence us, voices melt us, looks subdue us, deeds inflame us. Many a man will live and die upon a dogma; no man will be a martyr for a conclusion." [33]

This notion, that men ordinarily reason not from propositions to propositions but from things to things, from concrete to concrete, dealing with things directly as they stand, one by one, is at the heart of Newman's theory and practice of preaching. Hence preaching is not intended to win notional assent, though it might include it. Rather, preaching intends to move the whole man toward real assent, to that religious certitude which is infinitely more decisive than mere intellectual certainty, and in which "a thousand difficulties do not make one doubt." And since men are more affected by the concrete than by the abstract, Newman rejects in preaching the primacy of the intellect or the dominance of reason, particularly in the form of logic. In one of his own superb university sermons, Newman exhibits his realistic understanding of how an audience actually responds, of how completely the mental processes move to conviction, to belief, and finally to the condition of real assent. He asserts: "The mind ranges to and fro, and spreads out, and advances forward with a quickness which has become a proverb, and a subtlety and versatility which baffle investigation. It passes on from point to point, gaining one by some indications; another on a probability; then availing itself of an association; then falling back on some received law; next seizing on testimony; then committing itself to some popular impression, or some inward instinct, or some obscure memory; and thus it makes a progress not unlike a clamberer on a steep cliff, who, by quick eye, prompt hand, and firm foot, ascends how he knows

[33] John Henry Newman, *An Essay in Aid of a Grammar of Assent* (London: Longmans, Green & Co., 1909), pp. 92–93.

not by himself, by personal endowments and by practice, rather than by rule, leaving no track behind him, and unable to teach another. It is not too much to say that the stepping by which great geniuses scale the mountains of truth is as unsafe and precarious to men in general, as the ascent of a skillful mountaineer up a literal crag. It is a way which they alone can take; and its justification lies in their success. And such mainly is the way in which all men, gifted or not gifted, commonly reason,—not by rule, but by an inward faculty." [34]

Such a commitment to the specific—a definite aim, a particular audience, a clearly defined subject, a mode that rejects the abstract idea for the concrete instance—such a commitment no doubt explains to a great extent why Newman succeeded so admirably in bringing his audiences to *realize* and appropriate for themselves his own insight and spiritual grace.

Finally, a word must be said about Newman's understanding of one other particular dimension in preaching, the irreducibly personal element. He puts it this way: "A definite hearer . . . a definite topic . . . a definite speaker. Nothing that is anonymous will preach." [35] This is true, first of all, because language itself is a uniquely personal and human phenomenon. Speech is not the production or result attained by the partnership of several persons, but the work of one individual. Hence a sermon belongs to the preacher himself, and is the expression of the preacher's ideas and feelings; ideas and feelings that, though parallel and similar to those of others, nevertheless are "proper to himself, in the same sense as his voice, his air, his countenance, his carriage, and his action, are personal." [36] In this sense the very style of a preacher is a kind of extension or projection of his interior life or self. His style is not only the image of his subject, but of his mind; it belongs to no one but himself. His thought and feeling are

34 John Henry Newman, "Implicit and Explicit Reason," in *Oxford University Sermons* (London: Longmans, Green & Co., 1909), p. 257.
35 "University Preaching," p. 218.
36 "Literature," p. 274.

personal, and so his language is personal. "His language expresses not only his . . . thoughts, but his . . . self." [37] Hence the fundamental importance of *hearing sermons preached,* of the auditory experience, rather than merely reading them. "There is something more than composition in a sermon; there is something personal in preaching; people are drawn and moved, not simply by what is said, but by who says it. The same things said by one man are not the same as when said by another. The same things when read are not the same as when they are preached." [38]

It is the case, of course, that associations that gather around a preacher can work for good or for ill; but the point is that the case is altered in any discourse precisely by the associations the audience brings to the person of the speaker. "Take a preacher and he shall deliver a sermon; then let it be considered how differently the sermon seems to persons who know him well and those who do not. Very different for better or for worse; let him be a man of pomp and parade, or of smoothness and artifice, and strangers will be taken in, and admire the very words, turns of speech and gestures, which make those who know him well only cry out, 'How like so-and-so!' On the other hand, the deep feeling and reality of another sort of man go clean over the heads of those who do not know him, while friends are pierced by every word. Let the very same speech or sentiment come from two persons, and it has quite a different meaning, according to the speaker, and takes a different form in our minds." [39]

This notion of the primacy of human personality and personal influence runs through much of Newman's thought, and it is crucial for his theory of preaching. The unconsciously communicated ethos of the preacher is its own most cogent and persuasive argument. Hence the immediacy of preaching,

[37] *Ibid.,* p. 280.

[38] "University Preaching," pp. 216–17.

[39] John Henry Newman, "The Reformation of the Eleventh Century," in *Essays Critical and Historical,* II, 251.

the personal confrontation which it represents. In the oral tradition, of which preaching partakes, the personal presence of the teacher is the great instrument or organ for propagating truth. In 1830 Newman wrote his friend the Reverend S. Rickards from Oriel: "Men live after their death—they live not only in their writings or their chronicled history, but still more in . . . a school of pupils who trace their moral parentage to them. As moral truth is discovered, not by reasoning, but by habituation, so it is recommended not by books, but by oral instruction. Socrates wrote nothing. Authorship is the second best way." [40] The great instrument of religious persuasion has always been the personal presence of the teacher or prophet; it is the living voice, the breathing form, the expressive countenance, which preaches, which catechizes. Hence the signal importance of human personality in preaching, and the significance of the moral character of the preacher. What the preacher himself is, is communicated on depth levels to his hearers; traits of a moral nature hidden in the preacher are nevertheless cognizable by the hearer. And "the common sense of the world decides that it is safer . . . to commit oneself to the judgment of men of character, than to any considerations addressed merely to the feelings or the reason." [41]

This explains why Newman makes such a clear distinction between the minister's service as a *priest* and as a *preacher*. As a priest, he loses his individuality: his words are impersonal, his tones, his actions, his presence, all lose their personality; his vestments are sacerdotal; making the same genuflections, chanting the same notes, giving one peace and one blessing, every priest is like another, since each is but a representative of Christ from whom he derives his commission. But when the liturgy is over, then the celebrant "resumes himself, and comes to us in the gifts and associations which

40 John Henry Newman, *Letters and Correspondence,* ed. Anne Mozley (London: Longmans, Green & Co., 1903), I, 203.

41 "University Preaching," p. 191.

43

attach to his person. He knows his sheep, and they know him, and it is this direct bearing of the teacher on the taught, of his mind upon their minds, and the mutual sympathy which exists between them, which is his strength and influence, when he addresses them." [42] Religion is best kindled and intensified not by argument or by academic discourse but by appeals to the whole man, to his conscience, his affections, his imagination—all in themselves reached ultimately by personal influences.

Newman gave the classic statement—we might say the definitive statement—of this lifelong conviction in his sermon at Oxford as select preacher to the university on January 22, 1832. He opens the sermon by referring to the apostles and the problems they faced in an indifferent or hostile world. Then he puts the question around which the sermon is organized: "Whence, then, was it, that in spite of all these impediments to their success, still they succeeded? How did they gain that lodgment in the world, which they hold down to this day, enabling them to perpetuate principles distasteful to the majority even of those who profess to receive them? What is that hidden attribute of the truth, and how does it act, prevailing, as it does, single-handed, over the many and multi-form errors, by which it is simultaneously and incessantly attached?" [43]

One by one and in careful argument Newman raises popular and possible answers, only to show them each and altogether as inadequate. Finally he himself answers his own question. Truth, he says, "has been upheld in the world not as a system, not by books, not by argument, nor by temporal power, but by the personal influence of such men as have already been described, who are at once the teachers and the patterns of it." [44] This is so, Newman contends, because the

[42] *Ibid.*, pp. 217–18.

[43] John Henry Newman, "Personal Influence, the Means of Propagating the Truth," in *Oxford University Sermons*, p. 76.

[44] *Ibid.*, pp. 91–92.

peculiar natural beauty and majesty of virtue concretely seen in human personality is the most persuasive of forces. All but the most abandoned of men feel this beauty, and are subject to its power. Personal holiness cannot be ignored. "Men persuade themselves, with little difficulty, to scoff at principles, to ridicule books, to make sport of the names of good men; but they cannot bear their presence: it is holiness embodied in personal form, which they cannot steadily confront and bear down: so that the silent conduct of a conscientious man secures for him from beholders a feeling different in kind from any which is created by the mere versatile and garrulous reason." [45]

Hence, it is no surprise that the greatest preachers have been the greatest men, have indeed been saints and apostles. For such qualities are not only communicated to the hearers unconsciously, but are indeed requisite to deep spiritual awareness. And such personal holiness illumines all areas of human understanding, and enhances all other human excellencies. St. Paul embodies for Newman these qualities shared with the great saints and preachers of all ages: "They are versed in human knowledge; they are busy in human society; they understand the human heart; they can throw themselves into the minds of other men; and all this in consequence of natural gifts and secular education. While they themselves stand secure in the blessedness of purity and peace, they can follow in imagination the ten thousand aberrations of pride, passion, and remorse. The world is to them a book, to which they are drawn not for its own sake, which they read fluently, which interests them naturally—though by reason of the grace which dwells within them, they study it and hold converse with it for the glory of God and the salvation of souls. Thus they have the thoughts, feelings, frames of mind, attractions, antipathies of other men, so far as these are not sinful, only they have these properties of human nature purified, sanctified, and exalted; and they are only made more elo-

45 *Ibid.*, p. 92.

quent, more poetical, more profound, more intellectual by reason of their being more holy." [46]

One French critic, impressed by Newman's emphasis upon the power of personal influence, suggests that Newman's exaltation of the heroes of the faith was, whether consciously or not, a way of holding up himself to view through the heroes of his choice. Not that in the patriarch Jacob, or in St. Paul or St. John Chrysostom or St. Athanasius, Newman is *exalting* himself. On the contrary, he does not admire or love himself in them. "But he describes himself in them, because he finds in them either what he is, what he wishes to be, or what he is on the point of becoming." [47] Since we are in the process of becoming forever what we are loving most and freely choosing now, perhaps we could do worse than to join Newman in his veneration of the heroes of the faith.

## 4. *Newman's Continuing Significance for Preaching*

In February of 1828 Newman was named vicar of St. Mary's, once the church of Oriel College but in 1828 the University Church and the parish for the local shopkeepers and university servants. For the next fifteen years from St. Mary's pulpit he was to preach week after week at the four o'clock service on Sunday afternoon and on feast days. In 1883, in introducing his American lecture on Emerson, Matthew Arnold remembered that time: "Forty years ago, when I was an undergraduate at Oxford, voices were in the air there which haunt my memory still. Happy the man who in that susceptible season of youth hears such voices! They are a possession to him for ever. No such voices as those which we heard in our youth at Oxford are sounding there now. Oxford

[46] John Henry Newman, "St. Paul's Characteristic Gift," in *Sermons on Various Occasions* (London: Longmans, Green & Co., 1908), pp. 92–93.

[47] Henri Bremond, *The Mystery of Newman,* trans. H. C. Corrance (London: Williams and Norgate, 1907), p. 9.

has more criticism now, more knowledge, more light; but such voices as those of our youth it has no longer. The name of Cardinal Newman is a great name to the imagination still; his genius and his style are still things of power. But he is over eighty years of age; he is in the Oratory at Birmingham; he has adopted, for the doubts and difficulties which beset men's minds today, a solution which, to speak frankly, is impossible. Forty years ago he was in the very prime of life; he was close at hand to us at Oxford; he was preaching in St. Mary's pulpit every Sunday; he seemed about to renew what was for us the most national and natural institution in the world, the Church of England. Who could resist the charm of that spiritual apparition, gliding in the dim afternoon light through the aisles of St. Mary's, rising into the pulpit, and then, in the most entrancing of voices, breaking the silence with words and thoughts which were a religious music— subtle, sweet, mournful?" [1]

After a century of silence, Newman speaks again. While sermon reading has gone out of fashion, reading Newman's sermons has not. The problems and their solutions to which Newman addressed himself are of great immediacy to modern Christians. These sermons are contemporary; they are existential; in a genuine sense they are perennial. Hence it is no surprise that new editions of the sermons in English are now appearing; [2] and it is no surprise that the recent German and French translations of the *Parochial and Plain Sermons,* in whole and in part respectively, are being received with great enthusiasm by priests and monks, ministers and intelligent

[1] Quoted by Basil Willey, "Newman and the Oxford Movement," in *Nineteenth Century Studies* (New York: Columbia University Press, 1949), p. 73.

[2] These include Vincent F. Blehl (ed.), *Cardinal Newman's Best Plain Sermons* (New York: Herder and Herder, 1964); Vincent F. Blehl (ed.), *Realizations: Newman's Selection of His Parochial and Plain Sermons* (London: Darton, Longman and Todd, 1964); Lawrence F. Barmann (ed.), *Newman at St. Mary's* (Westminster, Md.: The Newman Press, 1962); and Armel J. Coupet (ed.), *A Newman Companion to the Gospels* (London: Burns & Oates, 1966).

laymen who are seeking for more adequate answers to the religious and human dilemmas of our time.[3] In his classic *Christian Spirituality* Pierre Pourrat speaks of Newman as one who "must be particularly recommended to people of understanding who are lost in the darkness of unbelief and seek the light of faith." [4] The novelist Muriel Spark, speaking of her own reading, assigns a very high priority to Newman's sermons. She says: "Over the past twelve years, at times when I have felt my mind becoming congested from hearing too many voices, including my own, I have turned to the sermons which Newman delivered to the undergraduates of Oxford when he was Vicar at St. Mary's. His voice from the pulpit was, by all accounts, something very special indeed. I am sure nothing has been lost in the past hundred and twenty years, only gained; for if there is one comprehensive thing that can be said about Newman's writings, it is that he has a 'voice'; it is his own and no one else's. To me, at least, it is a voice that never fails to start up, radioactive from the page, however musty the physical book." [5] She continues, "I read Newman's sermons because they are Newman's, not because they are sermons. He was as sincere as light." [6] And again, "In his own time his persuasive power was greatly feared. But what did it consist of? Simplicity of intellect and speech. Simplicity is the most suspect of qualities; it upsets people a great deal." [7] Again, she points up the peculiar force of Newman's continuing power. "Serious-minded people still call, from time to time, for a 'return to the moral standards of Christianity,' by which they mean those codes of decency

---

[3] See Charles Stephen Dessain, "Newman's Spirituality and Its Value Today," *The Clergy Review* (London), XLV (May, 1960), 257–82.

[4] Barmann (ed.), *Newman at St. Mary's*, p. xii, citing Pierre Pourrat, *La Spiritualité Chrétienne* (Paris, 1947), IV, 559–60.

[5] See Blehl (ed.), *Cardinal Newman's Best Plain Sermons*, p. v.

[6] *Ibid.*

[7] *Ibid.*, p. ix.

which evolved in the chivalrous West from the Christian faith. Many hold that it is the morals that count, Christianity can go. I am not an expert in such matters, but I always sense, underlying these moralistic appeals and urges, a demand for something showy. Let us show the spirit of service, the people say, let us have some austerity, work harder, clean up our streets; morality must not only be done, it must be seen to be done; let us return to the hypocrisy of our forefathers—God used to like it so much when everyone went to church and didn't commit adultery. Newman's contribution to this field of study is to say that conscientious people of high moral principle may be on the side of evil. He says that, however inspired, however honourable, they may be Satan's instruments in seducing and enfeebling the people of God. Moreover those who are genuinely pleasing in God's sight, only God knows. The disposition of every soul is a secret matter, not easily discernible." [8]

The question must be put, what is Newman's "secret"? How does it happen that he yet speaks? The answer to this might indeed be suggested when we look at the sources of his peculiar power in his own time, at what was unique or different about him then. It is clear, of course, that only Newman in his complex and variegated qualities of excellence can finally answer the question of his secret. His superb intelligence, his astute knowledge of language and his creative, disciplined use of it, his utter abandonment of all human ambition and desire for personal aggrandizement in his austere pursuit of truth, his lucid and intense spirituality—all these clearly are part of the Newman portrait. But other men of his day participated in greater or lesser degree in all these qualities; and their unique and concrete convergence in Newman the man is, of course, unrepeatable. Can we find some other qualities that set Newman apart as a preacher, and that can continue to reenforce the efficacy of the preaching vocation in our time?

[8] *Ibid.,* pp. vii–viii.

It seems to me that we can. The first such quality that is prominent is his rejection of "topical" or "timely" preaching —what we might call his rejection of the urgency of relevance in preaching. As he insisted that the attempt to be earnest is the surest way to appear false, so he no doubt would insist that a nervous concern for relevancy reveals a growing doubt that the Christian gospel can address itself to the concrete realities of human existence. Horton Davies has shown that one of the striking qualities of much Victorian preaching was its attempt to wrestle seriously with such immediate problems of the day.[9] But Newman is concerned with topical issues only in a very indirect and oblique way. To be sure, his preaching is almost always apologetic. The sermons preached to the university were deliberately given to apologetic and, to some degree, to polemical purposes. They were primarily concerned with the relationship of faith and reason, always a topical interest in the university and particularly so in Newman's Oxford.[10] On certain occasions, particularly in the last years of his Anglican life, Newman delivered sermons that must be called topical.[11] But the very fact that Newman published these separately, and under the title he chose, indicates that they were exceptions to his general practice. His parochial sermons are deliberately given to the enduring verities of the Christian faith, to the centuries-old tradition found in the fathers of the first five centuries and in the biblical deposit of revealed truth in both the Old Testament and the New. Indeed, Newman eschewed the popular appeal which topical preaching seemed to have with masses of his contemporaries. He would have thought of this method of preaching,

[9] Davies, *Worship and Theology in England: From Newman to Martineau*, pp. 287–90.

[10] These sermons were first published in 1834 as *Sermons Preached Before the University of Oxford*.

[11] These are found in *Sermons on Subjects of the Day*, first published in 1843. For a perceptive analysis of these, see Maisie Ward, *Young Mr. Newman* (New York: Sheed & Ward, 1948), pp. 383–403.

when it was regularly and deliberately employed, as a reflection of the spirit of the age, a spirit which he strongly resisted. While aware of the necessity for accomodation to his audience, Newman was nevertheless actively suspicious of what he termed "indulgence to the evil principles of the age." He was persuaded that often, "when one accommodates the age, one hurts posterity." [12] For better or for worse, in this regard Newman had the wisdom of a later liberal, Dean Inge, who warned: "If you marry the Spirit of your generation, you will be a widow in the next." [13] Newman deliberately rejected the spirit of his age, whether it was met as the tendency to exalt human reason to a position of primacy, or to extol utility as the guiding system of values for human life, or to rely on private judgment in doctrinal issues and the stirring of the religious affections in devotional exercises, or to embrace the promises and hopes implicit in the developing science and technology of the day. In short, his whole life was given over to resisting and refuting the great threat which he saw in "liberalism," [14] particularly as this spirit opposed itself to the dogmatic principle underlying Christianity.

One of the enigmas of Newman is found precisely at this point. Through reading his parochial sermons one would never discover that a newly developing critical approach to the Bible was an issue in his time, though it is true that indirectly he attacks what Coleridge called "bibliolatry"; and through his insistence on tradition apart from Scripture, and on the church as interpreter of Scripture, he was in fact freeing the church from many of the apparent threats which the

[12] See Newsome, "Justification and Sanctification," p. 37, quoting a Newman letter to Samuel Wilberforce.

[13] Cited by Davies, *Worship and Theology in England: From Newman to Martineau,* p. 205, quoting W. R. Inge, *The Diary of a Dean* (London: Hutchinson & Co., 1949), p. 12.

[14] For Newman's own definition of "liberalism," see "Note A" appended to his *Apologia Pro Vita Sua,* ed. A. Dwight Culler (Riverside Editions, Boston: Houghton Mifflin Co., 1956), pp. 269-77.

new approach to the Bible seemed to pose to traditional Christianity. From Newman's sermons having to do with Jesus of Nazareth one would never guess that a Strauss or a Renan was dealing with the same materials, but in a radically different way. From Newman's preaching based on Old Testament texts, one would never guess that anyone in his time had raised any critical questions concerning their historicity or any of the other questions normally raised with reference to ancient literature. Insofar as the sermons are concerned, from them one could hardly get a glimpse of the storms and explosions going on all about: the repeal of corn laws, the passing of reform bills, the extension of the franchise and of free public education, the mass shifting of populations to the new industrial cities, the squalor and poverty of the developing slums, the inhuman exploitation of children and women in mine and factory, the conflicts between labor and capital, the rising tide of indignation against the corruption of the slave traffic in its various manifestations. No one would ever guess from Newman's parochial sermons that the same England that produced him also produced in the same century a Marx and a Darwin and a Lyell and a Chambers and a Maurice.[15] Apes and geology do not appear in Newman's sermons! One would never discover from Newman's sermons that the whole culture of which he was a part was in fact in a succession of major revolutions of gigantic proportions—unless the sheer apocalyptic dimension of his preaching would indirectly suggest this.

The fact that Newman deliberately refused to come to grips with such topical issues as these, issues which many of the great preachers were in fact directly engaging, makes him stand out from his contemporaries as atypical. Indeed, his

[15] Strauss published *Das Leben Jesu* in two volumes in 1835–36, which was translated into English by the novelist George Eliot; Renan published *Vie de Jesus* in 1863; Darwin published the *Origin of Species* in 1859; Lyell published *Principles of Geology* in 1830–33; Chambers published *The Vestiges of the Natural History of Creation* in 1844; Marx published *Das Kapital* in 1848, the same year that Maurice helped organize the Christian Socialists.

aloofness from such topical concerns has brought him into much criticism, in his own day and in subsequent times. On the surface it is easy to charge him with an excessive other-worldliness, or even with having deliberately set over against his own time the spirit of another and no-longer-relevant age. He appears to be blind to the deep conflicts and struggles brought sharply into focus for many Christians, intellectuals and ordinary men as well, by the apparent contradictions between the developing sciences and religion, between the emerging biblical criticism and traditional Christianity. Newman rejected such immediately topical concerns, almost as if he were unaware that the new floods of human knowledge seemed to be eroding the citadels of Christian dogma and that the claims to uniqueness for the Christian faith, the claim for a particular divine providence in the affairs of men and history, and even the humanistic as well as Christian claim to a peculiar role in the universe for the human animal, were in ostensible danger of being swept away. One can only conclude that Newman was naively unaware of the major intellectual forces of his own time—of the immense battle underway for men's minds and hearts—or that he was gripped by an obsessive obscurantism, or possessed by a supremely confident and historically orthodox dogmatism.

We can dismiss at once the possibility that Newman was naively unaware of the life-and-death struggle in which the church found itself in his time. He was deeply conscious, perhaps more than any man of his time, of the desperate need in such a revolutionary age for firm standards of belief and clear guides to conduct. The more difficult question is whether Newman was a proud obscurantist, who in refusing to come to terms with modern thought simply adopted for his motto "Remove not the ancient landmarks"—and then employed his shrewd intelligence and subtle literary powers in making such a reaction intellectually feasible and personally viable. This is essentially the point of view taken by Newman's detractors, both in his own day and until our own time. But such a judgment will not stand, either before a careful analysis of Newman's own works, or before the judgment bar of history.

One of the ironies of the Newman story is that in his refusal to adopt the spirit of the age, or to engage the topical problems of his day, he was in fact expressing in a profound but possibly unknowing sense his own modernity. His lifelong experience of only partial acceptance by his contemporaries is to be explained primarily by the fact that he was born "out of time." And he was ahead of his age, not behind it. What Newman, in effect, refused to do was to let the enemy choose the time or the place of battle—to say nothing of the weapons to be employed. He had the wisdom to recognize that in any conflict with the spirit of the age, if the spirit of the age were to choose the weapons and lay down the rules, revealed religion was sure to lose.

Newman had a lifelong preoccupation with the prospect of a great modern movement to unbelief, and his life work, at least as he saw it, was to erect barriers against the onslaught of such a tidal wave. In this sense he was deeply concerned with the immediate issues of his day, and in this sense his preaching is almost without exception apologetic. But Newman held that a secure fortress against the tidal wave of unbelief, against those giants, the intellect and the pride of modern men, could be built only out of the foundations of the historic faith, only by the recovery of the forgotten truths of revealed religion. Hence his hold on a religion of authority rather than of experience; hence his lifelong struggle against "liberalism," the anti-dogmatic principle, in the conviction that this route of accomodation to the spirit of the age leads inevitably to mere private judgment or to the loss of faith. As he himself once said, he had a profound grasp of the significance of *first principles* and their implications. In refusing to engage the modern temper on its own terms he was in fact rejecting the adequacy of its first principles. He would have held, for example, that in the matter of science and religion, the findings of science that stood in apparent conflict with religion would subsequently be found either to have been misunderstood or to be untrue, or that the real claims of revealed religion had not been properly understood. For Newman, the decisive issue always reverts back to first principles. This is suggested by the pointed query which he raises concerning an earlier science-religion controversy. He reminds us that Christians once thought the sun moved around the earth, whereas now we say that the earth moves around the sun. But how can we know which is correct, Newman asks, "until we know what motion is?"

In refusing to debate the issues of the day, Newman moved the whole discussion onto another level, a level that continues to be as significant for our time as it was for his own. In choosing his own grounds for doing battle Newman was not in fact ignoring the great intellectual issues of his day; he was rather developing quite indirectly, and in the context of revealed religion and dogma, a subtle new apologetic that would come into its own with its own particular force only when the immediate issues of his day had passed. In effect, Newman rejected the notion that biblical criticism and developing knowledge and theory in natural and social and biological sciences were in fact shaking the foundations of the Christian faith. They only appeared to do so, and they appeared most threateningly to do so to those who admitted the first principles upon which they operated. In Newman's day, topical preaching bravely took on the battle for men's minds. It was understandably popular when ably done. But Newman refused to follow this route. His refusal came neither from cowardly evasion of the issues of his day nor from a reactionary obscurantism. Rather, it came from his supreme confidence that in the end revealed religion would carry the day, and from his conviction that any accommodation to "liberalism" was an opening for infidelity.

To some degree, the wisdom of Newman's conviction was borne out even in his own time. Matthew Arnold, in his essay

"Sweetness and Light" (1869), pays moving tribute to Newman's triumph. He speaks of the Oxonian dedication to that "beauty and sweetness" which are "essential characters of a complete human perfection," and insists that "our sentiment for beauty and sweetness, our sentiment against hideousness and rawness, has been at the bottom of our attachment to so many beaten causes, of our opposition to so many triumphant movements." This sentiment, he continues, since it is true, "has never been wholly defeated, and has shown its power even in its defeat. We have not won our political battles, we have not carried our main points, we have not stopped our adversaries' advance, we have not marched victoriously with the modern world; but we have told silently upon the mind of the country, we have prepared currents of feeling which sap our adversaries' position when it seems gained, we have kept up our own communications with the future. Look at the course of the great movement which shook Oxford to its centre some thirty years ago! It was directed, as any one who reads Dr. Newman's *Apology* may see, against what in one word may be called 'Liberalism.' Liberalism prevailed; it was the appointed force to do the work of the hour; it was necessary, it was inevitable that it should prevail. The Oxford movement was broken, it failed; our wrecks are scattered on every shore. . . . But what was it, this liberalism, as Dr. Newman saw it, and as it really broke the Oxford movement? It was the great middle-class liberalism, which had for the cardinal points of its belief the Reform Bill of 1832, and local self-government, in politics; in the social sphere, free-trade, unrestricted competition, and the making of large industrial fortunes; in the religious sphere, the Dissidence of Dissent and the Protestantism of the Protestant religion. I do not say that other and more intelligent forces than this were not opposed to the Oxford movement: but this was the force which really beat it; this was the force which Dr. Newman felt himself fighting with; this was the force which till only the other day seemed to be the paramount force in this country, and to be in possession of the future. . . . And where is this great force of Philistinism now? It is thrust into the second rank, it is become a power of yesterday, it has lost the future. . . . And who will estimate how much the currents of feeling created by Dr. Newman's movement, the keen desire for beauty and sweetness which it nourished, the deep aversion it manifested to the hardness and vulgarity of middle-class liberalism, the strong light it turned on the hideous and grotesque illusions of middle-class Protestantism,—who will estimate how much all these contributed to swell the tide of secret dissatisfaction which has mined the ground under the self-confident liberalism of the last thirty years, and has prepared the way for its sudden collapse and supersession?" [16]

Newman's rejection of topical preaching, which was so widely popular in his own time, should at least raise the question in us of whether our own nervous anxiety for relevance is not symptomatic of a deeper malady. And of course Newman's rejection of this particular form of popularity was of one piece with his rejection of all forms of show, including cheap appeals to transient emotions, to rhetorical brilliance, to homely use of wit and humor, and to the widespread romantic notions concerning nature and natural beauty.[17] No doubt Newman's rejection of all these was rooted deeply in his own personality, in his fundamental reserve, and in his refined sensibilities. Yet it must be said that it also reflects his deep sense of awe and mystery before the vocation of preaching, his sense of reverence toward personal presences, both God and men. Can we not say that reverence is a prerequisite to faith? Our own generation will not perish for want of knowledge; it might well perish for lack of reverence. Preaching for reverence, preaching which is itself impregnated with the mystery of presences, and with a sense of awe before its

[16] Matthew Arnold, "Culture and Anarchy," in *The Complete Prose Works,* ed. R. H. Super (Ann Arbor: University of Michigan Press, 1965), V, 106–7.

[17] Horton Davies has shown that in addition to topical preaching, Victorian popular preaching moved largely on (1) appeals to emotion, (2) use of wit and humor, and (3) delight in natural, scenic grandeur. See *Worship and Theology in England: From Newman to Martineau,* pp. 287–301.

own vocation, only such preaching can ultimately be efficacious. Such was Newman's preaching. His sermons always
move solidly on a tough-minded dogmatic and biblical frame-
work; they have a clear intellectual formation and a precise
rational dimension. Yet they also evoke deep emotion; they
carry a depth of human feeling which is alive and vibrant.
There is throughout Newman's preaching an elegiac note, a
restrained anguish in the face of the glidingness of all things
temporal, a quiet joy in the greatness and a profound pathos
in the littleness of human life. His sermons pulsate with the
grand Augustinian awareness that we are made for God, and
that we know no rest until we rest in him.

Perhaps the most devastating criticism that can be made of
Newman has to do with his failure to recognize the demands
of the Christian faith for active social concern. The same
situations that produced *Das Kapital* in 1848 also brought
about, in the same year, the founding of the Christian Social-
ist movement, largely under the inspiration and leadership of
F. D. Maurice, an early admirer but later a critic of Newman.
Insofar as his sermons or his actions would indicate, Newman
was singularly lacking in that deep commitment of the Christian Socialists on the one hand and many of the Anglican
Evangelicals and dissenters on the other, to the amelioration
of human suffering and the social betterment of the poor and
the dispossessed. The unconscionable exploitation of children
in the mines and factories, the appalling conditions of poverty
and disease and filth in the slums, the indignities of prison
and other institutional life, the dehumanizing traffic in human
slavery—all of these seem to have escaped Newman's attention. While many ministers, both of the establishment and of
dissent, were providing their congregations with ethical guidance in the economic and industrial problems of the day—an
urgent responsibility in any period of moral and ethical rela-
tivism—Newman appeared singularly unconcerned with such
questions.

To be sure, Newman's influence might be seen as a healthy
corrective to those ministers who confused the realization of

mere social goals with the kingdom of God, or to those who wanted (as Matthew Arnold) to reduce the Christian faith to "morality tinged with emotion." No doubt Newman's eschatological depths, both in the *futuristic* and in the *realized* sense, served as a necessary challenge to those who encouraged only an earthbound religion or a passing feeling of sentimentality. Nevertheless, it must be pointed out that Newman never seemed to recognize, or to come to grips with, the profound this-worldly implications of biblical religion— particularly the radical social criticisms of the Old Testament prophets. While his preaching and his theology are christological, and indeed incarnational, it seems that the social imperatives of incarnational Christianity never penetrated Newman's understanding. He saw with great clarity the primary task of awakening and confirming faith, of bringing faith to white-hot *realization;* but he seems to have failed to grasp the secondary but also necessary task of asserting Christian ethical imperatives—except as these could be understood in individualistic and personalistic terms. In view of Newman's great sense of the corporate nature of the church, it is all the more surprising that in his ethical concerns he should have failed to see the corporate nature of social and economic evil. While his sermons deplore the mercenary spirit of the age, and reflect from time to time his personal feelings of compassion toward the poor, toward widows and orphans and outcasts, and while he himself practiced generous charities, he never seems to go beyond such gestures.

It might be said that Newman's strong anti-Pelagian conviction of human sin would have made him suspicious of any attempt to bring in the kingdom through social awakening. No doubt he took quite literally the words of Christ, "The poor you have with you always"; and in his passion to point men to their ultimate destiny, he was willing to think of this world as significant only as preparatory to the eternal world. In all this Newman exercised a necessary critique upon all this-worldly hopes, however noble and genuine. Yet it must be said that the most glaring limitation of Newman's genius is found in his apparent ignoring of the radical social needs of his time, in his failure to see the imperative of incarnational Christianity to take such needs seriously. And he cannot be acquitted for so grievous a fault. It is difficult to avoid the judgment that in this failure he was revealing a want of fundamental human sympathy and compassion.

Newman has also been criticized for the notes of fear and severity which run throughout his preaching. But it must be said that in the total output of his sermons there is an equal emphasis upon holy joy. Over against the semi-Pelagianism of much of the prudential and merely moralistic preaching of his predecessors, Newman's emphasis on the reality of human sin and its destructive consequences—in time and in eternity—was a necessary corrective. Over against the advocates of "cultural Christianity" and "cheap grace" in his own day, Newman's rediscovery and espousal of a costly *kerygma* was salutary. In his personal life, in the reserve of his preaching style, and in his sober insistence on holiness rather than peace, he succeeded in making attractive again, particularly to young intellectuals, the high severe ideal of chastity and the demanding vocation of celibacy. To him was given the consummate grace of making ancient dogma take on vibrant life.

Indeed, if there is a "secret" of Newman, it lies fundamentally in the lifelong unity of his mission: the revival and revitalizing of revealed religion in the modern world. The purity of heart of his single-minded will to this one end irradiates the whole of his life and work, from beginning to end. In its fundamental dogmatic basis, Newman's preaching must be seen as doctrinal, though not systematic; in its incarnational and christological emphases it is kerygmatic; in its insistence upon holiness of life and obedience to the will of God, it is highly moral and unsentimental; in its peculiar sense of urgency it is apocalyptic; in its awareness of the presence of God and its hope for beatitude it is eschatological; in its unrelenting probings of human motives and facades it is psychologically penetrating; in its critique of the spirit of the age it is prophetic; in its urgent longing for holiness and its exaltation of the heroes and martyrs of the faith it is moving and devotional; in its impregnation with biblical and patristic insights and sensibilities, it is genuinely Catholic; in its deep sense of the historic church and its worship it is ecclesiastical and liturgical; in its power to *realize* lost causes and forgotten truths, it is superbly apologetic. Newman's preaching is the product of his own spirituality, his scholarship and study, and his lively imagination. It is the classic and most characteristic expression of his genius and of the unity and singular purpose of his lifelong aim: the recovery and establishment and celebration of revealed religion.

Yet despite all these excellences, Newman has human limitations. He failed to see the force of the ethical imperatives of the gospel with reference to economic and social questions; he was sometimes guilty of unconscious pride and a somewhat narrow exclusivism; he failed to understand the force of his own polemical powers, and he sometimes was guilty of unfair caricature rather than accurate characterization of his opponents. Perhaps with some justification, Newman has been accused of a want of human sympathy—a lack which is reflected in the austerity of his life and to some degree in his preaching. No doubt he failed to see the full force of some of the new findings of the various sciences of his day. But however these limitations are understood, they appear inconsequential in the light of Newman's profound spirituality, his imaginative powers in *realizing* truth for his auditors, and in comparison with his lifelong and arduous venture of faith.

## 5. A Note on the Present Edition

The present edition is made up of thirteen sermons which Newman himself identified as amongst his best.[1] Newman

---

[1] In a letter to Ambrose St. John, January 26, 1846. See Charles Stephen Dessain (ed.), *The Letters and Diaries of John Henry Newman* (London: Thomas Nelson & Sons, 1961), XI, 98–99.

believed that a person could get interested in his sermons through reading selections of the best of them. The ones presented here are typical and representative. They reveal Newman's religious genius, his literary excellence, and his strikingly unique power as a preacher to penetrate deeper and deeper into a particular subject until it was concretely *exhibited* before and *realized* by his auditors. A careful study of these sermons will make sense of Bouyer's judgment that "of all Newman's many writings, the *Parochial and Plain Sermons* will probably always be assigned the highest place." [2] They also confirm the statement of Dean Church that the dominant quality of Newman's preaching was "a passionate and sustained earnestness after a high moral rule, seriously realized in conduct." [3]

Each of these sermons was first preached in Newman's regular parochial ministry at St. Mary's. They are not university sermons, and they are not sermons for special occasions. Some of them were repeated at St. Mary's and in other parish pulpits. As was Newman's custom as an Anglican, each of these was read from a carefully detailed manuscript, and then published virtually without change.

The text used in this collection is that of the uniform edition issued by W. J. Copeland in 1868 (after Newman became a Catholic), itself reproducing the text of the editions published when Newman was still a member of the Church of England. Quotations from the Authorized Version of the English Bible are left unchanged; in all other cases I have tried to bring the spelling and capitalization into general conformity with contemporary American practice. The date of each sermon, Newman's title for each, and the place of each in the eight-volume set of *Parochial and Plain Sermons*, are indicated in the table of contents. The main title shown for each

[2] Louis Bouyer, *Newman: His Life and Spirituality*, trans. J. Lewis May (New York: P. J. Kenedy & Sons, 1958), p. 178.

[3] Church, p. 21.

sermon is the editor's; subtitles are Newman's. Footnotes to the sermons are Newman's own.

It is hoped that many Christians of various traditions will be persuaded through the reading of these sermons to join Newman in his grand venture of faith.

*Parochial and Plain Sermons:*

*Newman's Selection of His Best*

# Freedom in Bondage to Christ

## The Strictness of the Law of Christ

*"Being then made free from sin, ye became the servants of righteousness."*—Rom. 6:18

IN THE PASSAGE OF which these words form a part, St. Paul insists again and again on the great truth which they declare, that Christians are not their own, but bought with a price, and, as being so, are become the servants or rather the slaves of God and his righteousness; and this, upon their being rescued from the state of nature. The great apostle is not content with speaking half the truth; he does not merely say that we are set free from guilt and misery, but he adds, that we have become the servants of Christ; nay, he uses a word which properly means *slaves*. Slaves are bought and sold; we were by nature slaves to sin and Satan; we are bought by the blood of Christ: we do not cease to be slaves. We no longer indeed belong to our old master; but a master we have, unless slaves on being bought become freemen. We are still slaves, but to a new master, and that master is Christ. He has not bought us, and then set us loose upon the world; but he has done for us what alone could complete his first benefit, bought us to be his servants or slaves. He has given us that only liberty which is really such, bond service to himself; lest if left to ourselves, we should fall back again, as we certainly should, to the cruel bondage from which he redeemed us. But anyhow, whatever be the consequences it involves, whatever the advantage, whatever the trial, we did not cease to be slaves on being set free from Satan; but we became subject to a new master, to him who bought us.

This needs insisting on; for a number of persons who are not unwilling to confess that they are slaves by nature, from some cause or other have learned to think that they are not bound to any real service at all, now that Christ has set them free. Now if by the word *slavery*, some cruel and miserable state of suffering is meant, such as human masters often inflict on their slaves, in that sense indeed Christians are not slaves, and the word is improper to apply to them; but if by being slaves, is meant that we cannot throw up our service, change our place, and do as we will, in that sense it is literally true, that we are more than servants to Christ, we are, as the text really words it, slaves. Men often speak as if the perfections of human happiness lay in our being free to do or not to do, to choose and to reject. Now we are indeed thus free, as far as this—that if we do not choose to be Christ's servants, we can go back to that old bondage from which he rescued us, and be slaves again to the powers of evil. But though we are free to make our situation worse, we are not free to be without service or post of any kind. It is not in man's nature to be out of all service and to be self-dependent. We may choose our master, but God or mammon we must serve. We cannot possibly be in a neutral or intermediate state. Such a state does not exist. If we will not be Christ's servants, we are forthwith Satan's; and Christ set us free from Satan only by making us His servants. Satan's kingdom touches upon Christ's, the world touches on the church; and we cease to be Satan's property by becoming Christ's. We cannot be without a master, such is the law of our nature; yet a number of persons, as I have said, overlook it, and think their Christian liberty lies in being free from all law, even from the law of

God. Such an error seems to have obtained even in St. Paul's time, and is noticed in the chapter before us. Men seem to have thought that, since the law of sin was annulled, and the terrors of the law of nature removed, that therefore they were under no law at all; that their own will was their law, and that faith stood instead of obedience. In opposition to this great mistake, St. Paul reminds his brethren in the text, that when they were "made free from *sin*," they "became the servants of *righteousness*." And again, "Sin shall not have dominion over you: for ye are not under the law," that is, the law of nature, "but under grace," or (as he elsewhere expresses it), "the law of faith," or, "the law of the Spirit of life." They were not without a master, but they had a gracious and bountiful one.

He says the same in other epistles. For instance, "He that is called, being free" (that is, free as regards this world), "is Christ's servant" or slave. "Ye are bought with a price; be not ye the servants of *men*," but, that is, be slaves of Christ. Again, after saying, "Servants, obey in all things your masters according to the flesh," he adds, "for ye serve the Lord Christ." Elsewhere he speaks of himself as "Paul a servant," or slave, as the word really means, "of Jesus Christ"; and again, as "not without law to God, but under the law to Christ." [1]

Religion then is a necessary service; of course it is a privilege too, but it becomes more and more of a privilege, the more we exercise ourselves in it. The perfect Christian state is that in which our duty and our pleasure are the same, when what is right and true is natural to us, and in which God's "service is perfect freedom." And this is the state towards which all true Christians are tending; it is the state in which the angels stand; entire subjection to God in thought and deed is their happiness; an utter and absolute captivity of their will to his will, is their fullness of joy and everlasting life. But it is not so with the best of us, except in part. Upon our regeneration indeed, we have a seed of truth and holiness planted within us, a new law introduced into our nature; but still we

[1] I Cor. 7:22, 23; Col. 3:22, 24; Rom. 1:1; I Cor. 9:21.

have that old nature to subdue, "the old man, which is corrupt according to the deceitful lusts." [2] That is, we have a work, a conflict all through life. We have to master and bring under all we are, all we do, expelling all disorder and insubordination, and teaching and impressing on every part of us, of soul and body, its due place and duty, till we are wholly Christ's in will, affections, and reason, as we are by profession; in St. Paul's words, "casting down imaginations, and every high thing that exalteth itself against the knowledge of God, and bringing into captivity every thought to the obedience of Christ." [3]

Now I may seem to have been saying what everyone will at once confess. And yet, after all, nothing perhaps is so rare among those who profess to be Christians as an assent in practice to the doctrine that they are under a law; nothing so rare as strict obedience, unreserved submission to God's will, uniform conscientiousness in doing their duty—as a few instances will at once show.

Most Christians then will allow in general terms that they are under a law, but then they admit it with a reserve; they claim for themselves some dispensing power in their observance of the law. What I am saying is quite independent of the question, what is the *standard* of obedience which each man proposes to himself? One man puts the line of his duty higher than another; some men take a low view of it, confining it to mere personal morality; others confine it to their social obligations; others limit it by some conventional law, which is received in particular classes or circles; others include religious observances. But whether men view the law of conscience as high or low, as broad or narrow, few indeed there are who make it a rule to themselves; few there are who make their own notion of it, whatever that be, binding on themselves; few who even profess to act up to it uniformly and consistently. Inquire of the multitude of men, as you meet

[2] Eph. 4:22.
[3] II Cor. 10:5.

them in the world, and you will find that one and all think it allowable at times to put themselves above the law, even according to their own standard of it; to make exceptions and reserves, as if they were absolute sovereigns of their conscience, and had a dispensing power upon occasions.

What is the sort of man whom the world accounts respectable and religious, in a high rank or a lower? At best he is such as this. He has a number of good points in his character; but some of these he has by nature, and if others have been acquired by trouble, it is either because outward circumstances compelled him to acquire them, or that he has from nature some active principle within him, of one kind or another, which has exerted itself, and brought other principles under, and rules him. He has acquired a certain self-command, because no one is respected without it. He has been forced into habits of diligence, punctuality, precision, and honesty. He is courteous and obliging; and has learned not to say all he thinks and feels, or to do all he wishes to do, on all occasions. The great mass of men of course are far from having in them so much that is really praiseworthy as this; but I am supposing the best. I am supposing then, that a man's character and station are such, that only now and then he will feel his inclinations or his interest to run counter to his duty. Such times constitute his trial; there is nothing to hinder him serving God in the ordinary course, but the proof of his sincerity lies in his conduct on these extraordinary occasions. Now this is the point to which I wish to draw attention; for these very occasions, which alone are his times of trial, are just the times on which he is apt to consider that he has a leave to dispense with the law. He dispenses with it at those very times when it is simply the law of God, without being also the law of self, and of the world. He does what is right, while the road of religion runs along the road of the world; when they part company awhile, he chooses the world, and calls his choice an exception. He does right for ninety-nine days, but on the hundredth he knowingly and willfully does wrong; and if he does not justify, at least he absolves himself in doing it.

For instance; he *generally* comes to church, it is his *practice*; but some urgent business at a certain time presses on him, or some scheme of pleasure tempts him—he omits his attendance; he knows this is wrong, and says so, but it is only once in a way.

Again; he is strictly honest in his dealings; he speaks the truth, that is, it is his rule to do so; but if hard pressed, he allows himself now and then in a falsehood, particularly if it is a slight one. He knows he should not lie; he confesses it; but he thinks it cannot be helped; it is unavoidable from circumstances, as being his only way of escaping some great difficulty. In *such* a case it is, as he says, all fair, and so he gets over it; that is, in a case where he must either disobey God, or incur some temporal disadvantage.

Again; he has learned to curb his temper and his tongue; but on some unusual provocation they get the better of him. He becomes angry, says what he should not, perhaps curses and swears. Are not all men subject to being overtaken with anger or ill temper? That is not the point: the point is this— that he does not feel compunction afterwards, he does not feel he has done anything which needs forgiveness. On the contrary, he defends himself to himself, on the plea that such language is very *unusual* with him; he does not understand that he is under a law, which he may not put himself above, which he may not dispense with.

Once more; he is in general sober and temperate; but he joins a party of friends and makes merry; he is tempted to exceed. Next day he says that it is a long time since such a thing happened to him; it is not at all his way; he hardly touches wine or the like in common. He does not understand he has any sin to repent of, because it is but once in a way.

And now, I suppose you quite understand what I mean, and I need not say more in explanation. Such men, being thus indulgent to themselves, are indulgent to each other; they make allowance for all around them, as taking what they give freely. This is the secret of being friends with the world, to have a sympathy and a share in its sins. They who are strict with themselves are strict with the world; but where men grant themselves a certain license of disobedience, they do not draw the line very rigidly as regards others. Conscious of what might be said against themselves, they are cautious what they say against others; and they meet them on the understanding of a mutual sufferance. They learn to say that the private habits of their neighbors are nothing to them; and they hold intercourse with them only as public men, or members of society, or in the way of business, not at all as with responsible beings having immortal souls. They desire to see and know nothing but what is on the surface; and they call a man's personal history sacred, because it is sinful. In their eyes, their sole duty to their neighbor is, not to offend him; whatever his morals, whatever his creed, is nothing to them. Such are they in mature and advanced life; in youth, they are pliable as well as indulgent, they readily fall in with the ways of the world, as they come across them. They are, and have the praise of being, pleasant, good-tempered, and companionable. They are not bad-principled, or evilly disposed, or flagrantly irregular, but they are lax. They in no sense live by rule. They have high spirits, and all the natural amiableness which youth has to show, and they generally go right; but, since they have no root in themselves, an accident from within or without, the stirring of a passion, or the incitement of a friend, makes them swerve at once. They swerve, and they have little compunction afterwards; they forget it. They shrink from the notion of being under a law, and think religion gloomy as imposing it. They like their own way, and without any great extreme of sin, or at least any habits of sin, follow it. They are orderly and well-conducted, when among well-conducted people—at home, for instance; but they indulge themselves abroad, when temptation comes in their way. They have the world at will; they are free; alas! what a melancholy freedom! yet in one sense a freedom it is. A religious man must withdraw his eyes from sights which inflame his heart, recollecting our Savior's caution; but a man of the world thinks it no harm to gaze where he should not, because he goes no further. A religious man watches his words; but the other utters whatever his heart prompts, and excuses himself for profane language, on the plea that he means nothing by it. A religious man will scruple about his society; but the other takes part in jests and excesses, though he condemns while he shares them, but not himself for sharing, and despises those with whom he shares them. He can see life, as it is called. He can go among all sorts of people, for he has no troublesome ceremonial, no rule of religion to shackle him. Perhaps he goes abroad, and then for a time he considers himself to be in disguise, as an unknown person in unknown countries, permitted to fall in with all things bad and good, as they come. Or again, he may be so circumstanced, whatever his station, as to find himself engaged in what are called politics; and then he thinks that though truth and religion are certainly all-commanding and all-important, yet still the world could not go on, public business would be at a stand, political parties would be unable to act, all that he really loves and reveres would become but of secondary concern, if religion refused at all times to give way ever so little. Again; a religious man carries his religion into his conduct throughout the day; but lax persons will do many things in private, which they would not like to be known. They will overreach, if they can do it without noise. They will break promises when made to an inferior. Or, if they have time on their hands, they will be curious and meddlesome; they will speak against others and spread scandals. They will pry into things which do not concern them, according to their station in life. They will listen where they have no right to listen; they will read what they have no right to read. Or they will allow themselves in petty thefts, where they think they do no injury, excusing themselves on the plea that what they take will never be missed. Or in matters of trade, they think a certain sort and degree of double-dealing allowable, and no dishonesty. They argue with themselves as if it were not their business to be true and just, but of others to find them out; and as if fraud and cheating did not imply sin in the one party, but dullness in the other. If in humble life, they think it no harm to put on an appearance; to profess what is not strictly true, if they are to gain by it; to color a story; or to affect to be more religious than they are; or to pretend to agree in religion with persons from whom they hope something; or to take up a religion if it is their interest to do so; or to profess two or three religions at once, when any alms or other benefit is to be given away.

These are a few out of a multitude of traits which mark an easy religion—the religion of the world; which would cast in its lot with Christian truth, were not that truth so very strict, and quarrels with it and its upholders, not as if it were not good and right, but because it is so unbending—because it will not suit itself to times and emergencies, and to the private and occasional likings and tastes of individuals. This is the kind of religion which St. Paul virtually warns us against, as often as he speaks of the gospel as really being a law and a servitude. He indeed glories in its being such; for, as the happiness of all creatures lies in their performing their parts well, where God has placed them, so man's greatest good lies in obedience to God's law and in imitation of God's perfections. But the apostle knew that the world would not think so, and therefore he insists on it. Therefore it is that he insists on the necessity of Christians "*fulfilling* the righteousness of the law"; fulfilling it, because till we aim at complete, unreserved obedience in all things, we are not really Christians at all. Hence St. James says, "Whosoever shall keep the whole law, and yet offend in one point, he is guilty of all." And our Savior assures us that "whosoever shall break one of these least commandments, and shall teach men so, he shall be called the least in the kingdom of heaven"; and that "except your righteousness shall exceed the righteousness of the scribes and Pharisees," which was thus partial and circumscribed, "ye shall in no case enter into the kingdom of heaven." And when the young man came to him, saying that he had kept all the commandments, and asking what he lacked, he pointed out the "one thing" wanting in him; and when he would not complete his obedience by that one thing, but went away sorrowful, then, as if all his obedience in other points availed him nothing, Christ added, "Children, how hard is it for them that trust in riches to enter into the kingdom of God!" [4] Let us not then deceive ourselves; what God demands of us is to fulfill his law, or at least to aim at fulfilling it; to be content with nothing short of perfect obedience—to attempt everything—to avail ourselves of the aids given us, and throw ourselves, not first, but afterwards on God's mercy for our shortcomings. This is, I know, at first hearing a startling doctrine; and so averse are our hearts to it that some men even attempt to maintain that it is an unchristian doctrine. A forlorn expedient indeed, with the Bible to refer to, and its statements about the strait gate and the narrow way. Still men would fain avail themselves of it, if they could; they argue that all enforcement of religion as a service or duty is erroneous, or what they call legal, and that no observance is right but what proceeds from impulse, or what they call the heart. They would fain prove that the law is not binding on us, because Christ has fulfilled it; or because, as is the case, faith would be accepted instead of obedience in those who had not yet had time to begin fulfilling it.

Such persons appeal to Scripture, and they must be refuted, as is not difficult, from Scripture; but the multitude of men do not take so much trouble about the matter. Instead of even professing to discover what God has said, they take what they call a common-sense view of it. They maintain it is impossible that religion should really be so strict according to God's design. They condemn the notion as overstrained and morose. They profess to admire and take pleasure in religion as a whole, but think that it should not be needlessly pressed in details, or, as they express it, carried too far. They complain only of its particularity, if I may use the term, or its want of indulgence and consideration in little things; that is, in other words, they like religion before they have experience of it—in

[4] Rom. 8:1–4; Jas. 2:10; Matt. 5:19–20; Mark 10:21, 24.

prospect—at a distance—*till* they have to be religious. They like to talk of it, they like to see men religious; they think it commendable and highly important; but directly religion comes home to them in real particulars of whatever kind, they like it not. It suffices them to have seen and praised it; they feel it a burden whenever they feel it at all, whenever it calls upon them to do what otherwise they would not do. In a word, the state of the multitude of men is this—their hearts are going the wrong way; and their real quarrel with religion, if they know themselves, is not that it is strict, or engrossing, or imperative, not that it goes too far, but that it *is* religion. It is religion itself which we all by nature dislike, not the excess merely. Nature tends towards the earth, and God is in heaven. If I want to travel north, and all the roads are cut to the east, of course I shall complain of the roads. I shall find nothing but obstacles; I shall have to surmount walls, and cross rivers, and go round about, and after all fail of my end. Such is the conduct of those who are not bold enough to give up a profession of religion, yet wish to serve the world. They try to reach Babylon by roads which run to Mount Zion. Do you not see that they necessarily must meet with thwartings, crossings, disappointments, and failure? They go mile after mile, watching in vain for the turrets of the City of Vanity, because they are on the wrong road; and, unwilling to own what they are really seeking, they find fault with the road as circuitous and wearisome. They accuse religion of interfering with what they consider their innocent pleasures and wishes. But religion is a bondage only to those who have not the heart to like it, who are not cast into its mold. Accordingly, in the verse before the text, St. Paul thanks God that his brethren had "obeyed from the *heart* that *form* of doctrine into which they had been delivered." We Christians are cast into a certain mold. So far as we keep within it, we are not sensible that it is a mold, or has an outline. It is when our hearts would overflow in some evil direction, then we discover that we are confined, and consider ourselves in prison. It is the law in our members warring against the law of the Spirit which brings us into a distressing bondage. Let us then see where we stand, and what we must do. Heaven cannot change; God is without "variableness, neither shadow of turning." His "word endureth for ever in heaven," his law is from everlasting to everlasting. *We* must change. We must go over to the side of heaven. Never had a soul true happiness but in conformity to God, in obedience to his will. We must become what we are not; we must learn to love what we do not love, and practice ourselves in what is difficult. We must have the law of the Spirit of life written and set up in our hearts, "that the righteousness of the law might be fulfilled in us," and that we may learn to please and to love God.

Lastly, as some men defend their want of strictness on what they consider the authority of Scripture, and others, that is, the majority, try to persuade themselves that religion cannot really be strict, whatever strong expressions or statements may be found in Scripture, others again there are, who take a more candid, but a more daring course. Instead of making excuses, such as I have been considering, they frankly admit the fact, and then go on to urge it as a valid argument against religion altogether. Instead of professing to like religion, *all but* its service, they boldly object that religion is altogether unnatural, and therefore cannot be incumbent on us. They say that it is very well for its ministers and teachers to set up a high doctrine, but that men are men, and the world is the world, and that life was not meant to be a burden, and that God sent us here for enjoyment, and that he will never punish us hereafter for following the law of our nature. I answer, doubtless this life was meant to be enjoyment; but why not a rejoicing in the Lord? We were meant to follow the law of our nature; but why of our old nature, why not of our new? Were we indeed in the state of our first nature, under the guilt and defilement of our birth-sin, then this argument might be urged speciously, though not conclusively of course then; but how does it apply to Christians? Now that God has opened the doors of our prison-house, and brought us into the kingdom of his Son, if men are still carnal men, and the world a sinful world, and the life of angels a burden, and the law of our nature not the law of God, whose fault is it?

We Christians are indeed under the law as other men, but, as I have already said, it is the new law, the law of the Spirit of Christ. We are under grace. That law, which to nature is a grievous bondage, is to those who live under the power of God's presence, what it was meant to be, a rejoicing. When then we feel reluctant to serve God, when thoughts rise within us as if he were a hard master, and that his promises are not attractive enough to balance the strictness of his commandments, let us recollect that we, as being Christians, are not in the flesh, but in the Spirit, and let us act upon the conviction of it. Let us go to him for grace. Let us seek his face. Let us come where he gives grace. Let us come to the ordinances of grace, in which Christ gives his Holy Spirit, to enable us to do that which by nature we cannot do, and to be "the servants of righteousness." They who pray for his saving help to change their likings and dislikings, their tastes, their views, their wills, their hearts, do not indeed all at once gain what they seek—they do not gain it at once asking; they do not *perceive* they gain it while they gain it, but if they come continually day by day to him, if they come humbly, if they come in faith—if they come, not as a trial how they shall like God's service, but throwing (as far as may be) their whole hearts and souls into their duty as a sacrifice to him—if they come, not seeking a sign, but determined to go on seeking him, honoring him, serving him, trusting him, whether they see light, or feel comfort, or discern their growth, or no—such men *will* gain, though they know it not; they will find, even while they are still seeking; before they call, he will answer them, and they will in the end find themselves saved wondrously, to their surprise, how they know not, and when their crown seemed at a distance. "They that wait upon the Lord," says the prophet, "shall renew their strength; they shall mount up with wings as eagles; they shall run, and not be weary; and they shall walk, and not faint." [5]

[5] Isa. 40:31.

# TWO

# Hollow Obedience

## Obedience Without Love, as Instanced in the Character of Balaam

*"The word that God putteth in my mouth, that shall I speak."—*
Num. 22:38

WHEN WE CONSIDER THE
Old Testament as written by divine inspiration, and preserved, beyond the time of its own dispensation, for us Christians—as acknowledged and delivered over to us by Christ
himself, and pronounced by St. Paul to be "profitable for
doctrine, for reproof, for correction, for instruction in righteousness" [1]—we ought not surely to read any portion of it
with indifference, nay, without great and anxious interest.
"Lord, what wilt thou have me to do?" is the sort of inquiry
which spontaneously arises in the serious mind. Christ and his
apostle cannot have put the Law and the Prophets into our
hands for nothing. I would this thought were more carefully
weighed than it commonly is. We profess indeed to revere the
Old Testament; yet, for some reason or other, at least one
considerable part of it, the historical, is regarded by the mass,
even of men who think about religion, as merely historical, as
a relation of facts, as antiquities; not in its divine characters,
not in its practical bearings, not in reference to themselves.
The notion that God speaks in it to them personally, the
question, *"What* does he say?" "What must I *do*?" does not
occur to them. They consider that the Old Testament con-

[1] II Tim. 3:16.

cerns them only as far as it can be made typical of one or two of the great Christian doctrines; they do not consider it in its fullness, and in its literal sense, as a collection of deep moral lessons, such as are not vouchsafed in the New, though St. Paul expressly says that it is "profitable for instruction in righteousness."

If the Old Testament history generally be intended as a permanent instruction to the church, much more, one would think, must such prominent and remarkable passages in it as the history of Balaam. Yet I suspect a very great number of readers carry off little more from it than the impression of the miracle which occurs in it, the speaking of his ass. And not unfrequently they talk more lightly on the subject than is expedient. Yet I think some very solemn and startling lessons may be drawn from the history, some of which I shall now attempt to set before you.

What is it which the chapters in question present to us? The first and most general account of Balaam would be this —that he was a very eminent person in his age and country, that he was courted and gained by the enemies of Israel, and that he promoted a wicked cause in a very wicked way; that, when he could do nothing else for it, he counseled the Moabites to employ their women as means of seducing the chosen people into idolatry; and that he fell in battle in the war which ensued. These are the chief points, the prominent features of his history as viewed at a distance—and repulsive indeed they are. He took on him the office of a tempter, which is especially the Devil's office. But Satan himself does not seem so hateful near as at a distance; and when we look into Balaam's history closely, we shall find points of character which may well interest those who do not consider his beginning and his end. Let us then approach him more nearly, and forget for a moment the summary account of him, which I have just been giving.

Now first he was blessed with God's especial favor. You will ask at once, How could so bad a man be in God's favor? but I wish you to put aside reasonings, and contemplate facts.

81

I say he was especially favored by God; God has a store of favors in his treasure-house, and of various kinds—some for a time, some forever—some implying his approbation, others not. He showers favors even on the bad. He makes his sun to rise on the unjust as well as on the just. He willeth not the death of a sinner. He is said to have loved the young ruler, whose heart, notwithstanding, was upon the world. His loving-mercy extends over all his works. How he separates in his own divine thought, kindness from approbation, time from eternity, what he does from what he foresees, we know not and need not inquire. At present he is loving to all men, as if he did not foresee that some are to be saints, others reprobates to all eternity. He dispenses his favors variously—gifts, graces, rewards, faculties, circumstances being indefinitely diversified, nor admitting of discrimination or numbering on our part. Balaam, I say, was in his favor; not indeed for his holiness' sake, not forever; but in a certain sense, according to His inscrutable purpose—who chooses whom he will choose, and exalts whom he will exalt, without destroying man's secret responsibilities or his own governance, and the triumph of truth and holiness, and his own strict impartiality in the end. Balaam was favored in an especial way above the mere heathen. Not only had he the grant of inspiration, and the knowledge of God's will, an insight into the truths of morality, clear and enlarged, such as even we Christians cannot surpass; but he was even admitted to conscious inter-course with God, such as we Christians have not. In our Sunday services, you may recollect, we read the chapters which relate to this intercourse; and we do not read those which record the darker passages of his history. Now, do you not think that most persons, who know only so much of him as our Sunday lessons contain, form a very mild judgment about him? They see him indeed to be on the wrong side, but still view him as a prophet of God. Such a judgment is not incorrect as far as it goes; and I appeal to it, if it be what I think it is, as a testimony how highly Balaam was in God's favor.

But again, Balaam was, in the ordinary and commonly received sense of the word, without straining its meaning at all, a very conscientious man. That this is so, will be plain from some parts of his conduct and some speeches of his, of which I proceed to remind you; and which will show also his enlightened and admirable view of moral and religious obligation. When Balak sent to him to call him to curse Israel, he did not make up his mind for himself, as many a man might do, or according to the suggestions of avarice and ambition. No, he brought the matter before God in prayer. He *prayed* before he did what he did, as a religious man ought to do. Next, when God forbade his going, he at once, as he ought, positively refused to go. "Get you into your land," he said, "for the Lord refuseth to give me leave to go with you." Balak sent again a more pressing message and more lucrative offers, and Balaam was even more decided than before. "If Balak," he said, "would give me his house full of silver and gold, I cannot go beyond the word of the Lord my God, to do less or more." Afterwards God gave him leave to go. "If the men come to call thee, rise up, and go with them." [2] Then, and not till then, he went.

Almighty God added, "Yet the word which I shall say unto thee, that shalt thou do." Now, in the next place, observe how strictly he obeyed this command. When he first met Balak, he said, in the words of the text, "Lo, I am come unto thee: have I now any power at all to say anything? the word that God putteth in my mouth, that shall I speak." Again, when he was about to prophesy, he said, "Whatsoever he sheweth me I will tell thee";[3] and he did so, in spite of Balak's disappointment and mortification to hear him bless Israel. When Balak showed his impatience, he only replied calmly, "Must I not take heed to speak that which the Lord hath put in my mouth?" Again he prophesied, and again it was a blessing; again Balak was angered, and again the prophet firmly and serenely answered, "Told not I thee, saying, All that the Lord

[2] Num. 22.
[3] Num. 23.

83

speaketh, that I must do?" A third time he prophesied blessing; and now Balak's anger was kindled, and he smote his hands together, and bade him depart to his place. But Balaam was not thereby moved from his duty. "The wrath of a king is as messengers of death." [4] Balak might have instantly revenged himself upon the prophet; but Balaam, not satisfied with blessing Israel, proceeded, as a prophet should, to deliver himself of what remained of the prophetic burden, by foretelling more pointedly than before, destruction to Moab and the other enemies of the chosen people. He prefaced his prophecy with these unacceptable words—

> Spake I not also to thy messengers which thou sentest unto me, saying, If Balak would give me his house full of silver and gold, I cannot go beyond the commandment of the Lord, to do either good or bad of mine own mind; but what the Lord saith, that will I speak? And now, behold, I go unto my people: come, therefore, and I will advertise thee what this people shall do to thy people in the latter days.

After delivering his conscience, he "rose up, and went and returned to his place."

All this surely expresses the conduct and the feelings of a high-principled, honorable, conscientious man. Balaam, I say, was certainly such, in that very sense in which we commonly use those words. He said, and he did; he professed, and he acted according to his professions. There is no inconsistency in word and deed. He obeys as well as talks about religion; and this being the case, we shall feel more intimately the value of the following noble sentiments which he lets drop from time to time, and which, if he had shown less firmness in his conduct, might have passed for mere words, the words of a maker of speeches, a sophist, moralist, or orator. "Let me die the death of the righteous, and let my last end be like his!" "God is not a man, that he should lie; neither the son of man, that he should repent. . . . Behold, I have received commandment to bless: and he hath blessed; and I cannot

[4] Prov. 16:14.

reverse it." "I shall see him, but not now: I shall behold him, but not nigh." It is remarkable that these declarations are great and lofty in their mode of expression; and the saying of his recorded by the prophet Micah is of the same kind. Balak asked what sacrifices were acceptable to God. Balaam answered "He hath shewed thee, O man, what is good; and what doth the Lord require of thee, but to do justly, and to love mercy, and to walk humbly with thy God?" [5]

Viewing then the inspired notices concerning Balaam in all their parts, we cannot deny to him the praise which, if those notices have a plain meaning, they certainly do convey that he was an honorable and religious man, with a great deal of what was great and noble about him; a man whom any one of us at first sight would have trusted, sought out in our difficulties, perhaps made the head of a party, and anyhow spoken of with great respect. We may indeed, if we please, say that he fell away afterwards from all this excellence: though, after all, there is something shocking in such a notion. Nay, it is not natural even that ordinarily honorable men should suddenly change; but however this *may* be said—it may be said he fell away; but, I presume, it *cannot* be said that he was other than a high-principled man (in the language of the world) *when* he so spoke and acted.

But now the strange thing is, that at this very time, *while* he so spoke and acted, he seems, as in one sense to be in God's favor, so in another and higher to be under his displeasure. If this be so, the supposition that he fell away will not be in point; the difficulty it proposes to solve will remain; for it will turn out that he was displeasing to God *amid* his many excellences. The passage I have in mind is this, as you will easily suppose. "God's anger was kindled because he went" with the princes of Moab; "and the angel of the Lord stood in the way for an adversary against him." Afterwards, when God opened his eyes, "he saw the angel of the Lord standing in the way, and his sword drawn in his hand" . . . "And Balaam

[5] Mic. 6:8.

said, I have *sinned;* for I knew not that thou stoodest in the way against me: now therefore, if it displease thee, I will get me back again." You observe Balaam said, "I have sinned," *though* he avers he did not *know* that God was his adversary. What makes the whole transaction the more strange is this— that Almighty God had said before, "If the men come to call thee, rise up, and go with them"; and that when Balaam offered to go back again, the angel repeated, "Go with the men." And afterwards we find in the midst of his heathen enchantments "God met Balaam," and "put a word in his mouth"; and afterwards "the spirit of God came upon him."

Summing up then what has been said, we seem, in Balaam's history, to have the following remarkable case, that is, re-markable according to our customary judgment of things: a man divinely favored, visited, influenced, guided, protected, eminently honored, illuminated—a man possessed of an en-lightened sense of duty, and of moral and religious acquire-ments, educated, high-minded, conscientious, honorable, firm; and yet on the side of God's enemies, personally under God's displeasure, and in the end (if we go on to that) the direct instrument of Satan, and having his portion with the unbelievers. I do not think I have materially overstated any part of this description; but if it be correct only in substance, it certainly is most fearful, after allowing for incidental exag-geration—most fearful to every one of us, the more fearful the more we are conscious to ourselves in the main of purity of intention in what we do, and conscientious adherence to our sense of duty.

And now it is natural to ask, what is the *meaning* of this startling exhibition of God's ways? Is it really possible that a conscientious and religious man should be found among the enemies of God, nay, should be personally displeasing to him, and that at the very time God was visiting him with extraor-dinary favor? What a mystery is this! Surely, if this be so, revelation has added to our perplexities, not relieved them! What instruction, what profit, what correction, what doctrine is there in such portions of inspired Scripture?

In answering this difficulty, I observe in the first place that it certainly is impossible, quite impossible, that a really conscientious man should be displeasing to God; at the same time it is possible to be *generally* conscientious, or what the world calls honorable and high-principled, yet to be destitute of that religious fear and strictness, which God calls conscientiousness, but which the world calls superstition or narrowness of mind. And bearing this in mind, we shall, perhaps, have a solution of our perplexities concerning Balaam.

And here I would make a remark: that when a passage of Scripture, descriptive of God's dealings with man, is obscure or perplexing, it is as well to ask ourselves whether this may not be owing to some insensibility, in ourselves or in our age, to certain peculiarities of the divine law or government therein involved. Thus, to those who do not understand the nature and history of religious truth, our Lord's assertion about sending a sword on earth is an obscurity. To those who consider sin a light evil, the doctrine of eternal punishment is a difficulty. In like manner the history of the flood, of the call of Abraham, of the plagues of Egypt, of the wandering in the desert, of the judgment on Korah, Dathan, and Abiram, and a multitude of other occurrences, may be insuperable difficulties, except to certain states and tempers of mind, to which, on the contrary, they will seem quite natural and obvious. I consider that the history of Balaam is a striking illustration of this remark. Those whose hearts, like Josiah's, are "tender," scrupulous, sensitive in religious matters, will see with clearness and certainty what the real state of the case was as regards him; on the other hand, our difficulties about it, if we have them, are a presumption that the age we live in has not the key to a certain class of divine providences, is deficient in a certain class of religious principles, ideas, and sensibilities. Let it be considered, then, whether the following remarks may not tend to lessen our perplexity.

Balaam obeyed God from a sense of its being right to do so, but not from a *desire to please him*, not from *fear and love*. He had other ends, aims, wishes of his own, distinct from God's will and purpose, and he would have effected these if he could. His endeavor was not to please God, but to please self without displeasing God; to pursue his own ends *as far* as was consistent with his duty. In a word, he did not give his heart to God, but obeyed him, as a man may obey human law, or observe the usages of society or his country, as something external to himself, because he knows he ought to do so, from a sort of rational good sense, a conviction of its propriety, expediency, or comfort, as the case may be.

You will observe he *wished* to go with Balak's messengers, only he felt he *ought not* to go; and the problem which he attempted to solve was *how* to go and yet not offend God. He was quite resolved he *would* anyhow act religiously and conscientiously; he was too honorable a man to break any of his engagements; if he had given his word, it was sacred; if he had duties, they were imperative: he had a character to maintain, and an inward sense of propriety to satisfy; but he would have given the world to have gotten rid of his duties; and the question was *how* to do so without violence; and he did not care about walking on the very brink of transgression, so that he could keep from falling over. Accordingly he was not content with *ascertaining* God's will, but he attempted to *change* it. He inquired of him a *second time,* and this was to tempt him. Hence, while God bade him go, his anger was kindled against him because he went.

This surely is no uncommon character; rather, it is the common case even with the more respectable and praiseworthy portion of the community. I say plainly, and without fear of contradiction, though it is a serious thing to say, that the aim of most men esteemed conscientious and religious, or who are what is called honorable, upright men, is, to all appearance, not how to please God, but how to please themselves without displeasing him. I say confidently—that is, if we may judge of men in general by what we see—that they make this world the first object in their minds, and use religion as a corrective, a restraint, upon *too much* attachment to the world. They think that religion is a negative thing, a sort of moderate love of the world, a moderate luxury, a moderate avarice, a moderate ambition, and a moderate selfishness. You see this in numberless ways. You see it in the course of trade, of public life, of literature, in all matters where men have objects to pursue. Nay, you see it in religious exertions; of which it too commonly happens that the chief aim is to attain *anyhow* a certain definite end, religious indeed, but of man's own choosing; not to please God, and *next*, if possible, to attain it; not to attain it religiously, or not at all.

This surely is so plain that it is scarcely necessary to enlarge upon it. Men do not take for the object towards which they act, God's will, but certain maxims, rules, or measures, right perhaps as far as they go, but defective because they admit of being subjected to certain other ultimate ends, which are not religious. Men are just, honest, upright, trustworthy; but all this not from the love and fear of God, but from a mere feeling of obligation to be so, and in subjection to certain worldly objects. And thus they are what is popularly called moral, without being religious. Such was Balaam. He was in a popular sense a strictly moral, honorable, conscientious man; that he was not so in a heavenly and true sense is plain, if not from the considerations here insisted on, at least from his after-history, which (we may presume) brought to light his secret defect, in whatever it consisted.

And here we see why he spoke so much and so vauntingly of his determination to follow God's direction. He made a great *point* of following it; his end was not to please God, but to keep straight with him. He who loves does not act from calculation or reasoning; he does not in his cool moments reflect upon or talk of what he is doing, as if it were a great sacrifice. Much less does he pride himself on it; but this is what Balaam seems to have done.

I have been observing that his defect lay in this, that he had not a single eye towards God's will, but was ruled by other objects. But moreover, this evil heart of unbelief showed itself in a peculiar way, to which it is necessary to draw your attention, and to which I alluded just now in saying that the difficulties of Scripture often arose from the defective moral condition of our hearts.

*Why* did Almighty God give Balaam leave to go to Balak, and then was angry with him for going? I suppose for this reason, because his asking twice was tempting God. God is a jealous God. Sinners as we are, nay as creatures of his hands, we may not safely intrude upon him, and make free with him. We may not dare to do that, which we should not dare to do with an earthly superior, which we should be punished, for instance, for attempting in the case of a king or noble of this world. To rush into His presence, to address him familiarly, to urge him, to strive to make our duty lie in one direction when it lies in another, to handle rudely and practice upon his holy word, to trifle with truth, to treat conscience lightly, to take liberties (as it may be called) with anything that is God's, all irreverence, profaneness, unscrupulousness, wantonness, is represented in Scripture not only as a sin, but as felt, noticed, quickly returned on God's part (if I may dare use such human words of the almighty and all-holy God, without transgressing the rule I am myself laying down—but he vouchsafes in Scripture to represent himself to us in that only way in which we can attain to the knowledge of him), I say all irreverence towards God is represented as being jealously and instantly and fearfully noticed and visited, as friend or stranger among men might resent an insult shown him. This should be carefully considered; we are apt to act towards God and the things of God as towards a mere system, a law, a name, a religion, a principle, not as against a person, a living, watchful, present, prompt and powerful eye and arm. That all this is a great error, is plain to all who study Scripture; as is sufficiently shown by the death of that multitude of persons for looking into the ark—the death of the prophet by the lion, who was sent to Jeroboam from Judah, and did not minutely obey the instructions given him—the slaughter of the children at Bethel by the bears, for mocking Elisha—the exclusion of Moses from the promised land, for smiting the rock twice—and the judgment on Ananias and Sapphira. Now Balaam's fault seems to have been of this nature. God told him distinctly not to go to Balak. He was rash enough to ask a second time, and God as a punishment gave him leave to ally himself with His enemies, and to take part against His people. With this presumptuousness and love of self in his innermost heart, his prudence, firmness, wisdom, illumination, and general conscientiousness availed him nothing.

A number of reflections crowd upon the mind on the review of this awful history, as I may well call it; and with a brief notice of some of these I shall conclude.

(1) First, we see how little we can depend, in judging of right and wrong, on the apparent excellence and high character of individuals. There *is* a right and a wrong in matters of conduct, in spite of the world; but it is the world's aim and Satan's aim to take our minds off from the indelible distinctions of things, and to fix our thoughts upon man, to make us the slaves of man, to make us dependent on his opinion, his patronage, his honor, his smiles, and his frowns. But if Scripture is to be our guide, it is quite plain that the most conscientious, religious, high-principled, honorable men (I use the words in their ordinary, not in their scriptural sense), may be on the side of evil, may be Satan's instruments in cursing, if that were possible, and at least in seducing and enfeebling the people of God. For in the world's judgment, even when most refined, a person is conscientious and consistent, who acts up to his standard, *whatever that is*, not he only who aims at taking the highest standard. This is the world's highest flight; but in its ordinary judgment, a man is conscientious and consistent, who is only inconsistent and goes against conscience in any extremity, when hardly beset, and when he must cut the knot or remain in present difficulties. That is, *he* is thought to obey conscience, who only disobeys it when it is a praise and merit to obey it. This, alas! is the way with some of the most honorable of mere men of the world, nay of the mass of (so-called) respectable men. They never tell untruths, or break their word, or profane the Lord's Day, or are dishonest in trade, or falsify their principles, or insult religion, except in

91

very great straits or great emergencies, when driven into a corner; and then perhaps they force themselves, as Saul did when he offered sacrifice instead of Samuel—they force themselves, and (as it were) undergo their sin as a sort of unpleasant self-denial or penance, being ashamed of it all the while, getting it over as quickly as they can, shutting their eyes and leaping blindfolded, and then forgetting it, as something which is bitter to think about. And if memory is ever roused and annoys them, they console themselves that after all they have only gone against their conscience now and then. This is their view of themselves and of each other, taken at advantage; and if anyone come across them who has lived more out of the world than themselves, and has a truer sense of right and wrong, and who fastens on some one point in them, which to his mind is a token and warning to himself against them, such a one seems, of course, narrow-minded and over-strict in his notions. For instance; supposing some such man had fallen in with Balaam, and had been privy to the history of his tempting God, it is clear that Balaam's general correctness, his nobleness of demeanor, and his enlightened view of duty, would not have availed one jot or tittle to overcome such a man's repugnance to him. He would have been startled and alarmed, and would have kept at a distance, and in consequence he would have been called by the world uncharitable and bigoted.

(2) A second reflection which rises in the mind has relation to the wonderful secret providence of God, while all things seem to go on according to the course of this world. Balaam did not see the angel, yet the angel went out against him as an adversary. He had no open denunciation of God's wrath directed against him. He had sinned, and nothing happened outwardly, but wrath was abroad and in his path. *This* again is a very serious and awful thought. God's arm is not shortened. What happened to Balaam is as if it took place yesterday. God is what he ever was; we sin as man has ever sinned. We sin without being aware of it. God is our enemy without our being aware of it; and when the blow falls, we

turn our thoughts to the creature, we ill-treat our ass, we lay the blame on circumstances of this world, instead of turning to him. "Lord, when thy hand is lifted up, they will not see: but they shall see," in the next world if not here, "and be ashamed for their envy at the people; yea, the fire of thine enemies shall devour them." [6]

(3) Here too is a serious reflection, if we had time to pursue it, that when we have begun an evil course, we cannot retrace our steps. Balaam was forced to go with the men; he offered to draw back—he was not allowed—yet God's wrath followed him. This is what comes of committing ourselves to an evil line of conduct; and we see daily instances of it in our experience of life. Men get entangled, and are bound hand and foot in unadvisable courses. They make imprudent marriages or connections; they place themselves in dangerous situations; they engage in unprofitable or harmful undertakings. Too often indeed they do not discern their evil plight; but when they do, they cannot draw back. God seems to say, "Go with the men." They are in bondage, and they must make the best of it; being the slave of the creature, without ceasing to be the responsible servants of God; under his displeasure, yet bound to act as if they could please him. All this is very fearful.

(4) Lastly, I will but say this in addition—God gives us warnings now and then, but does not repeat them. Balaam's sin consisted in not acting upon what was told him *once for all*. In like manner, you, my brethren, now hear what you may never hear again, and what perchance in its substance is the word of God. You may never hear it again, though with your outward ears you hear it a hundred times, because you may be impressed with it now, but never may again. You may be impressed with it now, and the impression may die away; and some time hence, if you ever think about it, you may then speak of it thus—that the view struck you at the time, but somehow the more you thought about it, the less you liked or valued it. True; this *may* be so, and it *may* arise, as you think,

[6] Isa. 26:11.

from the doctrine I have been setting before you not being true and scriptural; but it *may* also arise from your having heard God's voice and not obeyed it. It may be that you have become blind, not the doctrine been disproved. Beware of trifling with your conscience. It is often said that second thoughts are best; so they are in matters of judgment, but not in matters of conscience. In matters of duty first thoughts are commonly best—they have more in them of the voice of God. May he give you grace so to hear what has been said, as you will wish to have heard, when life is over; to hear in a practical way, with a desire to profit by it, to learn God's will, and to do it!

# THREE

# The Centrality
# of Charity

## Love, the One Thing Needful

*"Though I speak with the tongues of men and of angels, and have not charity, I am become as sounding brass, or a tinkling cymbal."*
—I Cor. 13:1

I SUPPOSE THE GREATER number of persons who try to live Christian lives, and who observe themselves with any care, are dissatisfied with their own state on this point, viz., that, whatever their religious attainments may be, yet they feel that their motive is not the highest—that the love of God, and of man for His sake, is not their ruling principle. They may do much, nay, if it so happen, they may suffer much; but they have little reason to think that they love much, that they do and suffer for love's sake. I do not mean that they thus express themselves exactly, but that they are dissatisfied with themselves, and that when this dissatisfaction is examined into, it will be found ultimately to come to this, though they will give different accounts of it. They may call themselves cold, or hardhearted, or fickle, or double-minded, or doubting, or dim-sighted, or weak in resolve, but they mean pretty much the same thing, that their affections do not rest on Almighty God as their great object. And this will be found to be the complaint of religious men among ourselves, not less than others; their reason and their heart not going together; their reason tending heavenwards, and their heart earthwards.

I will now make some remarks on the defect I have described, as thinking that the careful consideration of it may serve as one step towards its removal.

Love, and love only, is the fulfilling of the law, and they only are in God's favor in whom the righteousness of the law is fulfilled. This we know full well; yet, alas! at the same time, we cannot deny that whatever good thing we have to show, whether activity, or patience, or faith, or fruitfulness in good works, love to God and man is not ours, or, at least, in very scanty measure; not at all proportionately to our apparent attainments. Now, to enlarge upon this.

In the first place, love clearly does not consist merely in great sacrifices. We can take no comfort to ourselves that we are God's own, merely on the ground of great deeds or great sufferings. The greatest sacrifices without love would be nothing worth, and that they are great does not necessarily prove they are done with love. St. Paul emphatically assures us that his acceptance with God did not stand in any of those high endowments, which strike us in him at first sight, and which, did we actually see him, doubtless would so much draw us to him. One of his highest gifts, for instance, was his spiritual knowledge. He shared, and felt the sinfulness and infirmities of human nature; he had a deep insight into the glories of God's grace, such as no natural man can have. He had an awful sense of the realities of heaven, and of the mysteries revealed. He could have answered ten thousand questions on theological subjects, on all those points about which the church has disputed since his time, and which we now long to ask him. He was a man whom one could not come near without going away from him wiser than one came; a fount of knowledge and wisdom ever full, ever approachable, ever flowing, from which all who came in faith gained a measure of the gifts which God had lodged in him. His presence inspired resolution, confidence, and zeal, as one who was the keeper of secrets, and the revealer of the whole counsel of

God; and who, by look, and word, and deed encompassed, as it were, his brethren with God's mercies and judgments, spread abroad and reared aloft the divine system of doctrine and precept, and seated himself and them securely in the midst of it. Such was this great servant of Christ and teacher of the Gentiles; yet he says, "Though I speak with the tongues of men and of angels, though I have the gift of prophecy, and understand all mysteries, and all knowledge, and have not charity, I am become as sounding brass, or a tinkling cymbal. . . . I am nothing." Spiritual discernment, an insight into the gospel covenant, is no evidence of love.

Another distinguishing mark of his character, as viewed in Scripture, is his faith, a prompt, decisive, simple assent to God's word, a deadness to motives of earth, a firm hold of the truths of the unseen world, and keenness in following them out; yet he says of his faith also, "Though I have all faith, so that I could remove mountains, and have not charity, I am nothing." Faith is no necessary evidence of love.

A tender consideration of the temporal wants of his brethren is another striking feature of his character, as it is a special characteristic of every true Christian; yet he says, "Though I bestow all my goods to feed the poor, and have not charity, it profiteth me nothing." Self-denying almsgiving is no necessary evidence of love.

Once more. He, if any man, had the spirit of a martyr; yet he implies that even martyrdom, viewed in itself, is no passport into the heavenly kingdom. "Though I give my body to be burned, and have not charity, it profiteth me nothing." Martyrdom is no necessary evidence of love.

I do not say that at this day we have many specimens or much opportunity of such high deeds and attainments; but in our degree we certainly may follow St. Paul in them—in spiritual discernment, in faith, in works of mercy, and in confessorship. We may, we ought, to follow him. Yet though we do, still, it may be, we are not possessed of the one thing needful, of the spirit of love, or in a very poor measure; and this is what serious men feel in their own case.

Let us leave these sublimer matters, and proceed to the humbler and continual duties of daily life; and let us see whether these too may not be performed with considerable exactness, yet with deficient love. Surely they may; and serious men complain of themselves here, even more than when they are exercised on greater subjects. Our Lord says, "If ye love me, keep my commandments"; but they feel that though they are, to a certain point, keeping God's commandments, yet love is not proportionate, does not keep pace, with their obedience; that obedience springs from some source short of love. This they perceive; they feel themselves to be hollow; a fair outside, without a spirit within it.

I mean as follows: It is possible to obey, not from love towards God and man, but from a sort of conscientiousness short of love; from some notion of acting up to a *law;* that is, more from the fear of God than from love of him. Surely this is what, in one shape or other, we see daily on all sides of us; the case of men, living to the world, yet not without a certain sense of religion, which acts as a restraint on them. They pursue ends of this world, but not to the full; they are checked, and go a certain way only, because they dare not go further. This external restraint acts with various degrees of strength on various persons. They all live to this world, and act from the love of it; they all allow their love of the world a certain range; but, at some particular point, which is often quite arbitrary, this man stops, and that man stops. Each stops at a different point in the course of the world, and thinks everyone else profane who goes further, and superstitious who does not go so far—laughs at the latter, is shocked at the former. And hence those few who are miserable enough to have rid themselves of all scruples, look with great contempt on such of their companions as have any, be those scruples more or less, as being inconsistent and absurd. They scoff at the principle of mere fear, as a capricious and fanciful principle; proceeding on no rule, and having no evidence of its authority, no claim on our respect; as a weakness in our nature, rather than an essential portion of that nature, viewed in its perfection and entireness. And this being all the notion which their experience gives them of religion, as not knowing really religious men, they think of religion only as a principle which interferes with our enjoyments unintelligibly and irrationally. Man is made to love. So far is plain. They see that clearly and truly; but religion, as far as they conceive of it, is a system of fear. It repels and forbids, and thus seems to destroy the proper function of man, or, in other words, to be unnatural. And it is true that this sort of fear of God, or rather slavish dread, as it may more truly be called, *is* unnatural; but then it is not religion, which really consists, not in the mere fear of God, but in his love; or if it be religion, it is but the religion of devils, who believe and tremble; or of idolaters, whom devils have seduced, and whose worship is superstition—the attempt to appease beings whom they love not; and, in a word, the religion of the children of this world, who would, if possible, serve God and mammon, and, whereas religion consists of love *and* fear, give to God their fear, and to mammon their love.

And what takes place so generally in the world at large, this, I say, serious men will feel as happening, in its degree, in their own case. They will understand that even strict obedience is no evidence of fervent love, and they will lament to perceive that they obey God far more than they love him. They will recollect the instance of Balaam, who was even exemplary in his obedience, yet had not love; and the thought will come over them as a perplexity, what proof they have that they are not, after all, deceiving themselves, and thinking themselves religious when they are not. They will indeed be conscious to themselves of the sacrifice they make of their own wishes and pursuits to the will of God; but they are conscious also that they sacrifice them because they know they *ought* to do so, not simply from love of God. And they ask, almost in a kind of despair, how are we to learn, not merely to obey, but to love?

They say, how are we to fulfill St. Paul's words, "The life which I now live in the flesh I live by the faith of the Son of

God, who loved me, and gave himself for me"? And this would seem an especial difficulty in the case of those who live among men, whose duties lie amid the engagements of this world's business, whose thoughts, affections, exertions, are directed towards things which they see, things present and temporal. In their case it seems to be a great thing, even if their *rule* of life is a heavenly one, if they *act* according to God's will; but how can they hope that heavenly objects should fill their heart, when there is no room left for them? How shall things absent displace things present, things unseen the things that are visible? Thus they seem to be reduced, as if by a sort of necessity, to that state, which I just now described as the state of men of the world, that of having their hearts set on the world, and being only restrained outwardly by religious rules.

To proceed. Generally speaking, men will be able to bring against themselves positive charges of want of love, more unsatisfactory still. I suppose most men, or at least a great number of men, have to lament over their hardness of heart, which, when analyzed, will be found to be nothing else but the absence of love. I mean that hardness which, for instance, makes us unable to repent as we wish. No repentance is truly such without love; it is love which gives it its efficacy in God's sight. Without love there may be remorse, regret, self-reproach, self-condemnation, but there is not saving penitence. There may be conviction of the reason, but not conversion of the heart. Now, I say, a great many men lament in themselves this want of love in repenting; they are hard-hearted; they are deeply conscious of their sins; they abhor them; and yet they can take as lively an interest in what goes on around them as if they had no such consciousness; or they mourn this minute, and the next are quite impenetrable. Or, though, as they think and believe, they fear God's anger, and are full of confusion at themselves, yet they find (to their surprise, I may say) that they cannot abstain from any indulgence ever so trivial, which would be (as their reason tells them) a natural way of showing sorrow. They eat and drink with as good a heart as if they had no distress upon their minds; they find no difficulty in entering into any of the recreations or secular employments which come in their way. They sleep as soundly; and, in spite of their grief, perhaps find it most difficult to persuade themselves to rise early to pray for pardon. These are signs of want of love.

Or, again, without reference to the case of penitence, they have a general indisposition towards prayer and other exercises of devotion. They find it most difficult to get themselves to pray; most difficult, too, to rouse their minds to attend to their prayers. At very best they do but feel satisfaction in devotion *while* they are engaged in it. Then perhaps they find a real pleasure in it, and wonder that they can ever find it irksome; yet if any chance throws them out of their habitual exercises, they find it most difficult to return to them. They do not like them well enough to seek them *from* liking them. They are kept in them by habit, by regularity in observing them; not by love. When the regular course is broken, there is no inward principle to act at once in repairing the mischief. In wounds of the body, nature works towards a recovery, and, left to itself, would recover; but we have no spiritual principle strong and healthy enough to set religious matters right in us when they have got disordered, and to supply for us the absence of rule and custom. Here, again, is obedience, more or less mechanical, or without love.

Again—a like absence of love is shown in our proneness to be taken up and engrossed with trifles. Why is it that we are so open to the power of excitement? Why is it that we are looking out for novelties? Why is it that we complain of want of variety in a religious life? Why is it that we cannot bear to go on in an ordinary round of duties year after year? Why is it that lowly duties, such as condescending to men of low estate, are distasteful and irksome? Why is it that we need powerful preaching, or interesting and touching books, in order to keep our thoughts and feelings on God? Why is it that our faith is so dispirited and weakened by hearing casual objections urged against the doctrine of Christ? Why is it that we are so impatient that objections should be answered? Why are we so afraid of worldly events, or the opinions of men? Why do we so dread their censure or ridicule?—Clearly because we are deficient in love. He who loves cares little for anything else. The world may go as it will; he sees and hears it not, for his thoughts are drawn another way; he is solicitous mainly to walk with God, and to be found with God; and is in perfect peace because he is stayed in him.

And here we have an additional proof of how weak our love is; viz., when we consider how little adequate our professed principles are found to be, to support us in affliction. I suppose it often happens to men to feel this, when some reverse or unexpected distress comes upon them. They indeed most especially will feel it, of course, who have let their words, nay their thoughts, much outrun their hearts; but numbers will feel it too, who have tried to make their reason and affections keep pace with each other. We are told of the righteous man, that "he shall not be afraid of evil tidings," for "his heart is fixed, trusting in the Lord. His heart is established, he shall not be afraid." [1] Such must be the case of everyone who realizes his own words, when he talks of the shortness of life, the wearisomeness of the world, and the security of heaven. Yet how cold and dreary do all such topics prove, when a man comes into trouble? And why, except that he has been after all set upon things visible, not on God, while he has been speaking of things invisible? There has been much profession and little love.

These are some of the proofs which are continually brought home to us, if we attend to ourselves, of our want of love to God; and they will readily suggest others to us. If I must, before concluding, remark upon the mode of overcoming the evil, I must say plainly this, that, fanciful though it may appear at first sight to say so, the comforts of life are the main cause of it; and, much as we may lament and struggle against it, till we learn to dispense with them in good measure, we shall not overcome it. Till we, in a certain sense,

[1] Ps. 112:7–8.

detach ourselves from our bodies, our minds will not be in a state to receive divine impressions, and to exert heavenly aspirations. A smooth and easy life, an uninterrupted enjoyment of the goods of providence, full meals, soft raiment, well-furnished homes, the pleasures of sense, the feeling of security, the consciousness of wealth—these, and the like, if we are not careful, choke up all the avenues of the soul, through which the light and breath of heaven might come to us. A hard life is, alas! no certain method of becoming spiritually minded, but it is one out of the means by which Almighty God makes us so. We must, at least at seasons, defraud ourselves of nature, if we would not be defrauded of grace. If we attempt to force our minds into a loving and devotional temper, without this preparation, it is too plain what will follow —the grossness and coarseness, the affectation, the effeminacy, the unreality, the presumption, the hollowness (suffer me, my brethren, while I say plainly, but seriously, what I mean), in a word, what Scripture calls the hypocrisy, which we see around us; that state of mind in which the reason, seeing what we should be, and the conscience enjoining it, and the heart being unequal to it, some pretence or other is set up, by way of compromise, that men may say, "Peace, peace," when there is no peace.

And next, after enjoining this habitual preparation of heart, let me bid you cherish, what otherwise it were shocking to attempt, a constant sense of the love of your Lord and Savior in dying on the cross for you. "The love of Christ," says the apostle, "constraineth us"; not that gratitude leads to love, where there is no sympathy (for, as all know, we often reproach ourselves with not loving persons who yet have loved us), but where hearts are in their degree renewed after Christ's image, there, under his grace, gratitude to him will increase our love of him, and we shall rejoice in that goodness which has been so good to us. Here, again, self-discipline will be necessary. It makes the heart tender as well as reverent. Christ showed his love in deed, not in word, and you will be touched by the thought of his cross far more by bearing it after him, than by glowing accounts of it. All the modes by which you bring it before you must be simple and severe; "excellency of speech," or "enticing words," to use St. Paul's language, is the worst way of any. Think of the cross when you rise and when you lie down, when you go out and when you come in, when you eat and when you walk and when you converse, when you buy and when you sell, when you labor and when you rest, consecrating and sealing all your doings with this one mental action, the thought of the Crucified. Do not talk of it to others; be silent, like the penitent woman, who showed her love in deep subdued acts. She "stood at his feet behind him weeping, and began to wash his feet with tears, and did wipe them with the hairs of her head, and kissed his feet, and anointed them with the ointment." And Christ said of her, "Her sins, which are many, are forgiven; for she loved much: but to whom little is forgiven, the same loveth little." [2]

And, further, let us dwell often upon those his manifold mercies to us and to our brethren, which are the consequence of his coming upon earth; his adorable counsels, as manifested in our personal election—how it is that we are called and others not; the wonders of his grace towards us, from our infancy until now; the gifts he has given us; the aid he has vouchsafed; the answers he has accorded to our prayers. And, further, let us, as far as we have the opportunity, meditate upon his dealings with his church from age to age; on his faithfulness to his promises, and the mysterious mode of their fulfillment; how he has ever led his people forward safely and prosperously on the whole amid so many enemies; what unexpected events have worked his purposes; how evil has been changed into good; how his sacred truth has ever been preserved unimpaired; how saints have been brought on to their perfection in the darkest times. And, further, let us muse over the deep gifts and powers lodged in the church: what thoughts do his ordinances raise in the believing mind!—what wonder, what awe, what transport, when duly dwelt upon!

[2] Luke 7:38, 47.

It is by such deeds and such thoughts that our services, our repentings, our prayers, our intercourse with men, will become instinct with the spirit of love. Then we do everything thankfully and joyfully, when we are temples of Christ, with his image set up in us. Then it is that we mix with the world without loving it, for our affections are given to another. We can bear to look on the world's beauty, for we have no heart for it. We are not disturbed at its frowns, for we live not in its smiles. We rejoice in the house of prayer, because he is there "whom our soul loveth." We can condescend to the poor and lowly, for they are the presence of him who is invisible. We are patient in bereavement, adversity, or pain, for they are Christ's tokens.

Thus let us enter the forty days of Lent now approaching. For forty days we seek after love by means of fasting. May we find it more and more, the older we grow, till death comes and gives us the sight of Him who is at once its object and its author.

# FOUR

# The Joy of Christian Risk

## The Ventures of Faith

*"They say unto him, We are able."*—Matt. 20:22

THESE WORDS OF THE
holy apostles James and John were in reply to a very solemn
question addressed to them by their divine master. They coveted, with a noble ambition, though as yet unpracticed in the
highest wisdom, untaught in the holiest truth—they coveted
to sit beside him on his throne of glory. They would be content with nothing short of that special gift which he had come
to grant to his elect, which he shortly after died to purchase
for them, and which he offers to us. They ask the gift of
eternal life; and he in answer told them, not that they should
have it (though for them it was really reserved), but he reminded them what they *must venture for it*: "Are ye able to
drink of the cup that I shall drink of, and to be baptized with
the baptism that I am baptized with? They say unto him, We
are able." Here then a great lesson is impressed upon us, that
our duty as Christians lies in this, in making ventures for
eternal life without the absolute certainty of success.

Success and reward everlasting they will have, who persevere unto the end. Doubt we cannot that the ventures of all
Christ's servants must be returned to them at the Last Day

with abundant increase. This is a true saying—he returns far more than we lend to him, and without fail. But I am speaking of individuals, of ourselves one by one. No one among us knows for certain that he himself will persevere; yet everyone among us, to give himself even a chance of success at all, must make a venture. As regards individuals, then, it is quite true that all of us must for certain make ventures for heaven, yet without the certainty of success through them. This, indeed, is the very meaning of the word "venture"; for that is a strange venture which has nothing in it of fear, risk, danger, anxiety, uncertainty. Yes; so it certainly is; and in this consists the excellence and nobleness of *faith;* this is the very reason why *faith* is singled out from other graces, and honored as the especial means of our justification, because its presence implies that we have the heart to make a venture.

St. Paul sufficiently sets this before us in the eleventh chapter of his Epistle to the Hebrews, which opens with a definition of faith, and after that gives us examples of it, as if to guard against any possibility of mistake. After quoting the text, "The just shall live by faith," and thereby showing clearly that he is speaking of what he treats in his Epistle to the Romans as *justifying* faith, he continues, "Now faith is the substance," that is, the realizing, "of things hoped for, the evidence," that is, the ground of proof, "of things not seen." It is in its very essence the making present what is unseen; the acting upon the mere prospect of it, as if it really were possessed; the venturing upon it, the staking present ease, happiness, or other good, upon the chance of the future. And hence in another epistle he says pointedly, "If in this life only we have hope in Christ, we are of all men most miserable." [1] If the dead are not raised, we have indeed made a most signal miscalculation in the choice of life, and are altogether at fault. And what is true of the main doctrine itself is true also of our individual interest in it. This he shows us in his Epistle to the Hebrews, by the instance of the ancient saints, who thus risked their present happiness on the chance of future.

[1] I Cor. 15:19.

Abraham "went out, not knowing whither he went." He and the rest died "not having received the promises, but having seen them afar off, and were persuaded of them, and embraced them, and confessed that they were strangers and pilgrims on the earth." Such was the faith of the patriarchs: and in the text the youthful apostles, with an untaught but generous simplicity, lay claim to the same. Little as they knew what they said in its fullness, yet their words were anyhow expressive of their hidden hearts, prophetic of their future conduct. They say unto him, "We are able." They pledge themselves as if unawares, and are caught by one mightier than they, and, as it were, craftily made captive. But, in truth, their unsuspicious pledge was, after all, heartily made, though they knew not what they promised; and so was accepted. "Are ye able to drink of my cup, and to be baptized with my baptism? They say unto him, We are able." He in answer, without promising them heaven, graciously said, "Ye *shall* drink indeed of my cup, and be baptized with the baptism that I am baptized with."

Our Lord appears to act after the same manner towards St. Peter: he accepted his office of service, yet warned him how little he himself understood it. The zealous apostle wished to follow his Lord at once: but He answered, "Whither I go, thou canst not follow me now; but thou shalt follow me afterwards." [2] At another time, he claimed the promise already made to him; he said, "Follow thou me"; and at the same time explained it, "Verily, verily, I say unto thee, When thou wast young, thou girdedst thyself, and walkedst whither thou wouldest: but when thou shalt be old, thou shalt stretch forth thy hands, and another shall gird thee, and carry thee whither thou wouldest not." [3]

Such were the ventures made in faith, and in uncertainty, by apostles. Our Savior, in a passage of St. Luke's Gospel, binds upon us all the necessity of deliberately doing the like—"Which of you, intending to build a tower, sitteth not

[2] John 13:36.
[3] John 21:22, 18.

down first, and counteth the cost, whether he have sufficient to finish it? Lest haply, after he hath laid the foundation, and is not able to finish it, all that behold it begin to mock him, saying, This man began to build, and was not able to finish." And then he presently adds, "So likewise, whosoever he be of you that forsaketh not all that he hath, he cannot be my disciple": [4] thus warning us of the full sacrifice we must make. We give up our all to him; and he is to claim this or that, or grant us somewhat of it for a season, according to his good pleasure. On the other hand, the case of the rich young man, who went away sorrowful, when our Lord bade him give up his all and follow him, is an instance of one who had *not* faith to make the venture of this world for the next, upon His word.

If then faith be the essence of a Christian life, and if it be what I have now described, it follows that our duty lies in risking upon Christ's word what we have, for what we have not; and doing so in a noble, generous way, not indeed rashly or lightly, still without knowing accurately what we are doing, not knowing either what we give up, nor again what we shall gain; uncertain about our reward, uncertain about our extent of sacrifice, in all respects leaning, waiting upon him, trusting in him to fulfill his promise, trusting in him to enable us to fulfill our own vows, and so in all respects proceeding without carefulness or anxiety about the future.

Now I dare say that what I have said as yet seems plain and unexceptionable to most of those who hear me; yet surely, when I proceed to draw the practical inference which immediately follows, there are those who in their secret hearts, if not in open avowal, will draw back. Men allow us ministers of Christ to proceed in our preaching, while we confine ourselves to general truths, until they see that they themselves are implicated in them, and have to act upon them; and then they suddenly come to a stand; they collect themselves and draw back, and say, "They do not see *this*—or do not admit *that*"—and though they are quite unable to say

4 Luke 14:28–30, 33.

*why* that should not follow from what they already allow, which we show *must* follow, still they persist in saying that they do not see that it does follow; and they look about for excuses, and they say we carry things too far, and that we are extravagant, and that we ought to limit and modify what we say, that we do not take into account times, and seasons, and the like. This is what they pretend; and well has it been said, "Where there is a will there is a way"; for there is no truth, however overpoweringly clear, but men may escape from it by shutting their eyes; there is no duty, however urgent, but they may find ten thousand good reasons against it, in their own case. And they are sure to say we carry things too far, when we carry them home to themselves.

This sad infirmity of men, called Christians, is exemplified in the subject immediately before us. Who does not at once admit that faith consists in venturing on Christ's word without seeing? Yet in spite of this, may it not be seriously questioned whether men in general, even those of the better sort, venture anything upon his truth at all?

Consider for an instant. Let everyone who hears me ask himself the question, What stake has *he* in the truth of Christ's promise? How would he be a whit the worse off, supposing (which is impossible), but, supposing it to fail? We know what it is to have a stake in any venture of this world. We venture our property in plans which promise a return; in plans which we trust, which we have faith in. What have we ventured for Christ? What have we given to him on a belief of his promise? The apostle said that he and his brethren would be of all men most miserable if the dead were not raised. Can we in any degree apply this to ourselves? We think, perhaps, at present, we have some hope of heaven; well, *this* we should lose, of course; but after all, how should we be worse off as to our *present* condition? A trader, who has embarked some property in a speculation which fails, not only loses his prospect of gain, but somewhat of his own, which he ventured with the *hope* of the gain. This is the question, What have *we* ventured? I really fear, when we come to examine, it will be found that there is nothing we resolve, nothing we do, nothing we do not do, nothing we avoid, nothing we choose, nothing we give up, nothing we pursue, which we should not resolve, and do, and not do, and avoid, and choose, and give up, and pursue, if Christ had not died, and heaven were not promised us. I really fear that most men called Christians, whatever they may profess, whatever they may think they feel, whatever warmth and illumination and love they may claim as their own, yet would go on almost as they do, neither much better nor much worse, if they believed Christianity to be a fable. When young, they indulge their lusts, or at least pursue the world's vanities; as times goes on, they get into a fair way of business, or other mode of making money; then they marry and settle; and their interest coinciding with their duty, they seem to be, and think themselves, respectable and religious men; they grow attached to things as they are; they begin to have a zeal against vice and error; and they follow after peace with all men. Such conduct indeed, as far as it goes, is right and praiseworthy. Only I say, it has not necessarily anything to do with religion at all; there is nothing in it which is any proof of the presence of religious principle in those who adopt it; there is nothing they would not do still, though they had nothing to gain from it, except what they gain from it now: they do gain something now, they do gratify their present wishes, they are quiet and orderly, because it is their interest and taste to be so; but they *venture* nothing, they risk, they sacrifice, they abandon nothing on the faith of Christ's word.

For instance: St. Barnabas had a property in Cyprus; he gave it up for the poor of Christ. Here is an intelligible sacrifice. He did something he would not have done, unless the gospel were true. It is plain, if the gospel turned out to be a fable (which God forbid), but if so, he would have taken his line most unskillfully; he would be in a great mistake, and would have suffered a loss. He would be like a merchant whose vessels were wrecked, or whose correspondents had failed. Man has confidence in man, he trusts to the credit of his neighbor; but Christians do not risk largely upon their Savior's word; and this is the one thing they have to do. Christ tells us himself, "Make to yourselves friends of the mammon of unrighteousness; that, when ye fail, they may receive you into everlasting habitations"; [5] i.e., buy an interest in the next world with that wealth which this world uses unrighteously; feed the hungry, clothe the naked, relieve the sick, and it shall turn to "bags that wax not old, a treasure in the heavens that faileth not." [6] Thus almsdeeds, I say, are an intelligible *venture*, and an evidence of faith.

So again the man who, when his prospects in the world are good, gives up the promise of wealth or of eminence, in order to be nearer Christ, to have a place in his temple, to have more opportunity for prayer and praise, makes a sacrifice.

Or he who, from a noble striving after perfection, puts off the desire of worldly comforts, and is, like Daniel or St. Paul, in much labor and business, yet with a solitary heart, he too ventures something upon the certainty of the world to come.

Or he who, after falling into sin, repents in deed as well as in word; puts some yoke upon his shoulder, subjects himself to punishment; is severe upon his flesh; denies himself innocent pleasures; or puts himself to public shame—he too shows that his faith is the realizing of things hoped for, the warrant of things not seen.

Or again: he who only gets himself to pray against those things which the many seek after, and to embrace what the heart naturally shrinks from; he who, when God's will seems to tend towards worldly ill, while he deprecates it, yet prevails on himself to say heartily, "Thy will be done"; even he is not without his sacrifice. Or he who, being in prospect of wealth, honestly prays God that he may never be rich; or he who is in prospect of station, and earnestly prays that he may never have it; or he who has friends or kindred, and acquiesces with an entire heart in their removal while it is yet doubtful, who can say, "Take them away, if it be thy will, to thee I give

[5] Luke 16:9.
[6] Luke 12:33.

112

them up, to thee I commit them," who is willing to be taken at his word; he too risks somewhat, and is accepted.

Such a one is taken at his word, while he understands not, perhaps, what he says; but he is accepted, as meaning somewhat, and risking much. Generous hearts, like James and John, or Peter, often speak largely and confidently beforehand of what they will do for Christ, not insincerely, yet ignorantly; and for their sincerity's sake they are taken at their word as a reward, though they have yet to learn how serious that word is. "They say unto him, We are able"—and the vow is recorded in heaven. This is the case of all of us at many seasons. First, at confirmation; when we promise what was promised for us at baptism, yet without being able to understand how much we promise, but rather trusting to God gradually to reveal it, and to give us strength according to our day. So again they who enter holy orders promise they know not what, engage themselves they know not how deeply, debar themselves of the world's ways they know not how intimately, find perchance they must cut off from them the right hand, sacrifice the desire of their eyes and the stirring of their hearts at the foot of the cross, while they thought, in their simplicity, they were but choosing the quiet easy life of "plain men dwelling in tents." And so again, in various ways, the circumstances of the times cause men at certain seasons to take this path or that, for religion's sake. They know not whither they are being carried; they see not the end of their course; they know no more than this, that it is right to do what they are now doing; and they hear a whisper within them, which assures them, as it did the two holy brothers, that whatever their present conduct involves in time to come, they shall, through God's grace, be equal to it. Those blessed apostles said, "We are able"; and in truth they were enabled to do and suffer as they had said. St. James was given strength to be steadfast unto death, the death of martyrdom; being slain with the sword in Jerusalem. St. John, his brother, had still more to bear, dying last of the apostles, as St. James first. He had to bear bereavement, first, of his brother, then of the other apostles. He had to bear a length of years in loneliness, exile, and weakness. He had to experience the dreariness of being solitary, when those whom he loved had been summoned away. He had to live in his own thoughts, without familiar friend, with those only about him who belonged to a younger generation. Of him were demanded by his gracious Lord, as pledges of his faith, all his eye loved and his heart held converse with. He was as a man moving his goods into a far country, who at intervals and by portions sends them before him, till his present abode is well-nigh unfurnished. He sent forward his friends on their journey, while he stayed himself behind, that there might be those in heaven to have thoughts of him, to look out for him, and receive him when his Lord should call. He sent before him, also, other still more voluntary pledges and ventures of his faith—a self-denying walk, a zealous maintenance of the truth, fasting and prayers, labors of love, a virgin life, buffetings from the heathen, persecution, and banishment. Well might so great a saint say, at the end of his days, "Come, Lord Jesus!" as those who are weary of the night, and wait for the morning. All his thoughts, all his contemplations, desires, and hopes, were stored in the invisible world; and death, when it came, brought back to him the sight of what he had worshiped, what he had loved, what he had held intercourse with, in years long passed away. Then, when again brought into the presence of what he had lost, how would remembrance revive, and familiar thoughts long buried come to life? Who shall dare to describe the blessedness of those who find all their pledges safe returned to them, all their ventures abundantly and beyond measure satisfied?

Alas! that we, my brethren, have not more of this high and unearthly spirit! How is it that we are so contented with things as they are—that we are so willing to be let alone, and to enjoy this life—that we make such excuses, if anyone presses on us the necessity of something higher, the duty of bearing the cross, if we would earn the crown, of the Lord Jesus Christ?

I repeat it; what are our ventures and risks upon the truth of his word? For he says expressly, "Every one that hath forsaken houses, or brethren, or sisters, or father, or mother, or wife, or children, or lands, for my name's sake, shall receive an hundredfold, and shall inherit everlasting life. But many that are first shall be last; and the last shall be first." [7]

[7] Matt. 19:29–30.

# FIVE

# *Strength Perfect in Weakness*

## *The Weapons of Saints*

*"Many that are first shall be last; and the last shall be first."*—Matt. 19:30

THESE WORDS ARE fulfilled under the gospel in many ways. Our Savior in one place applies them to the rejection of the Jews and the calling of the Gentiles; but in the context, in which they stand as I have cited them, they seem to have a further meaning, and to embody a great principle, which we all indeed acknowledge, but are deficient in mastering. Under the dispensation of the Spirit all things were to become new and to be reversed. Strength, numbers, wealth, philosophy, eloquence, craft, experience of life, knowledge of human nature—these are the means by which worldly men have ever gained the world. But in that kingdom which Christ has set up, all is contrariwise. "The weapons of our warfare are not carnal, but mighty through God to the pulling down of strong holds." What was before in honor, has been dishonored; what before was in dishonor, has come to honor; what before was successful, fails; what before failed, succeeds. What before was great, has become little; what before was little, has become great. Weakness has conquered strength, for the hidden strength of

God "is made perfect in weakness." Death has conquered life, for in that death is a more glorious resurrection. Spirit has conquered flesh; for that spirit is an inspiration from above. A new kingdom has been established, not merely different from all kingdoms before it, but contrary to them; a paradox in the eyes of man—the visible rule of the invisible Savior.

This great change in the history of the world is foretold or described in very many passages of Scripture. Take, for instance, St. Mary's hymn, which we read every evening; she was no woman of high estate, the nursling of palaces and the pride of a people, yet she was chosen to an illustrious place in the kingdom of heaven. What God began in her was a sort of type of his dealings with his church. So she spoke of his "scattering the proud," "putting down the mighty," "exalting the humble and meek," "filling the hungry with good things," and "sending the rich empty away." This was a shadow or outline of that kingdom of the Spirit, which was then coming on the earth.

Again; when our Lord, in the beginning of his ministry, would declare the great principles and laws of his kingdom, after what manner did he express himself? Turn to the Sermon on the Mount. "He opened his mouth, and said, Blessed are the poor in spirit, blessed are they that mourn, blessed are the meek, blessed are they which are persecuted for righteousness' sake." [1] Poverty was to bring into the church the riches of the Gentiles; meekness was to conquer the earth; suffering was "to bind their kings with chains, and their nobles with fetters of iron."

On another occasion he added the counterpart:

Woe unto you that are rich! for ye have received your consolation. Woe unto you that are full! for ye shall hunger. Woe unto you that laugh now! for ye shall mourn and weep. Woe unto you, when all men shall speak well of you! for so did their fathers to the false prophets.[2]

[1] Matt. 5:2–10.
[2] Luke 6:24–26.

117

St. Paul addresses the Corinthians in the same tone:

Ye see your calling, brethren, how that not many wise men after the flesh, not many mighty, not many noble, are called: but God hath chosen the foolish things of the world to confound the wise; and God hath chosen the weak things of the world to confound the things which are mighty; and base things of the world, and things which are despised, hath God chosen, yea, and things which are not, to bring to nought things that are: that no flesh should glory in his presence.[3]

Once more; consider the Book of Psalms, which, if any part of the Old Testament, belongs immediately to gospel times, and is the voice of the Christian church; what is the one idea in that sacred book of devotion from beginning to end? This: that the weak, the oppressed, the defenseless shall be raised to rule the world in spite of its array of might, its threats, and its terrors; that "the first shall be last, and the last first."

Such is the kingdom of the sons of God; and while it endures, there is ever a supernatural work going on by which all that man thinks great is overcome, and what he despises prevails.

Yes, so it is; since Christ sent down gifts from on high, the saints are ever taking possession of the kingdom, and with the weapons of saints. The invisible powers of the heavens, truth, meekness, and righteousness, are ever coming in upon the earth, ever pouring in, gathering, thronging, warring, triumphing, under the guidance of him who "is alive and was dead, and is alive for evermore." The beloved disciple saw him mounted on a white horse, and going forth "conquering and to conquer." "And the armies which were in heaven followed him upon white horses, clothed in fine linen, white and clean. And out of his mouth goeth a sharp sword, that with it he should smite the nations: and he shall rule them with a rod of iron." [4]

Now let us apply this great truth to ourselves; for be it ever

[3] I Cor. 1:26–29.
[4] Rev. 19:14–15.

recollected, *we* are the sons of God, we are the soldiers of Christ. The kingdom is within us, and among us, and around us. We are apt to speak of it as a matter of history; we speak of it as at a distance; but really we are a part of it, or ought to be; and, as we wish to be a living portion of it, which is our only hope of salvation, we must learn what its characters are in order to imitate them. It is the characteristic of Christ's church, that the first should be last, and the last first; are we realizing in ourselves and taking part in this wonderful appointment of God?

Let me explain what I mean: We have most of us by nature longings more or less, and aspirations, after something greater than this world can give. Youth, especially, has a natural love of what is noble and heroic. We like to hear marvelous tales, which throw us out of things as they are, and introduce us to things that are not. We so love the idea of the invisible that we even build fabrics in the air for ourselves, if heavenly truth be not vouchsafed us. We love to fancy ourselves involved in circumstances of danger or trial, and acquitting ourselves well under them. Or we imagine some perfection, such as earth has not, which we follow, and render it our homage and our heart. Such is the state more or less of young persons before the world alters them, before the world comes upon them, as it often does very soon, with its polluting, withering, debasing, deadening influence, before it breathes on them, and blights and parches, and strips off their green foliage, and leaves them, as dry and wintry trees without sap or sweetness. But in early youth we stand with our leaves and blossoms on which promise fruit; we stand by the side of the still waters, with our hearts beating high, with longings after our unknown good, and with a sort of contempt for the fashions of the world; with a contempt for the world, even though we engage in it. Even though we allow ourselves in our degree to listen to it, and to take part in its mere gaieties and amusements, yet we feel the while that our happiness is not there; and we have not yet come to think, though we are in the way to think, that all that is beyond this world is after all an idle dream. We are on our way to think it, for no one stands where he was; his desires after what he has not, his earnest thoughts after things unseen, if not fixed on their true objects, catch at something which he does see, something earthly and perishable, and seduce him from God. But I am speaking of men *before* that time, before they have given their hearts to the world, which promises them true good, then cheats them, and then makes them believe that there is no truth anywhere, and that they were fools for thinking it. But before that time they have desires after things above this world, which they embody in some form of this world, because they have no other way at all of realizing them. If they are in humble life, they dream of becoming their own masters, rising in the world, and securing an independence; if in a higher rank, they have ambitious thoughts of gaining a name and exercising power. While their hearts are thus unsettled, Christ comes to them, if they will receive him, and promises to satisfy their great need, this hunger and thirst which wearies them. He does not wait till they have learned to ridicule high feelings as mere romantic dreams: he comes to the young; he has them baptized betimes, and then promises them, and in a higher way, those unknown blessings which they yearn after. He seems to say, in the words of the apostle, "What ye ignorantly worship, that declare I unto you." You are seeking what you see not, I give it you; you desire to be great, I will make you so; but observe how—just in the reverse way to what you expect; the way to real glory is to become unknown and despised.

He says, for instance, to the aspiring, as to his two apostles, "Whosoever will be great among you, let him be your minister; and whosoever will be chief among you, let him be your servant; even as the Son of man came not to be ministered unto, but to minister." [5] Here is our rule. The way to mount up is to go down. Every step we take downward makes us higher in the kingdom of heaven. Do you desire to be

[5] Matt. 20:26–28.

great? Make yourselves little. There is a mysterious connection between real advancement and self-abasement. If you minister to the humble and despised, if you feed the hungry, tend the sick, succor the distressed; if you bear with the froward, submit to insult, endure ingratitude, render good for evil, you are, as by a divine charm, getting power over the world and rising among the creatures. God has established this law. Thus he does his wonderful works. His instruments are poor and despised; the world hardly knows their names, or not at all. They are busied about what the world thinks petty actions, and no one minds them. They are apparently set on no great works; nothing is seen to come of what they do: they seem to fail. Nay, even as regards religious objects which they themselves profess to desire, there is no natural and visible connection between their doings and sufferings and these desirable ends; but there is an unseen connection in the kingdom of God. They rise by falling. Plainly so, for no condescension *can* be so great as that of our Lord *himself*. Now the more they abase themselves the more *like* they are to him; and the more like they are to him, the greater must be their power with him.

When we once recognize this law of God's providence we shall understand better, and be more desirous to imitate, our Lord's precepts, such as the following:

> Ye call me Master and Lord: and ye say well; for so I am. If I then, your Lord and Master, have washed your feet; ye also ought to wash one another's feet. For I have given you an example, that ye should do as I have done to you. Verily, verily, I say unto you, The servant is not greater than his lord; neither he that is sent greater than he that sent him.

And then our Lord adds, "If ye know these things, happy are ye if ye do them." [6] As if he should say to us of this day, You know well that the gospel was at the first preached and propagated by the poor and lowly against the world's power; you know that fishermen and publicans overcame the world.

[6] John 13:13-17.

You know it; you are fond of bringing it forward as an evidence of the truth of the gospel, and of enlarging on it as something striking, and a topic for many words; happy are ye if ye yourselves fulfill it; happy are ye if *ye* carry on the work of those fishermen; if ye in your generation follow them as they followed me, and triumph over the world and ascend above it by a like self-abasement.

Again,

> When thou art bidden of any man to a wedding, sit not down in the highest room; ... but when thou art bidden, go and sit down in the lowest room; that when he that bade thee cometh, he may say unto thee, Friend, go up higher: then shalt thou have worship in the presence of them that sit at meat with thee. For whosoever exalteth himself shall be abased; and he that humbleth himself shall be exalted.[7]

Here is a rule which extends to whatever we do. It is plain that the spirit of this command leads us, as a condition of being exalted hereafter, to cultivate here all kinds of little humiliations; instead of loving display, putting ourselves forward, seeking to be noticed, being loud or eager in speech, and bent on having our own way, to be content, nay, to rejoice in being made little of, to perform what to the flesh are servile offices, to think it enough to be barely suffered among men, to be patient under calumny; not to argue, not to judge, not to pronounce censures, unless a plain duty comes in; and all this because our Lord has said that such conduct is the very way to be exalted in his presence.

Again, "I say unto you, That ye resist not evil: but whosoever shall smite thee on thy right cheek, turn to him the other also." [8] What a precept is this? Why is this voluntary degradation? What good can come to it? Is it not an extravagance? Not to *resist* evil is going far; but to court it, to turn the left cheek to the aggressor and to offer to be insulted! What a wonderful command! What? Must we take pleasure in indignities? Surely we must; however difficult it be to understand

[7] Luke 14:8, 10–11.
[8] Matt. 5:39.

it, however arduous and trying to practice it. Hear St. Paul's words, which are a comment on Christ's: "Therefore I *take pleasure* in infirmities, in reproaches, in necessities, in persecutions, in distresses for Christ's sake"; he adds the reason; "*for when I am weak, then* am I strong." [9] As health and exercise and regular diet are necessary to strength of the body, so an enfeebling and afflicting of the natural man, a chastising and afflicting of soul and body, are necessary to the exaltation of the soul.

Again, St. Paul says, "Avenge not yourselves, but rather give place unto wrath: for it is written, Vengeance is mine; I will repay, saith the Lord. Therefore if thine enemy hunger, feed him; if he thirst, give him drink: for in so doing thou shalt heap coals of fire on his head." [10] As if he said, *This* is a *Christian's* revenge; *this* is how a *Christian* heaps punishment and suffering on the head of his enemy; viz., by returning good for evil. Is there pleasure in seeing an injurer and oppressor at your feet? Has a man wronged you, slandered you, tyrannized over you, abused your confidence, been ungrateful to you? Or to take what is more common, has a man been insolent to you, shown contempt of you, thwarted you, outwitted you, been cruel to you, and you feel resentment—and your feeling is this, "I wish him no ill, but I should like him just to be brought down for this, and to make amends to me"; rather say, hard though it be,

I will overcome him with love; except severity be a duty, I will say nothing, do nothing; I will keep quiet, I will seek to do him a service; I owe him a service, not a grudge; and I will be kind, and sweet, and gentle, and composed; and while I cannot disguise from him that I know well where he stands, and where I, still this shall be with all peaceableness and purity of affection.

O hard duty, but most blessed! for even to take into account the *pleasure* of revenge, such as it is, is there not greater gratification in thus melting the proud and injurious heart

[9] II Cor. 12:10.
[10] Rom. 12:19–20.

than in triumphing over it outwardly, without subduing it within? Is there not more of true enjoyment, in looking up to God, and calling him (so to speak), as a witness of what is done, and having his angels as conscious spectators of your triumph, though not a soul on earth knows anything of it, than to have your mere carnal retaliation of evil for evil known and talked of, in the presence of all, and more than all, who saw the insult or heard of the wrong?

The case is the same as regards poverty, which it is the fashion of the world to regard not only as the greatest of evils, but as the greatest *disgrace*. Men count it a disgrace, because it certainly does often arise from carelessness, sloth, imprudence, and other faults. But, in many cases, it is nothing else but the very state of life in which God has placed a man; but still, even then, it is equally despised by the world. Now if there is one thing clearly set forth in the Bible it is this, that "blessed are the poor." Our Savior was the great example of poverty; he was a poor man. St. Paul says, "Ye know the grace of our Lord Jesus Christ, that, though he was rich, yet for your sakes he became poor, that ye through his poverty might be rich." [11] Or consider St. Paul's very solemn language about the danger of wealth: "The love of money is the root of all evil: which while some coveted after, they have erred from the faith, and pierced themselves through with many sorrows." [12] Can we doubt that poverty is under the gospel *better* than riches? I say *under* the gospel, and *in* the regenerate, and *in* the true servants of God. Of course, out of the gospel, among the unregenerate, among the lovers of this world, it matters not whether one is rich or poor; a man is anyhow unjustified, and there is no better or worse in his outward circumstances. But, I say, *in Christ* the poor is in a more blessed lot than the wealthy. Ever since the eternal Son of God was born in a stable, and had not a place to lay his head, and died an outcast and as a malefactor, heaven has been won by poverty, by disgrace, and by suffering. Not by these

[11] II Cor. 8:9.
[12] I Tim. 6:10.

things in themselves, but by faith working in and through them.

These are a few out of many things which might be said on this most deep and serious subject. It is strange to say, but it is a truth which our own observation and experience will confirm, that when a man discerns in himself most sin and humbles himself most, when his comeliness seems to him to vanish away and all his graces to wither, when he feels disgust at himself, and revolts at the thought of himself—seems to himself all dust and ashes, all foulness and odiousness, then it is that he is really rising in the kingdom of God: as it is said of Daniel, "From the first day that thou didst set thine heart to understand, and to chasten thyself before thy God, thy words were heard, and I am come for thy words." [13]

Let us then, my brethren, understand our place, as the redeemed children of God. Some *must* be great in this world, but woe to those who make themselves great; woe to any who take one step out of their way with this object before them. Of course, no one is safe from the intrusion of corrupt motives; but I speak of persons *allowing* themselves in such a motive, and acting mainly from such a motive. Let this be the settled view of all who would promote Christ's cause upon earth. If we are true to ourselves, nothing can really thwart us. Our warfare is not with carnal weapons, but with heavenly. The world does not understand what our real power is, and where it lies. And until we put ourselves into its hands of our own act, it can do nothing against us. Till we leave off patience, meekness, purity, resignation, and peace, it can do nothing against that truth which is our birthright, that cause which is ours, as it has been the cause of all saints before us. But let all who would labor for God in a dark time beware of anything which ruffles, excites, and in any way withdraws them from the love of God and Christ, and simple obedience to him.

[13] Dan. 10:12.

This be our duty in the dark night, while we wait for the day; while we wait for him who is our day, while we wait for his coming, who is gone, who will return, and before whom all the tribes of the earth will mourn, but the sons of God will rejoice. "It doth not yet appear what we shall be: but we know that, when he shall appear, we shall be like him; for we shall see him as he is. And every man that hath this hope in him purifieth himself, even as he is pure." [14] It is our blessedness to be made like the all-holy, all-gracious, long-suffering, and merciful God; who made and who redeemed us; in whose presence is perfect rest, and perfect peace; whom the seraphim are harmoniously praising, and the cherubim tranquilly contemplating, and angels silently serving, and the church thankfully worshiping. All is order, repose, love, and holiness in heaven. There is no anxiety, no ambition, no resentment, no discontent, no bitterness, no remorse, no tumult. "Thou wilt keep him in perfect peace, whose mind is stayed on thee: because he trusteth in thee. Trust ye in the Lord for ever: for in the Lord Jehovah is everlasting strength." [15]

[14] I John 3:2–3.
[15] Isa. 26:3–4.

# SIX

# *Toward Christian Honesty*

## *Unreal Words*

*"Thine eyes shall see the king in his beauty: they shall behold the land that is very far off."*—Isa. 33:17

THE PROPHET TELLS US that under the gospel covenant God's servants will have the privilege of seeing those heavenly sights which were but shadowed out in the law. Before Christ came was the time of shadows; but when he came, he brought truth as well as grace; and as he who is the truth has come to us, so does he in return require that we should be true and sincere in our dealings with him. To be true and sincere is really to see with our minds those great wonders which he has wrought in order that we might see them. When God opened the eyes of the ass on which Balaam rode, she saw the angel and acted upon the sight. When he opened the eyes of the young man, Elisha's servant, he too saw the chariots and horses of fire, and took comfort. And in like manner, Christians are now under the protection of a divine presence, and that more wonderful than any which was vouchsafed of old time. God revealed himself visibly to Jacob, to Job, to Moses, to Joshua, and to Isaiah; to us he reveals himself not visibly, but more wonderfully and truly; not without the cooperation of our own will, but upon our faith, and for that very reason more truly; for faith is the special means of gaining spiritual blessings. Hence St. Paul prays for the Ephesians "that Christ may dwell in their hearts by faith," and that "the eyes of their understanding may be enlightened." And St. John declares that "the Son of God hath given us an understanding, that we may know him that is true, and we are in him that is true, even in his Son Jesus Christ." [1]

We are no longer then in the region of shadows: we have the true Savior set before us, the true reward, and the true means of spiritual renewal. We know the true state of the soul by nature and by grace, the evil of sin, the consequences of sinning, the way of pleasing God, and the motives to act upon. God has revealed himself clearly to us; he has "destroyed the face of the covering cast over all people, and the vail that is spread over all nations." "The darkness is past, and the true light now shineth." [2] And therefore, I say, he calls upon us in turn to "walk in the light, as he is in the light." The Pharisees might have this excuse in their hypocrisy, that the plain truth had not been revealed to them; we have not even this poor reason for insincerity. We have no opportunity of mistaking one thing for another: the promise is expressly made to us that "our teachers shall not be removed into a corner any more, but our eyes shall see our teachers"; that "the eyes of them that see shall not be dim"; that everything shall be called by its right name; that "the vile person shall be no more called liberal, nor the churl said to be bountiful"; [3] in a word, as the text speaks, that "our eyes shall see the king in his beauty: we shall behold the land that is very far off." Our professions, our creeds, our prayers, our dealings, our conversation, our arguments, our teaching must henceforth be sincere, or, to use an expressive word, must be *real*. What St. Paul says of himself and his

[1] Eph. 3:17; 1:18; I John 5:20.
[2] Isa. 25:7; I John 2:8.
[3] Isa. 30:20; 32:3, 5.

fellow laborers, that they were true because Christ is true, applies to all Christians:

> Our rejoicing is this, the testimony of our conscience, that in simplicity and godly sincerity, not with fleshly wisdom, but by the grace of God, we have had our conversation in the world, and more abundantly to you-ward. . . . The things that I purpose, do I purpose according to the flesh, that with me there should be yea yea, and nay nay? But as God is true, our word toward you was not yea and nay. For the Son of God, Jesus Christ, . . . was not yea and nay, but in him was yea. For all the promises of God in him are yea, and in him Amen, unto the glory of God by us.[4]

And yet, it need scarcely be said, nothing is so rare as honesty and singleness of mind; so much so, that a person who is really honest, is already perfect. Insincerity was an evil which sprang up within the church from the first; Ananias and Simon were not open opposers of the apostles, but false brethren. And, as foreseeing what was to be, our Savior is remarkable in his ministry for nothing more than the earnestness of the dissuasives which he addressed to those who came to him, against taking up religion lightly, or making promises which they were likely to break.

Thus he, "the true Light, which lighteth every man that cometh into the world," "the Amen, the faithful and true witness, the beginning of the creation of God," [5] said to the young ruler, who lightly called him "good master," "Why callest thou me good?" as bidding him weigh his words; and then abruptly told him, "One thing thou lackest." When a certain man professed that he would follow him whithersoever he went, he did not respond to him, but said, "The foxes have holes, and the birds of the air have nests, but the Son of man hath not where to lay his head." When St. Peter said with all his heart in the name of himself and brethren, "To whom shall we go? thou has the words of eternal life," he answered pointedly, "Have not I chosen you twelve, and

[4] II Cor. 1:12, 17–20.
[5] John 1:9; Rev. 3:14.

one of you is a devil?" as if he said, "Answer for thyself."
When the two apostles professed their desire to cast their lot
with him, he asked whether they could "drink of his cup,
and be baptized with his baptism." And when "there went
great multitudes with him," he turned and said, that unless
a man hated relations, friends, and self, he could not be his
disciple. And then he proceeded to warn all men to "count
the cost" ere they followed him. Such is the merciful severity with which he repels us that he may gain us more truly.
And what he thinks of those who, after coming to him, re-
lapse into a hollow and hypocritical profession, we learn from
his language towards the Laodiceans: "I know thy works,
that thou art neither cold nor hot: I would thou wert cold
or hot. So then because thou art lukewarm, and neither cold
nor hot, I will spue thee out of my mouth." [6]

We have a striking instance of the same conduct on the
part of that ancient saint who prefigured our Lord in name
and office, Joshua, the captain of the chosen people in entering Canaan. When they had at length taken possession of
that land which Moses and their fathers had seen "very far
off," they said to him, "God forbid that we should forsake
the Lord, to serve other gods. . . . We will serve the Lord;
for he is our God." He made answer, "Ye cannot serve the
Lord: for he is an holy God; he is a jealous God; he will not
forgive your transgressions nor your sins." [7] Not as if he
would hinder them from obeying, but to sober them in professing. How does his answer remind us of St. Paul's still
more awful words, about the impossibility of renewal after
utterly falling away!

And what is said of profession of *discipleship* applies un-
doubtedly in its degree to *all* profession. To make professions
is to play with edged tools, unless we attend to what we are
saying. Words have a meaning, whether we mean that mean-

[6] Mark 10:17–21; Matt. 8:20; John 6:68–70; Matt. 20:22; Luke
14:25–28; Rev. 3:15–16.
[7] Josh. 24:16–19.

ing or not; and they are imputed to us in their real meaning, when our not meaning it is our own fault. He who takes God's name in vain, is not counted guiltless because he means nothing by it—he cannot frame a language for himself; and they who make professions, of whatever kind, are heard in the sense of those professions, and are not excused because they themselves attach no sense to them. "By thy words thou shalt be justified, and by thy words thou shalt be condemned." [8]

Now this consideration needs especially to be pressed upon Christians at this day; for this is especially a day of professions. You will answer in my own words, that all ages have been ages of profession. So they have been, in one way or other, but this day in its own especial sense—because this is especially a day of individual profession. This is a day in which there is (rightly or wrongly) so much of private judgment, so much of separation and difference, so much of preaching and teaching, so much of authorship, that it involves individual profession, responsibility, and recompense in a way peculiarly its own. It will not then be out of place if, in connection with the text, we consider some of the many ways in which persons, whether in this age or in another, make unreal professions, or seeing see not, and hearing hear not, and speak without mastering, or trying to master, their words. This I will attempt to do at some length, and in matters of detail, which are not the less important because they are minute.

Of course, it is very common in all matters, not only in religion, to speak in an unreal way; viz., when we speak on a subject with which our minds are not familiar. If you were to hear a person who knew nothing about military matters giving directions how soldiers on service should conduct themselves, or how their food and lodging, or their marching, was to be duly arranged, you would be sure that his mistakes would be such as to excite the ridicule and contempt of

[8] Matt. 12:37.

men experienced in warfare. If a foreigner were to come to one of our cities, and without hesitation offer plans for the supply of our markets, or the management of our police, it is so certain that he would expose himself, that the very attempt would argue a great want of good sense and modesty. We should feel that he did not understand us, and that when he spoke about us he would be using words without meaning. If a dim-sighted man were to attempt to decide questions of a proportion and color, or a man without ear to judge musical compositions, we should feel that he spoke on and from general principles, on fancy, or by deduction and argument, not from a real apprehension of the matters which he discussed. His remarks would be theoretical and unreal.

This unsubstantial way of speaking is instanced in the case of persons who fall into any new company, among strange faces and amid novel occurrences. They sometimes form amiable judgments of men and things, sometimes the reverse— but whatever their judgments be, they are to those who know the men and the things strangely unreal and distorted. They feel reverence where they should not; they discern slights where none were intended; they discover meaning in events which have none; they fancy motives; they misinterpret manner; they mistake character; and they form generalizations and combinations which exist only in their own minds.

Again, persons who have not attended to the subject of morals, or to politics, or to matters ecclesiastical, or to theology, do not know the relative value of questions which they meet with in these departments of knowledge. They do not understand the difference between one point and another. The one and the other are the same to them. They look at them as infants gaze at the objects which meet their eyes, in a vague unapprehensive way, as if not knowing whether a thing is a hundred miles off or close at hand, whether great or small, hard or soft. They have no means of judging, no standard to measure by—and they give judgment at random, saying yea or nay on very deep questions, according to how their fancy is struck at the moment, or as some clever or specious argument happens to come across them. Consequently they are inconsistent; say one thing one day, another the next—and if they must act, act in the dark; or if they can help acting, do not act; or if they act freely, act from some other reason not avowed. All this is to be unreal.

Again, there cannot be a more apposite specimen of unreality than the way in which judgments are commonly formed upon important questions by the mass of the community. Opinions are continually given in the world on matters, about which those who offer them are as little qualified to judge as blind men about colors, and that because they have never exercised their minds upon the points in question. This is a day in which all men are obliged to have an opinion on all questions, political, social, and religious, because they have in some way or other an influence upon the decision; yet the multitude are for the most part absolutely without capacity to take their part in it. In saying this, I am far from meaning that this need be so—I am far from denying that there is such a thing as plain good sense, or (what is better) religious sense, which will see its way through very intricate matters, or that this is in fact sometimes exerted in the community at large on certain great questions; but at the same time this practical sense is so far from existing as regards the vast mass of questions which in this day come before the public that (as all persons who attempt to gain the influence of the people on their side know well) their opinions must be purchased by interesting their prejudices or fears in their favor—not by presenting a question in its real and true substance, but by adroitly coloring it, or selecting out of it some particular point which may be exaggerated, and dressed up, and be made the means of working on popular feelings. And thus government and the art of government becomes, as much as popular religion, hollow and unsound.

And hence it is that the popular voice is so changeable. One man or measure is the idol of the people today, another tomorrow. They have never gotten beyond accepting shadows for things.

What is instanced in the mass is instanced also in various ways in individuals, and in points of detail. For instance, some men are set perhaps on being eloquent speakers. They use great words and imitate the sentences of others; and they fancy that those whom they imitate had as little meaning as themselves or they perhaps contrive to think that they themselves have a meaning adequate to their words.

Another sort of unreality, or voluntary profession of what is above us, is instanced in the conduct of those who suddenly come into power or place. They affect a manner such as they think the office requires, but which is beyond them, and therefore unbecoming. They wish to act with dignity, and they cease to be themselves.

And so again, to take a different case, many men, when they come near persons in distress and wish to show sympathy, often condole in a very unreal way. I am not altogether laying this to their fault; for it is very difficult to know what to do, when on the one hand we cannot realize to ourselves the sorrow, yet withal wish to be kind to those who feel it. A tone of grief seems necessary, yet (if so be) cannot under our circumstances be genuine. Yet even here surely there is a true way, if we could find it, by which pretence may be avoided, and yet respect and consideration shown.

And in like manner as regards religious emotions. Persons are aware from the mere force of the doctrines of which the gospel consists, that they ought to be variously affected, and deeply and intensely too, in consequence of them. The doctrines of original and actual sin, of Christ's divinity and atonement, and of holy baptism, are so vast, that no one can realize them without very complicated and profound feelings. Natural reason tells a man this, and that if he simply and genuinely believes the doctrines, he must have these feelings; and he professes to believe the doctrines absolutely, and therefore he professes the correspondent feelings. But in truth he perhaps does *not* really believe them absolutely, because such absolute belief is the work of long time, and therefore his profession of feeling outruns the real inward existence of feeling, or he becomes unreal. Let us never lose sight of two truths—that we ought to have our hearts penetrated with the love of Christ and full of self-renunciation; but that if they be not, professing that they are does not make them so.

Again, to take a more serious instance of the same fault, some persons pray, not as sinners addressing their God, not as the publican smiting on his breast, and saying, "God be merciful to me a sinner," but in such a way as they conceive to be becoming *under* circumstances of guilt, in a way becoming such a strait. They are self-conscious, and reflect on what they are about, and instead of actually approaching (as it were) the mercy seat, they are filled with the thought that God is great, and man his creature, God on high and man on earth, and that they are engaged in a high and solemn service, and that they ought to rise up to its sublime and momentous character.

Another still more common form of the same fault, yet without any definite pretence or effort, is the mode in which people speak of the shortness and vanity of life, the certainty of death, and the joys of heaven. They have commonplaces in their mouths, which they bring forth upon occasions for the good of others, or to console them, or as a proper and becoming mark of attention towards them. Thus they speak to clergymen in a professedly serious way, making remarks true and sound, and in themselves deep, yet unmeaning in their mouths; or they give advice to children or young men; or perhaps in low spirits or sickness they are led to speak in a religious strain as if it was spontaneous. Or when they fall into sin, they speak of man being frail, of the deceitfulness of the human heart, of God's mercy, and so on —all these great words, heaven, hell, judgment, mercy, repentance, works, the world that now is, the world to come, being little more than "lifeless sounds, whether of pipe or harp," in their mouths and ears, as the "very lovely song of one that hath a pleasant voice and can play well on an instrument"—as the proprieties of conversation, or the civilities of good breeding.

I am speaking of the conduct of the world at large, called Christian; but what has been said applies, and necessarily, to the case of a number of well-disposed or even religious men. I mean, that before men come to know the realities of human life, it is not wonderful that their view of religion should be unreal. Young people who have never known sorrow or anxiety, or the sacrifices which conscientiousness involves, want commonly that depth and seriousness of character, which sorrow only and anxiety and self-sacrifice can give. I do not notice this as a fault, but as a plain fact, which may often be seen, and which it is well to bear in mind. This is the legitimate use of this world, to make us seek for another. It does its part when it repels us and disgusts us and drives us elsewhere. Experience of it gives experience of that which is its antidote, in the case of religious minds; and we become real in our view of what is spiritual by the contact of things temporal and earthly. And much more are men unreal when they have some secret motive urging them a different way from religion, and when their professions therefore are forced into an unnatural course in order to subserve their secret motive. When men do not like the conclusions to which their principles lead, or the precepts which Scripture contains, they are not wanting in ingenuity to blunt their force. They can frame some theory, or dress up certain objections, to defend themselves withal; a theory, that is, or objections, which it is difficult to refute perhaps, but which any rightly ordered mind, nay, any common bystander, perceives to be unnatural and insincere.

What has been here noticed of individuals takes place even in the case of whole churches, at times when love has waxed cold and faith failed. The whole system of the church,

its discipline and ritual, are all in their origin the spontaneous and exuberant fruit of the real principle of spiritual
religion in the hearts of its members. The invisible church
has developed itself into the church visible, and its outward
rites and forms are nourished and animated by the living
power which dwells within it. Thus every part of it is real,
down to the minutest details. But when the seductions of
the world and the lusts of the flesh have eaten out this divine
inward life, what is the outward church but a hollowness
and a mockery, like the whited sepulchers of which our
Lord speaks, a memorial of what was and is not? And though
we trust that the church is nowhere thus utterly deserted
by the Spirit of truth, at least according to God's ordinary
providence, yet may we not say that in proportion as it approaches to this state of deadness, the grace of its ordinances,
though not forfeited, at least flows in but a scanty or uncertain stream?

And lastly, if this unreality may steal over the church
itself, which is in its very essence a practical institution,
much more is it found in the philosophies and literature of
men. Literature is almost in its essence unreal; for it is the
exhibition of thought disjoined from practice. Its very home
is supposed to be ease and retirement; and when it does
more than speak or write, it is accused of transgressing its
bounds. This indeed constitutes what is considered its true
dignity and honor, viz., its abstraction from the actual affairs of life; its security from the world's currents and
vicissitudes; its saying without doing. A man of literature
is considered to preserve his dignity by doing nothing; and
when he proceeds forward into action, he is thought to lose
his position, as if he were degrading his calling by enthusiasm, and becoming a politician or a partisan. Hence mere
literary men are able to say strong things against the opinions of their age, whether religious or political, without
offense; because no one thinks they mean anything by them.
They are not expected to go forward to act upon them,
and mere words hurt no one.

Such are some of the more common or more extended specimens of profession without action, or of speaking without really seeing and feeling. In instancing which, let it be observed, I do not mean to say that such profession, as has been described, is always culpable and wrong; indeed I have implied the contrary throughout. It is often a misfortune. It takes a long time really to feel and understand things as they are; we learn to do so only gradually. Profession beyond our feelings is only a fault when we might help it —when either we speak when we need not speak, or do not feel when we might have felt. Hard, insensible hearts, ready and thoughtless talkers, these are they whose unreality, as I have termed it, is a sin; it is the sin of every one of us, in proportion as our hearts are cold, or our tongues excessive.

But the mere fact of our saying more than we feel is not necessarily sinful. St. Peter did not rise up to the full meaning of his confession, "Thou art the Christ," yet he was pronounced blessed. St. James and St. John said, "We are able," without clear apprehension, yet without offense. We ever promise things greater than we master, and we wait on God to enable us to perform them. Our promising involves a prayer for light and strength. And so again we all say the creed, but who comprehends it fully? All we can hope is, that we are in the way to understand it; that we partly understand it; that we desire, pray, and strive to understand it more and more. Our creed becomes a sort of prayer. Persons are culpably unreal in their way of speaking, not when they say more than they feel, but when they say things different from what they feel. A miser praising almsgiving, or a coward giving rules for courage, is unreal; but it is not unreal for the less to discourse about the greater, for the liberal to descant upon munificence, or the generous to praise the noble-minded, or the self-denying to use the language of the austere, or the confessor to exhort to martyrdom.

What I have been saying comes to this—be in earnest, and you will speak of religion where, and when, and how you should; aim at things, and your words will be right without aiming. There are ten thousand ways of looking at this world, but only one right way. The man of pleasure has his way, the man of gain his, and the man of intellect his. Poor men and rich men, governors and governed, prosperous and discontented, learned and unlearned, each has his own way of looking at the things which come before him, and each has a wrong way. There is but one right way; it is the way in which God looks at the world. Aim at looking at it in God's way. Aim at seeing things as God sees them. Aim at forming judgments about persons, events, ranks, fortunes, changes, objects, such as God forms. Aim at looking at this life as God looks at it. Aim at looking at the life to come, and the world unseen, as God does. Aim at "seeing the King in his beauty." All things that we see are but shadows to us and delusions, unless we enter into what they really mean.

It is not an easy thing to learn that new language which Christ has brought us. He has interpreted all things for us in a new way; he has brought us a religion which sheds a new light on all that happens. Try to learn this language. Do not get it by rote, or speak it as a thing of course. Try to understand what you say. Time is short, eternity is long; God is great, man is weak; he stands between heaven and hell; Christ is his Savior; Christ has suffered for him. The Holy Ghost sanctifies him; repentance purifies him, faith justifies, works save. These are solemn truths, which need not be actually spoken, except in the way of creed or of teaching; but which must be laid up in the heart. That a thing is true is no reason that it should be said, but that it should be done; that it should be acted upon; that it should be made our own inwardly.

Let us avoid talking, of whatever kind; whether mere empty talking, or censorious talking, or idle profession, or descanting upon gospel doctrines, or the affectation of philosophy, or the pretence of eloquence. Let us guard against frivolity, love of display, love of being talked about, love of singularity, love of seeming original. Let us aim at meaning what we say, and saying what we mean; let us aim at knowing when we understand a truth, and when we do not. When we do not, let us take it on faith, and let us profess to do so. Let us receive the truth in reverence, and pray God to give us a good will, and divine light, and spiritual strength, that it may bear fruit within us.

# SEVEN

# Thankfulness as Remembrance

## Remembrance of Past Mercies

*"I am not worthy of the least of all the mercies, and of all the truth, which thou hast shewed unto thy servant."*—Gen. 32:10

THE SPIRIT OF HUMBLE thankfulness for past mercies which these words imply is a grace to which we are especially called in the gospel. Jacob, who spoke them, knew not of those great and wonderful acts of love with which God has since visited the race of man. But though he might not know the depths of God's counsels, he knew himself so far as to know that he was worthy of no good thing at all, and he knew also that Almighty God had shown him great mercies and great truth: mercies, in that He had done for him good things, whereas he had deserved evil; and truth, in that He had made him promises, and had been faithful to them. In consequence, he overflowed with gratitude when he looked back upon the past; marveling at the contrast between what he was in himself and what God had been to him.

Such thankfulness, I say, is eminently a Christian grace, and is enjoined on us in the New Testament. For instance, we are exhorted to be "thankful," and to let "the word of Christ dwell in us richly in all wisdom; teaching and admonishing one another in psalms and hymns and spiritual songs, singing with grace in our hearts to the Lord."

Elsewhere, we are told to "speak to ourselves in psalms and hymns and spiritual songs, singing and making melody in our heart to the Lord; giving thanks always for all things unto God and the Father in the name of our Lord Jesus Christ."

Again: "Be careful for nothing; but in every thing by prayer and supplication with thanksgiving let your requests be made known unto God."

Again: "In every thing give thanks: for this is the will of God in Christ Jesus concerning you." [1]

The apostle, who writes all this, was himself an especial pattern of a thankful spirit: "Rejoice in the Lord alway," he says, "and again I say, Rejoice." "I have learned, in whatsoever state I am, therewith to be content. I have all and abound; I am full." Again:

I thank Christ Jesus our Lord, who hath enabled me, for that he counted me faithful, putting me into the ministry; who was before a blasphemer, and a persecutor, and injurious: but I obtained mercy, because I did it ignorantly in unbelief. And the grace of our Lord was exceeding abundant with faith and love which is in Christ Jesus. [2]

O great apostle! how could it be otherwise, considering what he had been and what he was—transformed from an enemy to a friend, from a blind Pharisee to an inspired preacher? And yet there is another saint, besides the patriarch Jacob, who is his fellow in this excellent grace—like them, distinguished by great vicissitudes of life, and by the adoring love and the tenderness of heart with which he looked back upon the past: I mean, "David the son of Jesse, the man who was raised up on high, the anointed of the God of Jacob, and the sweet psalmist of Israel." [3]

The Book of Psalms is full of instances of David's thankful

[1] Col. 3:15, 16; Eph. 5:19–20; Phil. 4:6; I Thess. 5:18.
[2] Phil. 4:4, 11, 18; I Tim. 1:12–14.
[3] II Sam. 23:1.

spirit, which I need not cite here, as we are all so well acquainted with them. I will but refer to his thanksgiving, when he set apart the precious materials for the building of the Temple, as it occurs at the end of the First Book of Chronicles; when he rejoiced so greatly, because he and his people had the heart to offer freely to God, and thanked God for his very thankfulness.

> David the king ... rejoice with great joy. Wherefore David blessed the Lord before all the congregation: and David said, Blessed be thou, Lord God of Israel our father, for ever and ever. ... Both riches and honour come of thee, and thou reignest over all; and in thine hand is power and might; and in thine hand it is to make great, and to give strength unto all. Now therefore, our God, we thank thee, and praise thy glorious name. But who am I, and what is my people, that we should be able to offer so willingly after this sort? for all things come of thee, and of thine own have we given thee.[4]

Such was the thankful spirit of David, looking back upon the past, wondering and rejoicing at the way in which his almighty protector had led him on, and at the works he had enabled him to do; and praising and glorifying him for his mercy and truth. David, then, Jacob, and St. Paul, may be considered the three great patterns of thankfulness, which are set before us in Scripture; saints, all of whom were peculiarly the creation of God's grace, and whose very life and breath it was humbly and adoringly to meditate upon the contrast between what, in different ways, they had been, and what they were. A perishing wanderer had unexpectedly become a patriarch; a shepherd, a king; and a persecutor, an apostle: each had been chosen, at God's inscrutable pleasure, to fulfill a great purpose, and each, while he did his utmost to fulfill it, kept praising God that he was made his instrument. Of the first, it was said, "Jacob have I loved, but Esau have I hated"; of the second, that "he refused the tabernacle of Joseph, and chose not the tribe of Ephraim: but chose the tribe of Judah, the mount Zion which he loved:

[4] I Chron. 29:9–14.

he chose David also his servant, and took him away from the sheepfolds." And St. Paul says of himself, "Last of all he was seen of me also, as of one born out of due time." [5]

These thoughts naturally come over the mind at this season, when we are engaged in celebrating God's grace in making us his children, by the incarnation of his only-begotten Son, the greatest and most wonderful of all his mercies. And to the patriarch Jacob our minds are now particularly turned, by the First Lessons for this day,[6] taken from the prophet Isaiah, in which the church is addressed and comforted under the name of Jacob. Let us then, in this season of thankfulness, and at the beginning of a new year, take a brief view of the character of this patriarch; and though David and Isaiah be the prophets of grace, and St. Paul its special herald and chief pattern, yet, if we wish to see an actual specimen of a habit of thankfulness occupied in the remembrance of God's mercies, I think we shall not be wrong in betaking ourselves to Jacob.

Jacob's distinguishing grace then, as I think it may be called, was a habit of affectionate musing upon God's providences towards him in times past, and of overflowing thankfulness for them. Not that he had not other graces also, but this seems to have been his distinguishing grace. All good men have in their measure all graces; for He, by whom they have any, does not give one apart from the whole: He gives the root, and the root puts forth branches. But since time, and circumstances, and their own use of the gift, and their own disposition and character, have much influence on the mode of its manifestation, so it happens that each good man has his own distinguishing grace, apart from the rest, his own particular hue and fragrance and fashion, as a flower may have. As, then, there are numberless flowers on the earth, all of them flowers, and so far like each other; and all springing from the same earth, and nourished by

[5] Rom. 9:13; Ps. 78:67–71; I Cor. 15:8.
[6] Second Sunday after Christmas.

the same air and dew, and none without beauty; and yet some are more beautiful than others; and of those which are beautiful, some excel in color, and others in sweetness, and others in form; and then, again, those which are sweet have such perfect sweetness, yet so distinct, that we do not know how to compare them together, or to say which is the sweeter: so is it with souls filled and nurtured by God's secret grace. Abraham, for instance, Jacob's forefather, was the pattern of faith. This is insisted on in Scripture, and it is not here necessary to show that he was so. It will be sufficient to say, that he left his country at God's word; and, at the same word, took up the knife to slay his own son. Abraham seems to have had something very noble and magnanimous about him. He could realize and make present to him things unseen. He followed God in the dark as promptly, as firmly, with as cheerful a heart, and bold a stepping, as if he were in broad daylight. There is something very great in this; and, therefore, St. Paul calls Abraham *our* father, the father of Christians as well as of Jews. For we are especially bound to walk by faith, not by sight; and are blessed in faith, and justified by faith, as was faithful Abraham. Now (if I may say it, with due reverence to the memory of that favored servant of God, in whose praise I am now speaking) that faith in which Abraham excelled was not Jacob's characteristic excellence. Not that he had not faith, and great faith, else he would not have been so dear to God. His buying the birthright and gaining the blessing from Esau were proofs of faith. Esau saw nothing or little precious in them—he was profane; easily parted with the one, and had no high ideas of the other. However, Jacob's faith, earnest and vigorous as it was, was not like Abraham's. Abraham kept his affections loose from everything earthly, and was ready, at God's word, to slay his only son. Jacob had many sons, and may we not even say that he indulged them overmuch? Even as regards Joseph, whom he so deservedly loved, beautiful and touching as his love of him is, yet there is a great contrast between his feelings towards the "son of his old age" and those of Abraham towards Isaac, the unexpected offspring of his hundredth year—nor only such, but his long-promised only son, with whom were the promises. Again: Abraham left his country—so did Jacob; but Abraham, at God's word—Jacob, from necessity on the threat of Esau. Abraham, from the first, felt that God was his portion and his inheritance, and, in a great and generous spirit, he freely gave up all he had, being sure that he should find what was more excellent in doing so. But Jacob, in spite of his really living by faith, wished (if we may so say), as one passage of his history shows, to see before he fully believed. When he was escaping from Esau and came to Bethel, and God appeared to him in a dream and gave him promises, but not yet the performance of them—what did he do? Did he simply accept them? He says, "*If* God will be with me, and will keep me in this way that I go, and will give me bread to eat, and raiment to put on, so that I come again to my father's house in peace; *then* shall the Lord be my God." [7] He makes his obedience, in some sense, depend on a condition; and although we must not, and need not, take the words as if he meant that he would not serve God *till* and *unless* He did for him what He had promised, yet they seem to show a fear and anxiety, gentle indeed, and subdued, and very human (and therefore the more interesting and winning in the eyes of us common men, who read his words), yet an anxiety which Abraham had not. We feel Jacob to be more like ourselves than Abraham was.

What, then, was Jacob's distinguishing grace, as faith was Abraham's? I have already said it: I suppose, thankfulness. Abraham appears ever to have been looking forward in *hope* —Jacob looking back in *memory*: the one rejoicing in the future, the other in the past; the one setting his affections on the future, the other on the past; the one making his way towards the promises, the other musing over their fulfillment. Not that Abraham did not look back also, and

[7] Gen. 28:20–21.

Jacob, as he says on his deathbed, did not "wait for the salvation" of God; but this was the difference between them, Abraham was a hero, Jacob "a plain man, dwelling in tents."

Jacob seems to have had a gentle, tender, affectionate, timid mind—easily frightened, easily agitated, loving God so much that he feared to lose him, and, like St. Thomas perhaps, anxious for sight and possession from earnest and longing desire of them. Were it not for faith, love would become impatient, and thus Jacob desired to possess, not from cold incredulity or hardness of heart, but from such a loving impatience. Such men are easily downcast, and must be treated kindly; they soon despond, they shrink from the world, for they feel its rudeness, which bolder natures do not. Neither Abraham nor Jacob loved the world. But Abraham did not fear, did not feel it. Jacob felt and winced, as being wounded by it. You recollect his touching complaints, "All these things are against me!"—"Then shall ye bring down my gray hairs with sorrow to the grave"—"If I am bereaved of my children, I am bereaved." Again, elsewhere we are told, "All his sons and all his daughters rose up to comfort him; but he refused to be comforted." At another time, "Jacob's heart fainted, for he believed them not." Again, "The spirit of Jacob their father revived." [8] You see what a childlike, sensitive, sweet mind he had. Accordingly, as I have said, his happiness lay, not in looking forward to the hope, but backwards upon the experience, of God's mercies towards him. He delighted lovingly to trace, and gratefully to acknowledge, what had been given, leaving the future to itself.

For instance, when coming to meet Esau, he brings before God in prayer, in words of which the text is part, what He had already done for him, recounting His past favors with great and humble joy in the midst of his present anxiety.

O God of my father Abraham [he says], and God of my father Isaac, the Lord which saidst unto me, Return unto thy country, and to thy kindred, and I will deal well with thee: I am not

[8] Gen. 42:36, 38; 43:14; 37:35; 45:26, 27.

worthy of the least of all the mercies, and of all the truth, *which thou hast shewed unto thy servant; for with my staff I passed over this Jordan; and now I am become two bands.*

Again, after he had returned to his own land, he proceeded to fulfill the promise he had made to consecrate Bethel as a house of God, "Let us arise, and go up to Bethel; and I will make there an altar unto God, *who answered me in the day of my distress, and was with me in the way which I went.*" Again, to Pharaoh, still dwelling on the past: "The days of the years of my pilgrimage are an hundred and thirty years: few and evil have the days of the years of my life been," he means, in themselves, and as separate from God's favor, "and have not attained unto the days of the years of the life of my fathers in the days of their pilgrimage." Again, when he was approaching his end, he says to Joseph, "God Almighty *appeared unto me* at Luz," that is, Bethel, "in the land of Canaan, and blessed me." Again, still looking back, "As for me, when I came from Padan, Rachel died by me in the land of Canaan in the way, when yet there was but a little way to come to Ephrath: and I buried her there in the way of Ephrath." Again, his blessing upon Ephraim and Manasseh: "God, before whom my fathers Abraham and Isaac did walk, *the God which fed me all my life long unto this day,* the Angel which redeemed me from all evil, bless the lads." Again he looks back on the land of promise, though in the plentifulness of Egypt: "Behold, I die: but God shall be with you, and bring you again unto the land of your fathers." And when he gives command about his burial, he says: "I am to be gathered unto my people: bury me with my fathers in the cave that is in the field of Ephron the Hittite." He gives orders to be buried with his fathers; this was natural, but observe, he goes on to *enlarge* on the subject, after his special manner: "There they buried Abraham and Sarah his wife; there they buried Isaac and Rebekah his wife; and *there I buried Leah.*" And further on, when he speaks of waiting for God's salvation, which is an act of hope, he so words it as at the same time to dwell upon the past: "I *have* waited," he says, that is, all my life long, "I have waited for thy salvation, O Lord." [9] Such was Jacob, living in memory rather than in hope, counting times, recording seasons, keeping days; having his history by heart, and his past life in his hand; and as if to carry on his mind into that of his descendants, it was enjoined upon them, that once a year every Israelite should appear before God with a basket of fruit of the earth, and call to mind what God had done for him and his father Jacob, and express his thankfulness for it.

A Syrian ready to perish was my father [he had to say, meaning Jacob], and he went down into Egypt, and sojourned there...and became there a nation, great, mighty, and populous. . . . And the Lord brought us forth out of Egypt . . . with an outstretched arm, and with great terribleness, and with signs, and with wonders: and he hath brought us into this place . . . that floweth with milk and honey. And now, behold, I have brought the firstfruits of the land, which thou, O Lord, hast given me.[10]

Well were it for us, if we had the character of mind instanced in Jacob, and enjoined on his descendants; the temper of dependence upon God's providence, and thankfulness under it, and careful memory of all he has done for us. It would be well if we were in the habit of looking at all we have as God's gift, undeservedly given, and day by day continued to us solely by his mercy. He gave; he may take away. He gave us all we have, life, health, strength, reason, enjoyment, the light of conscience; whatever we have good and holy within us; whatever faith we have; whatever of a renewed will; whatever love towards him; whatever power over ourselves; whatever prospect of heaven. He gave us relatives, friends, education, training, knowledge, the Bible, the church. All comes from him. He gave; he may take away. Did he take away, we should be called on to follow Job's pattern, and be resigned: "The Lord gave, and the Lord hath taken away;

[9] Gen. 32:9–10; 35:3; 47:9; 48:3, 7, 15–16, 21; 49:29–31, 18.
[10] Deut. 26:5–10.

blessed be the name of the Lord." [11] While he continues his blessings, we should follow David and Jacob, by living in constant praise and thanksgiving, and in offering up to him of his own.

We are not our own, any more than what we possess is our own. We did not make ourselves; we cannot be supreme over ourselves. We cannot be our own masters. We are God's property by creation, by redemption, by regeneration. He has a triple claim upon us. Is it not our happiness thus to view the matter? Is it any happiness, or any comfort, to consider that we *are* our own? It may be thought so by the young and prosperous. These may think it a great thing to have everything, as they suppose, their own way—to depend on no one—to have to think of nothing out of sight—to be without the irksomeness of continual acknowledgment, continual prayer, continual reference of what they do to the will of another. But as time goes on, they, as all men, will find that independence was not made for man—that it is an unnatural state—may do for a while, but will not carry us on safely to the end. No, we are creatures; and, as being such, we have two duties, to be resigned and to be thankful.

Let us then view God's providences towards us more religiously than we have hitherto done. Let us try to gain a truer view of what we are, and where we are, in his kingdom. Let us humbly and reverently attempt to trace his guiding hand in the years which we have hitherto lived. Let us thankfully commemorate the many mercies he has vouchsafed to us in time past, the many sins he has not remembered, the many dangers he has averted, the many prayers he has answered, the many mistakes he has corrected, the many warnings, the many lessons, the much light, the abounding comfort which he has from time to time given. Let us dwell upon times and seasons, times of trouble, times of joy, times of trial, times of refreshment. How did he cherish us as children! How did he guide us in that dangerous time when the mind began to

[11] Job 1:21.

think for itself, and the heart to open to the world! How did he with his sweet discipline restrain our passions, mortify our hopes, calm our fears, enliven our heavinesses, sweeten our desolateness, and strengthen our infirmities! How did he gently guide us towards the strait gate! How did he allure us along his everlasting way, in spite of its strictness, in spite of its loneliness, in spite of the dim twilight in which it lay! He has been all things to us. He has been, as he was to Abraham, Isaac, and Jacob, our God, our shield, and great reward, promising and performing, day by day. "Hitherto hath he helped us." "He hath been mindful of us, and he will bless us." He has not made us for nought; he has brought us thus far, in order to bring us further, in order to bring us on to the end. He will never leave us nor forsake us; so that we may boldly say, "The Lord is my helper; I will not fear what flesh can do unto me." We may "cast all our care upon him, who careth for us." What is it to us how our future path lies, if it be but his path? What is it to us whither it leads us, so that in the end it leads to him? What is it to us what he puts upon us, so that he enables us to undergo it with a pure conscience, a true heart, not desiring anything of this world in comparison of him? What is it to us what terror befalls us, if he be but at hand to protect and strengthen us? "Thou, Israel," he says, "art my servant, Jacob whom I have chosen, the seed of Abraham my friend." "Fear not, thou worm Jacob, and ye men of Israel; I will help thee, saith the Lord, and thy redeemer, the Holy One of Israel."

> Thus saith the Lord that created thee, O Jacob, and he that formed thee, O Israel, Fear not: for I have redeemed thee, I have called thee by thy name; thou art mine. When thou passest through the waters, I will be with thee; and through the rivers, they shall not overflow thee: when thou walkest through the fire, thou shalt not be burned; neither shall the flame kindle upon thee. For I am the Lord thy God, the Holy One of Israel, thy Saviour.[12]

12 Isa. 41:8, 14; 43:1-3.

# EIGHT

# God Hidden
# and Revealed

## Christ Hidden from the World

*"The light shineth in darkness; and the darkness comprehended it not."*—John 1:5

OF ALL THE THOUGHTS
which rise in the mind when contemplating the sojourn of
our Lord Jesus Christ upon earth,[1] none perhaps is more af-
fecting and subduing than the obscurity which attended it.
I do not mean his obscure condition, in the sense of its being
humble; but the obscurity in which he was shrouded, and the
secrecy which he observed. This characteristic of his first
advent is referred to very frequently in Scripture, as in the
text, "The light shineth in darkness; and the darkness comprehended it not"; and is in contrast with what is foretold
about his second advent. Then "every eye shall see him";
which implies that all shall recognize him; whereas, when he
came for the first time, though many saw him, few indeed
discerned him. It had been prophesied, "When we shall see
him, there is no beauty that we should desire him"; and at
the very end of his ministry he said to one of his twelve chosen
friends, "Have I been so long time with you, and yet hast
thou not known me, Philip?" [2]

[1] Preached on Christmas Day.
[2] Isa. 53:2; John 14:9.

I propose to set before you one or two thoughts which arise from this very solemn circumstance, and which may, through God's blessing, be profitable.

(1) And first, let us review some of the circumstances which marked his sojourn when on earth.

His condescension in coming down from heaven, in leaving his Father's glory and taking flesh, is so far beyond power of words or thought, that one might consider at first sight that it mattered little whether he came as a prince or a beggar. And yet after all, it *is* much more wonderful that he came in low estate, for this reason; because it might have been thought beforehand, that, though he condescended to come on earth, yet he would not submit to be overlooked and despised: now the rich are not despised by the world, and the poor are. If he had come as a great prince or noble, the world without knowing a whit more that he was God, yet would at least have looked up to him and honored him, as being a prince; but when he came in a low estate, he took upon him one additional humiliation, *contempt*—being contemned, scorned, rudely passed by, roughly profaned by his creatures.

What were the actual circumstances of his coming? His mother is a poor woman; she comes to Bethlehem to be taxed, traveling, when her choice would have been to remain at home. She finds there is no room in the inn; she is obliged to betake herself to a stable; she brings forth her firstborn son, and lays him in a manger. That little babe, so born, so placed, is none other than the creator of heaven and earth, the eternal Son of God.

Well, he was born of a poor woman, laid in a manger, brought up to a lowly trade, that of a carpenter; and when he began to preach the gospel he had not a place to lay his head: lastly, he was put to death, to an infamous and odious death, the death which criminals then suffered.

For the three last years of his life he preached the gospel, I say, as we read in Scripture; but he did not begin to do so till he was thirty years old. For the first thirty years of his life he seems to have lived just as a poor man would live now.

Day after day, season after season, winter and summer, one year and then another, passed on, as might happen to any of us. He passed from being a babe in arms to being a child, and then he became a boy, and so he grew up "like a tender plant," increasing in wisdom and stature; and then he seems to have followed the trade of Joseph, his reputed father; going on in an ordinary way without any great occurrence, till he was thirty years old. How very wonderful is all this! that he should live here, doing nothing great, so long; living here, as if for the sake of living; not preaching, or collecting disciples, or apparently in any way furthering the cause which brought him down from heaven. Doubtless there were deep and wise reasons in God's counsels for his going on so long in obscurity; I only mean that *we* do not know them.

And it is remarkable that those who were about him seem to have treated him as one of their equals. His brethren, that is, his near relations, his cousins, did not believe in him. And it is very observable, too, that when he began to preach and a multitude collected, we are told, "When his friends heard of it, they went out to lay hold on him: for they said, He is beside himself." [3] They treated him as we might be disposed, and rightly, to treat any ordinary person now, who began to preach in the streets. I say "rightly," because such persons generally preach a *new* gospel, and therefore must be wrong. Also, they preach without being sent, and against authority; all which is wrong, too. Accordingly we are often tempted to say that such people are "beside themselves," or mad, and not unjustly. It is often charitable to say so, for it is better to be mad than to be disobedient. Well, what we should say of such persons, this is what our Lord's friends said of him. They had lived so long with him, and yet did not know him; did not understand what he was. They saw nothing to mark a difference between him and them. He was dressed as others, he ate and drank as others, he came in and went out, and spoke, and walked, and slept, as others. He was in all respects a man, except that he did not sin; and this great difference the

[3] Mark 3:21.

many would not detect, because none of us understands those who are much better than himself: so that Christ, the sinless Son of God, might be living close to us, and we not discover it.

(2) I say that Christ, the sinless Son of God, might be living now in the world as our next-door neighbor, and perhaps we not find it out. And this is a thought that should be dwelt on. I do not mean to say that there are not a number of persons who we could be sure were not Christ; of course, no persons who lead bad and irreligious lives. But there are a number of persons who are in no sense irreligious or open to serious blame, who are very much like each other at first sight, yet in God's eyes are very different. I mean the great mass of what are called respectable men, who vary very much: some are merely decent and outwardly correct persons, and have no great sense of religion, do not deny themselves, have no ardent love of God, but love the world; and, whereas their interest lies in being regular and orderly, or they have no strong passions, or have early got into the way of being regular, and their habits are formed accordingly, they are what they are, decent and correct, but very little more. But there are others who look just the same to the world, who in their hearts are very different; they make no great show, they go on in the same quiet ordinary way as the others, but really they are training to be saints in heaven. They do all they can to change themselves, to become like God, to obey God, to discipline themselves, to renounce the world; but they do it in secret, both because God tells them so to do and because they do not like it to be known. Moreover, there are a number of others between these two with more or less of worldliness and more or less of faith. Yet they all look about the same, to common eyes, because true religion is a hidden life in the heart; and though it cannot exist without deeds, yet these are for the most part secret deeds, secret charities, secret prayers, secret self-denials, secret struggles, secret victories.

Of course, in proportion as persons are brought out into public life, they will be seen and scrutinized, and (in a certain sense) known more; but I am talking of the ordinary condition of people in private life, such as our Savior was for thirty years; and these look very like each other. And there are so many of them that unless we get very near them we cannot see any distinction between one and another; we have no means to do so, and it is no business of ours. And yet, though we have no right to judge others, but must leave this to God, it is very certain that a really holy man, a true saint, though he looks like other men, still has a sort of secret power in him to attract others to him who are like-minded, and to influence all who have anything in them like him. And thus it often becomes a test, whether we are like-minded with the saints of God, whether they have influence over us. And though we have seldom means of knowing at the time who are God's own saints, yet after all is over we have; and then on looking back on what is past, perhaps after they are dead and gone, if we knew them, we may ask ourselves what power they had over us, whether they attracted us, influenced us, humbled us, whether they made our hearts burn within us. Alas! too often we shall find that we were close to them for a long time, had means of knowing them, and knew them not; and that is a heavy condemnation on us, indeed. Now this was singularly exemplified in our Savior's history, by how much he was so very holy. The holier a man is, the less he is understood by men of the world. All who have any spark of living faith will understand him in a measure, and the holier he is, they will, for the most part, be attracted the more; but those who serve the world will be blind to him, or scorn and dislike him, the holier he is. This, I say, happened to our Lord. He was all-holy, but "the light shined in darkness; and the darkness comprehended it not." His near relations did not believe in him. And if this was really so, and for the reason I have said, it surely becomes a question whether we should have understood him better than they: whether though he had been our next-door neighbor, or one of our family, we should have distinguished him from anyone else, who was correct and quiet in his deportment; or rather, whether we should not, though we respected him (alas, what a word! what language towards the Most High God!), yet even if we went as far as this, whether we should not have thought him strange, eccentric, extravagant, and fanciful. Much less should we have detected any sparks of that glory which he had with the Father before the world was, and which was merely hidden not quenched by his earthly tabernacle. This, truly, is a very awful thought; because if he were near us for any long time, and we did not see anything wonderful in him, we might take it as a clear proof that we were not his, for "his sheep know his voice, and follow him"; we might take it as a clear proof that we should not know him, or admire his greatness, or adore his glory, or love his excellency, if we were admitted to his presence in heaven.

(3) And here we are brought to another most serious thought, which I will touch upon. We are very apt to wish we had been born in the days of Christ, and in this way we excuse our misconduct, when conscience reproaches us. We say that had we had the advantage of being with Christ we should have had stronger motives, stronger restraints against sin. I answer, that so far from our sinful habits being reformed by the presence of Christ, the chance is that those same habits would have hindered us from recognizing him. We should not have known he was present; and if he had even told us who he was we should not have believed him. Nay, had we seen his miracles (incredible as it may seem), even they would not have made any lasting impression on us. Without going into this subject, consider only the possibility of Christ being close to us, even though he did no miracle, and our not knowing it; yet I believe this literally would have been the case with most men. But enough on this subject. What I am coming to is this: I wish you to observe what a fearful light this casts upon our prospects in the next world. We think heaven must be a place of happiness to us, if we do but get there; but the great probability is, if we can judge by what goes on here below, that a bad man, if brought to heaven, would not know he was in heaven; I do not go to the further question, whether,

on the contrary, the very fact of his being in heaven with all his unholiness upon him, would not be a literal torment to him, and light up the fires of hell within him. This indeed would be a most dreadful way of finding out where he was. But let us suppose the lighter case: let us suppose he could remain in heaven unblasted, yet it would seem that at least he would not know that he was there. He would see nothing wonderful there. Could men come nearer to God than when they seized him, struck him, spit on him, hurried him along, stripped him, stretched out his limbs upon the cross, nailed him to it, raised it up, stood gazing on him, jeered him, gave him vinegar, looked close whether he was dead, and then pierced him with a spear? O dreadful thought, that the nearest approaches man has made to God upon earth have been in blasphemy! Whether of the two came closer to him, St. Thomas, who was allowed to reach forth his hand and reverently touch his wounds, and St. John, who rested on his bosom, or the brutal soldiers who profaned him limb by limb, and tortured him nerve by nerve? His blessed mother, indeed, came closer still to him; and we, if we be true believers, still closer, who have them really, though spiritually, within us; but this is another, an inward sort of approach. Of those who approached him externally, they came nearest, who knew nothing about it. So it is with sinners: they would walk close to the throne of God; they would stupidly gaze at it; they would touch it; they would meddle with the holiest things; they would go on intruding and prying, not meaning anything wrong by it, but with a sort of brute curiosity, till the avenging lightnings destroyed them; all because they have no *senses* to guide them in the matter. Our bodily senses tell us of the approach of good or evil on earth. By sound, by scent, by feeling we know what is happening to us. We know when we are exposing ourselves to the weather, when we are exerting ourselves too much. We have warnings, and feel we must not neglect them. Now, sinners have no spiritual senses; they can presage nothing; they do not know what is going to happen the next moment to them. So they go fearlessly further and further among precipices, till on a sudden they fall, or are smitten and perish. Miserable beings! and this is what sin does for immortal souls; that they should be like the cattle which are slaughtered at the shambles, yet touch and smell the very weapons which are to destroy them!

(4) But, you may say, how does this concern us? Christ is not here; *we* cannot thus or in any less way insult his majesty. Are we so sure of this? Certainly we cannot commit such open blasphemy; but it is another matter whether we cannot commit as great. For often sins are greater which are less startling; insults more bitter, which are not so loud; and evils deeper, which are more subtle. Do we not recollect a very awful passage? "Whosoever speaketh a word against the Son of man, it shall be forgiven him: but whosoever speaketh against the Holy Ghost, it shall not be forgiven him." [4] Now, I am not deciding whether or no his denunciation can be fulfilled in the case of Christians now, though when we recollect that we *are* at present under the ministration of that very Spirit of whom our Savior speaks, this is a very serious question; but I quote it to show that there may be sins greater even than insult and injury offered to Christ's person, though we should think that impossible, and though they could not be so flagrant or open. With this thought let it be considered:

First, that Christ is still on earth. He said expressly that he would come again. The Holy Ghost's coming is so really his coming that we might as well say that he was not here in the days of his flesh, when he was visibly in this world, as deny that he is here now, when he is here by his divine Spirit. This indeed is a mystery, how God the Son and God the Holy Ghost, two persons, can be one, how he can be in the Spirit and the Spirit in him; but so it is.

Next, if he is still on earth, yet is not visible (which cannot be denied), it is plain that he keeps himself still in the condition which he chose in the days of his flesh. I mean, he

[4] Matt. 12:32.

is a hidden Savior, and may be approached (unless we are careful) without due reverence and fear. I say, wherever he is (for that is a further question), still he is here, and again he is secret; and whatever be the tokens of his presence, still they must be of a nature to admit of persons doubting where it is; and if they will argue, and be sharpwitted and subtle, they may perplex themselves and others, as the Jews did even in the days of his flesh, till he seems to them nowhere present on earth now. And when they come to think him far away, of course they *feel* it to be impossible so to insult him as the Jews did of old; and if nevertheless he *is* here, they *are* perchance approaching and insulting him, though they so feel. And this was just the case of the Jews, for they too were ignorant what they were doing. It is probable, then, that we can now commit at least as great blasphemy towards him as the Jews did first, because we are under the dispensation of that Holy Spirit, against whom even more heinous sins *can* be committed; next, because his presence now as little witnesses of itself, or is impressive to the many, as his bodily presence formerly.

We see a further reason for this apprehension, when we consider what the tokens of his presence now are; for they will be found to be of a nature easily to lead men into irreverence, unless they be humble and watchful. For instance, the church is called "his body": what his material body was when he was visible on earth, such is the church now. It is the instrument of his divine power; it is that which we must approach, to gain good from him; it is that which by insulting we awaken his anger. Now, what is the church but, as it were, a body of humiliation, almost provoking insult and profaneness, when men do not live by faith? An earthen vessel, far more so even than his body of flesh, for that was at least pure from all sin, and the church is defiled in all her members. We know that her ministers at best are but imperfect and erring, and of like passions with their brethren; yet of them he has said, speaking not to the apostles merely but to all the seventy disciples (to whom Christian ministers are in office surely equal), "He that heareth you, heareth me; and he that despiseth you despiseth me; and he that despiseth me despiseth him that sent me."

Again: he has made the poor, weak, and afflicted, tokens and instruments of his presence; and here again, as is plain, the same temptation meets us to neglect or profane it. What he was, such are his chosen followers in this world; and as his obscure and defenseless state led men to insult and ill-treat him, so the like peculiarities, in the tokens of his presence, lead men to insult him now. That such are his tokens is plain from many passages of Scripture: for instance, he says of children, "Whoso shall receive one such little child in my name, receiveth me." Again: he said to Saul, who was persecuting His followers, "Why persecutest thou me?" And he forewarns us that at the Last Day he will say to the righteous, "I was an hungred, and ye gave me meat: I was thirsty, and ye gave me drink: I was a stranger, and ye took me in: Naked, and ye clothed me: I was sick and ye visited me: I was in prison, and ye came unto me." And he adds, "Inasmuch as ye have done it unto one of the least of these my brethren, ye have done it unto me." [5] He observes the same connection between himself and his followers in his words to the wicked. What makes this passage the more awful and apposite, is this, which has been before now remarked, [6] that neither righteous nor wicked *knew* what they had done; even the righteous are represented as unaware that they had approached Christ. They say, "Lord, *when* saw we thee an hungred, and fed thee, or thirsty, and gave thee drink?" In every age, then, Christ is both in the world, and yet not publicly so more than in the days of his flesh.

And a similar remark applies to his ordinances, which are at once most simple, yet most intimately connected with him. St. Paul, in his First Epistle to the Corinthians, shows both how easy and how fearful it is to profane the Lord's Supper, while he states how great the excess of the Corinthians had

[5] Matt. 18:5; Acts 9:4; Matt. 25:35-40.
[6] *Vide* Pascal's *Pensées*.

been, yet also that it was a want of "*discerning* the Lord's body." When he was born into the world, the world knew it not. He was laid in a rude manger, among the cattle, but "all the angels of God worshipped him." Now, too, he is present upon a table, homely perhaps in make, and dishonored in its circumstances; and faith adores, but the world passes by.

Let us then pray him ever to enlighten the eyes of our understanding, that we may belong to the heavenly host, not to this world. As the carnal-minded would not perceive him even in heaven, so the spiritual heart may approach him, possess him, see him, even upon earth.

# NINE

# The True Humanism

## The Greatness and Littleness of Human Life

*"The days of the years of my pilgrimage are an hundred and thirty years: few and evil have the days of the years of my life been, and have not attained unto the days of the years of the life of my fathers, in the days of their pilgrimage."*—Gen. 47:9

Why did the aged patriarch call his days few, who had lived twice as long as men now live, when he spoke? Why did he call them evil, seeing he had on the whole lived in riches and honor, and, what is more, in God's favor? Yet he described his time as short, his days as evil, and his life as but a pilgrimage. Or if we allow that his afflictions were such as to make him reasonably think cheaply of his life, in spite of the blessings which attended it, yet that he should call it short, considering he had so much more time for the highest purposes of his being than we have, is at first sight surprising. He alludes indeed to the longer life which had been granted to his fathers, and perhaps felt a decrepitude greater than theirs had been; yet this difference between him and them could hardly be the real ground of his complaint in the text, or more than a confirmation or occasion of it. It was not because Abraham had lived one hundred and seventy-five years, and Isaac one hundred and eighty, and he himself, whose life was not yet finished, but one hundred and thirty, that he made this mournful speech. For it matters not, when time is gone, what length it has been; and this doubtless was the real cause why the patriarch spoke as he did, not because his life was shorter than his fathers', but because it was well-nigh over. When life is past, it is all one whether it has lasted two hundred years or fifty. And it is this characteristic, stamped on human life in the days of its birth, viz., that it is mortal, which makes it under all circumstances and in every form equally feeble and despicable. All the points in which men differ, health and strength, high or low estate, happiness or misery, vanish before this common lot, mortality. Pass a few years, and the longest-lived will be gone; nor will what is past profit him then, except in its consequences.

And this sense of the nothingness of life, impressed on us by the very fact that it comes to an end, is much deepened when we contrast it with the capabilities of us who live it. Had Jacob lived Methuselah's age, he would have called it short. This is what we all feel, though at first sight it seems a contradiction, that even though the days as they go be slow, and be laden with many events, or with sorrows or dreariness, lengthening them out and making them tedious, yet the year passes quickly though the hours tarry, and time bygone is as a dream, though we thought it would never go while it was going. And the reason seems to be this; that, when we contemplate human life in itself, in however small a portion of it, we see implied in it the presence of a soul, the energy of a spiritual existence, of an accountable being; consciousness tells us this concerning it every moment. But when we look back on it in memory, we view it, but externally, as a mere lapse of time, as a mere earthly history. And the longest duration of this external world is as dust and weighs nothing, against one moment's life of the world within. Thus we are ever expecting great things from life, from our internal consciousness every moment of our having souls; and we are ever being disappointed, on considering what we have gained from time past, or can hope from time to come. And life is ever promising and never fulfilling; and hence, however long it be, our days are few and evil. This is the particular view of the subject on which I shall now dwell.

Our earthly life then gives promise of what it does not accomplish. It promises immortality, yet it is mortal; it contains life in death and eternity in time; and it attracts us by beginnings which faith alone brings to an end. I mean, when we take into account the powers with which our souls are gifted as Christians, the very consciousness of these fills us with a certainty that they must last beyond this life; that is in the case of good and holy men, whose present state I say, is to them who know them well, an earnest of immortality. The greatness of their gifts, contrasted with their scanty time for exercising them, forces the mind forward to the thought of another life, as almost the necessary counterpart and consequence of this life, and certainly implied in this life, provided there be a righteous Governor of the world who does not make man for nought.

This is a thought which will come upon us not always, but under circumstances. And many perhaps of those who at first hearing may think they never felt it, may recognize what I mean, while I describe it.

I mean, when one sees some excellent person, whose graces we know, whose kindliness, affectionateness, tenderness, and generosity—when we see him dying (let him have lived ever so long; I am not supposing a premature death; let him live out his days), the thought is forced upon us with a sort of surprise: "Surely, he is not to die yet; he has not yet had any opportunity of exercising duly those excellent gifts with which God has endowed him." Let him have lived seventy or eighty years, yet it seems as if he had done nothing at all, and his life were scarcely begun. He has lived all his days perhaps in a private sphere; he has been engaged in a number of petty matters which died with the day, and yielded no apparent fruit. He has had just enough of trial under various circumstances to evidence, but not adequately to employ, what was in him. He has, we perhaps perceive, a noble benevolence of mind, a warmth of heart, and a beneficent temper, which, had it the means, would scatter blessings on every side; yet he has never been rich—he dies poor. We have been accustomed to say to ourselves, "What would such a one be were he wealthy?" not as fancying he ever *will* have riches, but from feeling how he would become them; yet, when he actually does die as he lived, without them, we feel somehow disappointed—there has been a failure—his mind, we think, has never reached its scope—he has had a treasure within him which has never been used. His days have been but few and evil, and have become old unseasonably, compared with his capabilities; and we are driven by a sense of these, to look on to a future state as a time when they will be brought out and come into effect. I am not attempting by such reflections to prove that there is a future state; let us take that for granted. I mean, over and above our positive belief in this great truth, we are actually driven to a belief, we attain a sort of sensible conviction of that life to come, a certainty striking home to our hearts and piercing them, by this imperfection in what is present. The very greatness of our powers makes this life look pitiful; the very pitifulness of this life forces on our thoughts to another; and the prospect of another gives a dignity and value to this life which promises it; and thus this life is at once great and little, and we rightly contemn it while we exalt its importance.

And, if this life is short, even when longest, from the great disproportion between it and the powers of regenerate man, still more is this the case, of course, where it is cut short, and death comes prematurely. Men there are, who, in a single moment of their lives, have shown a superhuman height and majesty of mind which it would take ages for them to employ on its proper objects, and, as it were, to exhaust; and who by such passing flashes, like rays of the sun, and the darting of lightning, give token of their immortality, give token to us that they are but angels in disguise, the elect of God sealed for eternal life, and destined to judge the world and to reign with Christ forever. Yet they are suddenly taken away, and we have hardly recognized them when we lose them. Can we believe that they are not removed for higher things elsewhere? This is sometimes said with reference to our intellectual powers; but it is still more true of our moral nature. There is something in moral truth and goodness, in faith, in firmness, in heavenly-mindedness, in meekness, in courage, in loving-kindness, to which this world's circumstances are quite unequal, for which the longest life is insufficient, which makes the highest opportunities of this world disappointing, which must burst the prison of this world to have its appropriate range. So that when a good man dies, one is led to say, "He has not half showed himself, he has had nothing to exercise him; his days are gone like a shadow, and he is withered like grass."

I say the word "disappointing" is the only word to express our feelings on the death of God's saints. Unless our faith be very active, so as to pierce beyond the grave, and realize the future, we feel depressed at what seems like a failure of great things. And from this very feeling surely, by a sort of contradiction, we may fairly take hope; for if this life be so disappointing, so unfinished, surely it is not the whole. This feeling of disappointment will often come upon us in an especial way, on happening to hear of or to witness the deathbeds of holy men. The hour of death seems to be a season, of which, in the hands of Providence, much might be *made,* if I may use the term; much might be done for the glory of God, the good of man, and the manifestation of the person dying. And beforehand friends will perhaps look forward, and expect that great things are then to take place, which they shall never forget. Yet, "how dieth the wise man? as the fool." [1] Such is the preacher's experience, and our own bears witness to it. King Josiah, the zealous servant of the living God, died the death of wicked Ahab, the worshiper of Baal. True Christians die as other men. One dies by a sudden accident, another in battle, another without friends to see how he dies, a fourth is insensible or not himself. Thus the opportunity seems thrown away, and we are forcibly reminded

[1] Eccl. 2:16.

167

that "the manifestation of the sons of God" [2] is hereafter; that "the earnest expectation of the creature" is but waiting for it; that this life is unequal to the burden of so great an office as the due exhibition of those secret ones who shall one day "shine forth as the sun in the kingdom of their Father." [3]

But further (if it be allowable to speculate), one can even conceive the same kind of feeling, and a most transporting one, to come over the soul of the faithful Christian, when just separated from the body, and conscious that his trial is once for all over. Though his life has been a long and painful discipline, yet when it is over, we may suppose him to feel at the moment the same sort of surprise at its being ended, as generally follows any exertion in this life, when the object is gained and the anticipation over. When we have wound up our minds for any point of time, any great event, an interview with strangers, or the sight of some wonder, or the occasion of some unusual trial, when it comes, and is gone, we have a strange reverse of feeling from our changed circumstances. Such, but without any mixture of pain, without any lassitude, dullness, or disappointment, may be the happy contemplation of the disembodied spirit; as if it said to itself,

> So all is now over; this is what I have so long waited for; for which I have nerved myself; against which I have prepared, fasted, prayed, and wrought righteousness. Death is come and gone—it is over. Ah! is it possible? What an easy trial, what a cheap price for eternal glory! A few sharp sicknesses, or some acute pain awhile, or some few and evil years, or some struggles of mind, dreary desolateness for a season, fightings and fears, afflicting bereavements, or the scorn and ill-usage of the world—how they fretted me, how much I thought of them, yet how little really they are! How contemptible a thing is human life—contemptible in itself, yet in its effects invaluable! for it has been to me like a small seed of easy purchase, germinating and ripening into bliss everlasting.

Such being the unprofitableness of this life, viewed in itself, it is plain how we should regard it while we go through

[2] Rom. 8:19.
[3] Matt. 13:43.

it. We should remember that it is scarcely more than an accident of our being—that it is no part of ourselves, who are immortal; that we are immortal spirits, independent of time and space, and that this life is but a sort of outward stage, on which we act for a time, and which is only sufficient and only intended to answer the purpose of trying whether we will serve God or no. We should consider ourselves to be in this world in no fuller sense than players in any game are in the game; and life to be a sort of dream, as detached and as different from our real eternal existence as a dream differs from waking; a serious dream, indeed, as affording a means of judging us, yet in itself a kind of shadow without substance, a scene set before us, in which we seem to be, and in which it is our duty to act just as if all we saw had a truth and reality, because all that meets us influences us and our destiny. The regenerate soul is taken into communion with saints and angels, and its "life is hid with Christ in God"; [4] it has a place in God's court, and is not of this world—looking into this world as a spectator might look at some show or pageant, except when called from time to time to take a part. And while it obeys the instinct of the senses, it does so for God's sake, and it submits itself to things of time so far as to be brought to perfection by them, that, when the veil is withdrawn and it sees itself to be, where it ever has been, in God's kingdom, it may be found worthy to enjoy it. It is this view of life which removes from us all surprise and disappointment that it is so incomplete: as well might we expect any chance event which happens in the course of it to be complete, any casual conversation with a stranger, or the toil or amusement of an hour.

Let us then thus account of our present state: it is precious as revealing to us, amid shadows and figures, the existence and attributes of Almighty God and his elect people: it is precious, because it enables us to hold intercourse with immortal souls who are on their trial as we are. It is momentous, as being

4 Col. 3:3.

the scene and means of our trial; but beyond this it has no claims upon us. "Vanity of vanities, says the preacher, all is vanity." We may be poor or rich, young or old, honored or slighted, and it ought to affect us no more, neither to elate us nor depress us, than if we were actors in a play, who know that the characters they represent are not their own, and that though they may appear to be superior one to another, to be kings or to be peasants, they are in reality all on a level. The one desire which should move us should be, first of all, that of seeing him face to face, who is now hid from us; and next of enjoying eternal and direct communication, in and through him, with our friends around us, whom at present we know only through the medium of sense, by precarious and partial channels, which give us little insight into their hearts.

These are suitable feelings towards this attractive but deceitful world. What have we to do with its gifts and honors, who, having been already baptized into the world to come, are no longer citizens of this? Why should we be anxious for a long life, or wealth, or credit, or comfort, who know that the next world will be everything which our hearts can wish, and that not in appearance only, but truly and everlastingly? Why should we rest in this world, when it is the token and promise of another? Why should we be content with its surface, instead of appropriating what is stored beneath it? To those who live by faith, everything they see speaks of that future world; the very glories of nature, the sun, moon, and stars, and the richness and the beauty of the earth, are as types and figures witnessing and teaching the invisible things of God. All that we see is destined one day to burst forth into a heavenly bloom, and to be transfigured into immortal glory. Heaven at present is out of sight, but in due time, as snow melts and discovers what it lay upon, so will this visible creation fade away before those greater splendors which are behind it, and on which at present it depends. In that day shadows will retire, and the substance show itself. The sun will grow pale and be lost in the sky, but it will be before the radiance of him whom it does but image, the Sun of Righteousness, with healing on his wings, who will come forth in visible form, as a bridegroom out of his chamber, while his perishable type decays. The stars which surround it will be replaced by saints and angels circling his throne. Above and below, the clouds of the air, the trees of the field, the waters of the great deep will be found impregnated with the forms of everlasting spirits, the servants of God which do his pleasure. And our own mortal bodies will then be found in like manner to contain within them an inner man, which will then receive its due proportions, as the soul's harmonious organ, instead of that gross mass of flesh and blood which sight and touch are sensible of. For this glorious manifestation the whole creation is at present in travail, earnestly desiring that it may be accomplished in its season.

These are thoughts to make us eagerly and devoutly say, "Come, Lord Jesus, to end the time of waiting, of darkness, of turbulence, of disputing, of sorrow, of care." These are thoughts to lead us to rejoice in every day and hour that passes, as bringing us nearer the time of his appearing, and the termination of sin and misery. They are thoughts which ought thus to affect us; and so they would, were it not for the load of guilt which weighs upon us, for sins committed against light and grace. Oh that it were otherwise with us! Oh that we were fitted duly to receive this lesson which the world gives us, and had so improved the gifts of life, that while we felt it to be perishing, we might rejoice in it as precious! Oh that we were not conscious of deep stains upon our souls, the accumulations of past years, and of infirmities continually besetting us! Were it not for all this—were it not for our unprepared state, as in one sense it may truly be called, how gladly should we hail each new month and year as a token that our Savior is so much nearer to us than he ever has been yet! May he grant his grace abundantly to us, to make us meet for his presence, that we may not be ashamed before him at his coming! May he vouchsafe to us the full grace of his ordinances: may he feed us with his choicest gifts:

may he expel the poison from our souls: may he wash us clean in his precious blood, and give us the fullness of faith, love, and hope, as foretastes of the heavenly portion which he destines for us!

# TEN

# *The Christian*
# *Character of Waiting*

## *Waiting for Christ*

*"He which testifieth these things saith, Surely I come quickly. Amen. Even so, come, Lord Jesus."*—Rev. 22:20

WHEN OUR LORD WAS going away, he said he would quickly come again; yet knowing that by "quickly" he did not mean what would be at first sight understood by the word, he added, "suddenly," or "as a thief." "Behold, I come as a thief. Blessed is he that watcheth, and keepeth his garments." [1] Had his coming been soon, in our sense of the word, it could not well have been sudden. Servants who are bidden to wait for their master's return from an entertainment, could not, one should think, be overtaken by that return. It was because to us his coming would not *seem* soon, that it *was* sudden. What you expect to come, you wait for; what fails to come, you give up; while, then, Christ said that his coming would be soon, yet by saying it would be sudden, he said that to us it would seem long.

Yet though to us he seems to delay, yet he has declared that his coming is speedy, he has bid us ever look out for his coming; and his first followers, as the epistles show us, *were* ever looking out for it. Surely it is our duty to look out for

[1] Rev. 16:15.

it, as likely to come immediately, though hitherto for near two thousand years the church has been looking out in vain.

Is it not something significant that, in the last book of Scripture, which more than any other implies a long continuance to the Christian church—that there we should have such express and repeated assurances that Christ's coming would be speedy? Even in the last chapter we are told it three times. "Behold, I come quickly: blessed is he that keepeth the sayings of the prophecy of this book." "Behold, I come quickly; and my reward is with me." And again, in the text, "He which testifieth these things saith, Surely I come quickly." Such is the announcement; and, in consequence, we are commanded to be ever looking out for the great day, to "wait for his Son from heaven"; [2] to "look and haste unto the coming of the day of God." [3]

It is true, indeed, that in one place St. Paul cautions his brethren against expecting the immediate coming of Christ; but he does not say more than that Christ will send a sign immediately before his coming—a certain dreadful enemy of the truth—which is to be followed by himself at once, and therefore does not stand in our way, or prevent eager eyes from looking out for him. And, in truth, St. Paul seems rather to be warning his brethren against being disappointed if Christ did not come, than hindering them from expecting him.

Now it may be objected that this is a kind of paradox; how is it possible, it may be asked, ever to be expecting what has so long been delayed? What has been so long coming, may be longer still. It was possible, indeed, for the early Christians, who had no experience of the long period which the church was to remain on earth, to look out for Christ; but we cannot help using our reason: there are no more grounds to expect Christ now than at those many former times, when, as the event showed, he did not come. Christians have ever been expecting the last day, and ever meeting with disappointment. They have seen what they thought symptoms of his coming,

2 I Thess. 1:10.
3 II Pet. 3:12.

174

and peculiarities in their own times, which a little more knowledge of the world, a more enlarged experience, would have shown them to be common to all times. They have ever been frightened without good reason, fretting in their narrow minds, and building on their superstitious fancies. What age of the world has there been in which people did not think the Day of Judgment coming? Such expectation has but evidenced and fostered indolence and superstition; it is to be considered as a mere weakness.

Now I shall attempt to say something in answer to this objection.

(1) And first, considered as an objection to a habit of continual waiting (to use the common phrase), it proves too much. If it is consistently followed up, no age ought ever to expect the day of Christ; the age in which he shall come (whenever it is) ought not to expect him; which is the very thing he has warned us against. He nowhere warns us against what is contemptuously called superstition; but he expressly warns us against high-minded security. If it be true that Christians have expected him when he did not come, it is quite as true that when he does come, the world will not expect him. If it be true that Christians have fancied signs of his coming, when there were none, it is equally true that the world will not see the signs of his coming when they are present. His signs are not so plain but you have to search for them; not so plain but you may be mistaken *in* your search; and your choice lies between the risk of thinking you see what is not and of not seeing what is. True it is, that many times, in many ages, have Christians been mistaken in thinking they discerned Christ's coming; but better a thousand times think him coming when he is not than once think him not coming when he is. Such is the difference between Scripture and the world; judging by Scripture, you would ever be expecting Christ; judging by the world, you would never expect him. Now he must come one day, sooner or later. Worldly men have their scoff at our failure of discernment now; but whose will be the want of discernment, whose the

triumph then? And what does Christ think of their present scoff? He expressly warns us, by his apostle, of scoffers, who shall say,

> Where is the promise of his coming? for since the fathers fell asleep, all things continue as they were from the beginning of the creation. . . . But, beloved [continues St. Peter], be not ignorant of this one thing, that one day is with the Lord as a thousand years, and a thousand years as one day.[4]

It should be recollected, too, that the enemies of Christ have ever been expecting the downfall of his religion, age after age; and I do not see why the one expectation is more unreasonable than the other; indeed they illustrate each other. So it is, undeterred by the failure of former anticipations, unbelievers are ever expecting that the church and the religion of the church are coming to an end. They thought so in the last century. They think so now. They ever think the light of truth is going out, and that their hour of victory is come. Now, I repeat, I do not see why it is reasonable to expect the overthrow of religion still, after so many failures; and yet unreasonable, because of previous disappointments, to expect the coming of Christ. Nay, Christians at least, over and above the aspect of things, can point to an express promise of Christ, that he will one day come; whereas unbelievers, I suppose, do not profess any grounds at all for expecting their own triumph, except the signs of the times. They are sanguine, because they seem so strong, and the church of God seems so weak; yet they have not enlarged their minds enough by the contemplation of past history to know that such apparent strength on the one side, and such apparent weakness on the other, has ever been the state of the world and the church; and that this has ever been one chief or rather the main reason, why Christians have expected the immediate end of all things, because the prospects of religion *were* so gloomy. So that, in fact, Christians and unbelievers have taken precisely the same view of the facts of the case; only they have drawn distinct conclusions from

4 II Pet. 3:4, 8.

them, according to their creed. The Christian has said, "All looks so full of tumult, that the world is coming to an end"; and the unbeliever has said, "All is so full of tumult, that the church is coming to an end"; and there is nothing, surely, more superstitious in the one opinion than in the other.

Now when Christians and unbelievers thus unite in expecting substantially the same thing, though they view it differently, according to their respective modes of thought, there cannot be anything very extravagant in the expectation itself; there must be something ever present in the world which warrants it. And I hold this to be the case. Ever since Christianity came into the world, it has been, in one sense, going out of it. It is so uncongenial to the human mind, it is so spiritual, and man is so earthly, it is apparently so defenseless, and has so many strong enemies, so many false friends, that every age, as it comes, may be called "the last time." It has made great conquests, and done great works; but still it has done all, as the apostle says of himself, "in weakness, and in fear, and in much trembling." [5] *How* it is that it is always failing, yet always continuing, God only knows who wills it—but so it is; and it is no paradox to say, on the one hand, that it has lasted eighteen hundred years, that it may last many years more, and yet that it draws to an end, nay, is likely to end any day. And God would have us give our minds and hearts to the latter side of the alternative, to open them to impressions *from* this side, viz., that the end is coming—it being a wholesome thing to live as if *that* will come in our day, which may come any day.

It was different during the ages before Christ came. The Savior was to come. He was to bring perfection, and religion was to grow *towards* that perfection. There was a system of successive revelations going on, first one and then another; each prophet in his turn adding to the store of divine truth, and gradually tending towards the full gospel. Time was measured out for believing minds before Christ came, by the word of

[5] I Cor. 2:3.

prophecy; so that he never could be expected in any age before the "fullness of time" in which he came. The chosen people were not bidden to expect him at once; but after a sojourning in Canaan, and a captivity in Egypt, and a wandering in the wilderness, and judges, and kings, and prophets, at length seventy long weeks were determined to introduce him into the world. Thus his delay was, as I may say, *recognized* then; and, *during* his delay, other doctrines, other rules, were given to fill the interval. But when once the Christ had come, as the Son over his own house, and with his perfect gospel, nothing remained but to gather in his saints. No higher priest could come—no truer doctrine. The Light and Life of men had appeared, and had suffered, and had risen again; and nothing more was left to do. Earth had had its most solemn event, and seen its most august sight; and therefore it was the last time. And hence, though time intervene between Christ's first and second coming, it is not *recognized* (as I may say) in the gospel scheme, but is, as it were, an accident. For so it was, that up to Christ's coming in the flesh, the course of things ran straight towards that end, nearing it by every step; but now, under the gospel, that course has (if I may so speak) altered its direction, as regards his second coming, and runs, not towards the end, but along it, and on the brink of it; and is at all times equally near that great event, which, did it run towards, it would at once run into. Christ, then, is ever at our doors; as near eighteen hundred years ago as now, and not nearer now than then; and not nearer when he comes than now. When he says that he will come soon, "soon" is not a word of time, but of natural order. This present state of things, "the present distress" as St. Paul calls it, is ever *close upon* the next world, and resolves itself into it. As when a man is given over, he may die any moment, yet lingers; as an implement of war may any moment explode, and must at some time; as we listen for a clock to strike, and at length it surprises us; as a crumbling arch hangs, we know not how, and is not safe to pass under; so creeps on this feeble weary world, and one day, before we know where we are, it will end.

And here I may observe in passing, on the light thus thrown upon the doctrine, that Christ is the sole priest under the gospel, or that the apostles ever sit on twelve thrones, judging the twelve tribes of Israel, or that Christ is with them always, even unto the end of the world. Do you not see the force of these expressions? The Jewish covenant, indeed, had "sundry times," which were ordered "in divers manners"; it had a long array of priests and a various history; one part of the series holier than another, and nearer heaven. But when Christ had come, suffered, and ascended, he was henceforth ever near us, ever at hand, even though he was not actually returned, ever scarcely gone, ever all but come back. He is the only ruler and priest in his church, dispensing gifts, and has appointed none to supersede him, because he is departed only for a brief season. Aaron took the place of Christ, and had a priesthood of his own; but Christ's priests have no priesthood but his. They are merely his shadows and organs, they are his outward signs; and what they do, he does; when they baptize, he is baptizing; when they bless, he is blessing. He is in all acts of his church, and one of its acts is not more truly his act than another, for all are his. Thus we are, in all times of the gospel, brought close to his cross. We stand, as it were, under it, and receive its blessings fresh from it; only that since, historically speaking, time has gone on, and the Holy One is away, certain outward forms are necessary, by way of bringing us again under his shadow; and we enjoy those blessings through a mystery, or sacramentally, in order to enjoy them really. All this witnesses to the duty both of remembering and of looking out for Christ, teaching us to neglect the present, to rely on no plans, to form no expectations, for the future, but so to live in faith, as if he had not left us, so in hope, as if he had returned to us. We must try to live as if the apostles were living, and we must try to muse upon our Lord's life in the gospels, not as a history, but as if a recollection.

(2) This leads me to remark upon a second aspect under which the objection in question may be urged; viz., that this

waiting for Christ is not only extravagant in its very idea, but becomes a superstition and weakness whenever carried into effect. The mind, intent upon the thought of an awful visitation close at hand, begins to fancy signs of it in the natural and moral world, and mistakes the ordinary events of God's providence for miracles. Thus Christians are brought into bondage, and substitute for the gospel a fond religion, in which imagination takes the place of faith, and things visible and earthly take the place of Scripture. This is the objection; yet the text, on the other hand, while it sanctions the expectation, in the words "Surely I come quickly," surely sanctions the temper of waiting also, by adding, "Amen. Even so, come, Lord Jesus."

I observe, then, that though Christians might be mistaken in what they took to be signs of Christ's coming, yet they were not wrong in their state of mind; they were not mistaken in looking out, and that for Christ. Whether credulous or not, they only acted as one acts towards some person beloved, or revered, or admired on earth. Consider the mode in which loyal persons look up to a good prince; you will find stories current, up and down the country, in his favor; people delight in believing that they have fallen in with tokens of his beneficence, nobleness, and paternal kindness. Many of these reports are false, yet others are true, and, on the whole, we should not think highly of that man who, instead of being touched at this mutual sympathy between sovereign and people, occupied himself merely in carping at what he called their credulity, and sifting the accuracy of this or that particular story. A great thing, truly, after all, to be able to detect a few misstatements, and to expose a few fictions, and to be without a heart! And forsooth, on the other hand, a sad deficiency in that people, I suppose, merely to be right on the whole, not in every particular, and to have the heart right! Who would envy such a man's knowledge? Who would not rather have that people's ignorance? And, in like manner, I had rather be he, who, from love of Christ and want of science, thinks some strange sight in the sky, comet or meteor, to be the sign of his coming, than the man, who, from more knowledge and from lack of love, laughs at the mistake.

Before now, religious persons have taken appearances in the heavens for signs of Christ's coming, which do not now frighten us at all. Granted, but what then? Let us consider the state of the case. Of old time it was not *known* generally that certain heavenly bodies moved and appeared at *fixed* times and by a rule; now it is known; that is, now men are *accustomed* to seeing them, then they were not accustomed. We know as little now as then *how* they come, or why; but then men were startled when they saw them, because they were strange, and now they are not strange, and therefore men are not startled. But how was it therefore absurd and ridiculous (for so it is that persons nowadays talk), why was it a foolish fond thing in a man to be impressed by what was rare and strange? Take a parallel case: traveling is common now, it was not common formerly. In consequence, we now travel without any serious emotion at parting from our friends; but then, because it was uncommon, even when risks were the same and the absence as long, persons did not go from home without much preparation, many prayers, and much leave-taking. I do not see anything very censurable in being more impressed at uncommon things than at common.

And you will observe, that in the case of which I am speaking, persons who are looking out for Christ are not only, *in that* they look out, acting in obedience to him, but are looking out—in their very *way* of looking out, through the very signs through which they look out—in obedience to Him. Always since the first, Christians have been looking out for Christ *in* the signs of the natural and moral world. If they have been poor and uneducated, strange sights in the sky, or tremblings of the ground, storms, failure of harvest, or disease, or anything monstrous and unnatural, has made them think that he was at hand. If they were in a way to take a view of the social and political world, then the troubles of states—wars, revolutions, and the like—have been additional circumstances which served to impress them, and kept their hearts awake for Christ. Now all these are nothing else but those very things which he himself has told us to dwell upon, and has given us as signs of his coming.

> There shall be signs [he says] in the sun, and in the moon, and in the stars; and upon the earth distress of nations, with perplexity; the sea and the waves roaring; men's hearts failing them for fear, and for looking after those things which are coming on the earth: for the powers of heaven shall be shaken.... And when these things begin to come to pass, then look up, and lift up your heads; for your redemption draweth nigh.[6]

One day the lights of heaven *will* be signs; one day the affairs of nations also *will* be signs; why, then, is it superstitious to *look* towards them? It is not. We may be wrong in the particulars we rest upon, and may show our ignorance in doing so; but there is nothing ridiculous or contemptible in our ignorance, and there is much that is religious in our watching. It is better to be wrong in our watching, than not to watch at all.

Nor does it follow that Christians were wrong, even in their particular anticipations, though Christ did not come, whereas they said, they saw his signs. Perhaps they *were* his signs, and he withdrew them again. Is there no such thing as countermanding? Do not skillful men in matters of this world sometimes form anticipations which turn out wrong, and yet we say that they *ought* to have been right? The sky threatens and then clears again. Or some military leader orders his men forward, and then for some reason recalls them; shall we say that informants were wrong who brought the news that he was moving? Well, in one sense Christ is ever moving forward, ever checking, the armies of heaven. Signs of the white horses are ever appearing, ever vanishing. "Clouds return after the rain"; and his servants are not wrong in pointing to them, and saying that the weather is breaking, though it does not break, for it is ever unsettled.

And another thing should be observed, that though Christians have ever been expecting Christ, ever pointing to his

[6] Luke 21:25-26, 28.

signs, they have never said that he was come. They have but said that he was just coming, *all but* come. And so he was and is. Enthusiasts, sectaries, wild presumptuous men, *they* have said that he was *actually* come, or they have pointed out the exact year and day in which he would come. Not so his humble followers. They have neither announced nor sought him, either in the desert or in the secret chambers, nor have they attempted to determine "the times or the seasons, which the Father has put in his own power." They have but waited; when he actually comes, they will not mistake him; and before then, they pronounce nothing. They do but see his forerunners.

Surely there can be no great harm, and nothing very ridiculous, where men are religious, in thus thinking the events of their day more than ordinary, in fancying that the world's matters are winding up, and that events are thickening for a final visitation; for, let it be observed, Scripture sanctions us in interpreting *all* that we see in the world in a religious sense, and as if all things were tokens and revelations of Christ, his providence, and will. I mean that if this lower world, which seems to go on in its own way, independently of him, governed by fixed laws or swayed by lawless hearts, will, nevertheless, one day in an awful way, herald his coming to judge it, surely it is not impossible that the same world, both in its physical order and its temporal course, speaks of him also in other manners. At first, indeed, one might argue that this world did but speak a language contrary to him; that in Scripture it is described as opposed to God, to truth, to faith, to heaven; that it is said to be a deceitful veil, misrepresenting things, and keeping the soul from God. How then, it may be asked, can this world have upon it tokens of his presence, or bring us near to him? Yet certainly so it is, that in spite of the world's evil, after all, he is in it and speaks through it, though not loudly. When he came in the flesh "He was in the world, and the world was made by him, and the world knew him not." Nor did he strive or cry, nor lift up his voice in the streets. So it is now. He still is here; he still whispers to us, he still makes signs to us. But his voice is so low, and the world's din is so loud, and his signs are so covert, and the world is so restless, that it is difficult to determine when he addresses us, and what he says. Religious men cannot but feel, in various ways, that his providence is guiding them and blessing them personally, on the whole; yet when they attempt to put their finger upon the times and places, the traces of his presence disappear. Who is there, for instance, but has been favored with answers to prayer, such that, at the time, he has felt he never could again be unbelieving? Who has not had strange coincidences in his course of life which brought before him, in an overpowering way, the hand of God? Who has not had thoughts come upon him with a sort of mysterious force, for his warning or his direction? And some persons, perhaps, experience stranger things still. Wonderful providences have before now been brought about by means of dreams; or in other still more unusual ways Almighty God has at times interposed. And then, again, things which come before our eyes, in such wise take the form of types and omens of things moral or future, that the spirit within us cannot but reach forward and presage what it is not told from what it sees. And sometimes these presages are remarkably fulfilled in the event. And then, again, the fortunes of men are so singularly various, as if a law of success and prosperity embraced a certain number, and a contrary law others. All this being so, and the vastness and mystery of the world being borne in upon us, we may well begin to think that there is nothing here below, but, for what we know, has a connection with everything else; the most distant events may yet be united, the meanest and highest may be parts of one; and God may be teaching us and offering us knowledge of his ways, if we will but open our eyes, in all the ordinary matters of the day. This is what thoughtful persons come to believe, and they begin to have a sort of faith in the divine meaning of the accidents (as they are called) of life, and a readiness to take impressions from them, which may easily become excessive, and which, whether excessive or not, is sure to be ridiculed by the world at large as superstition. Yet, considering Scripture tells us that the very hairs of our head are all numbered by God, that all things are ours, and that all things work together for our good, it does certainly encourage us in thus looking out for his presence in everything that happens, however trivial, and in holding that to religious ears even the bad world prophesies of him.

Yet, I say, this religious waiting upon God through the day, which is so like that spirit of watching which is under consideration, is just as open to objection and scoffing from the world. God does not so speak to us through the occurrences of life that you can persuade others that he speaks. He does not act upon such explicit laws that you can speak of them with certainty. He gives us sufficient tokens of himself to raise our minds in awe towards him; but he seems so frequently to undo what he has done, and to suffer counterfeits of his tokens, that a conviction of his wonder-working presence can but exist in the individual himself. It is not a truth that can be taught and recognized in the face of men; it is not of a nature to be urged upon the world at large, nay, even on religious persons, as a principle. God gives us enough to make us inquire and hope; not enough to make us insist and argue.

I have all along been speaking of thoughtful and conscientious persons; those who do their duty, and who study Scripture. It is quite certain that this regard to outward occurrences does become superstition, when it is found in men of irreligious lives, or of slender knowledge of Scripture. The great and chief revelation which God has made us of his will is through Christ and his apostles. They have given us a knowledge of the truth; they have sent forth heavenly principles and doctrines into the world; they have accompanied that revealed truth by divine sacraments, which convey to the heart what otherwise would be a mere outward and barren knowledge; and they have told us to practice what we know, and obey what we are taught, that the word of Christ may be formed and dwell in us. They have been inspired, moreover, to write Holy Scriptures for our learning and comfort; and in those Scriptures we find the history of this world interpreted for us by a heavenly rule. When, then, a man, thus formed and fortified within, with these living principles in his heart, with this firm hold and sight of things invisible, with likings, opinions, views, aims, molded upon God's revealed law, looks abroad into the world, he does not come to the world for a revelation—he has one already. He does not take his religion from the world, nor does he set an overvalue upon the tokens and presages which he sees there. But far different is the case when a man is not thus enlightened and informed by revealed truth. Then he is but a prey, he becomes the slave, of the occurrences and events, the sights and sounds, the omens and prodigies, which meet him in the world, natural and moral. His religion is a bondage to things perishable, and idolatry of the creature, and is, in the worst sense of the word, superstition. Hence it is a common remark that irreligious men are most open to superstition. For they have a misgiving that there is something great and divine somewhere: and since they have it not within them, they have no difficulty in believing that it is anywhere else, wherever men pretend to the possession of it. Thus you find in history men in high places practicing unlawful arts, consulting professed wizards, or giving heed to astrology. Others have had their lucky and unlucky days; others have been the sport of dreams, or of other idle fancies. And you have had others bowing themselves down to idols. For they have had no principle, no root in themselves. They have been ignorant, too, of Scripture, in which God has most mercifully removed the veil off a portion of this world's history, in order that we may see *how* he works. Scripture is the key by which we are given to interpret the world; but they who have it not, roam amid the shadows of the world, and interpret things at random.

The same want of inward religious principle is shown in the light, senseless way in which so many adopt wrong forms of religious profession. He who has the light of Christ within him, hears the voice of enthusiastic, mistaken, self-willed, or hypocritical men, calling him to follow them, without being moved. But when a man is conscious he is a willful sinner, and not at peace with God, when his own heart is against him, and he has no principle, no stay within him, then he is the prey of the first person who comes to him with strong language, and bids him believe in him. Hence you find numbers running eagerly after men who profess to work miracles, or who denounce the church as apostate, or who maintain that none are saved but those who agree with themselves, or anyone who, without any warrant of his being right, speaks confidently. Hence the multitude is so open to sudden alarms. You hear of their rushing out of a city in numbers at some idle prediction that the Day of Judgment is coming. Hence so many, in the private and lower ranks of life, are so full of small superstitions, which are too minute to mention; all because they have not the light of truth burning in their heart.

But the true Christian is not of these. To him apply St. Paul's words, "All things are lawful unto me, but all things are not expedient: all things are lawful for me, but I will not be brought under the power of any." [7] He knows how to "use this world as not abusing it." He *depends* on nothing in this world. He trusts not *its* sights against the revealed word. "Thou wilt keep him in perfect peace, whose mind is stayed on thee: because he trusteth in thee." Such is the promise made to him. And if he looks out into the world to seek, it is not to seek what he does not know, but what he does. He does not seek a Lord and Savior. He has "found the Messias" long since; and he is looking out for *him*. His Lord himself has *bid* him look for him in the signs of the world, and therefore he looks out. His Lord himself has shown him, in the Old Testament, how he, the Lord of Glory, condescends to humble himself to the things of heaven and earth. He knows that God's angels are about the earth. He knows that once they were even used to come in human shape. He knows that the Son of God, ere now, has come on earth. He knows that he promised to his church the presence of a miraculous agency, and has never recalled his promise. Again, he reads, in the

[7] I Cor. 6:12.

187

Book of the Revelation, quite enough, not to show him what is coming, but to show him that now, as heretofore, a secret supernatural system is going on *under* this visible scene. And therefore he looks out for Christ, for his present providences, and for his coming; and, though often deceived in his expectation, and fancying wonderful things are coming on the earth, when they still delay, he uses, and comforts him with the prophet's words,

> I will stand upon my watch, and set me upon the tower, and will watch to see what he will say unto me, and what I shall answer when I am reproved. And the Lord answered me, . . . The vision is yet for an appointed time, but at the end it shall speak, and not lie: though it tarry, wait for it; because it will surely come, it will not tarry. Behold, his soul, which is lifted up is not upright in him: but the just shall live by his faith.[8]

[8] Hab. 2:1–4.

# ELEVEN

# Christian Expectation

## Subjection of the Reason and Feelings to the Revealed Word

*"Bringing into captivity every thought to the obedience of Christ."*
—II Cor. 10:5

THE QUESTION MAY BE asked, How is it possible to live as if the coming of Christ were not far off, when our reason tells us that it probably is distant? It may be objected that there are no grounds for expecting it now, more than for the last eighteen hundred years; that if his long absence is a reason for expecting it now, yet his promise of a speedy return was a reason for expecting it in earlier times; and if the one reason has turned out insufficient, so may the other; that if, in spite of his promise to be speedy, he has tarried so long, he may tarry longer still; that no signs of his coming can be greater than were abroad soon after his departure; that, certainly, there are no such signs now; nay, that during the first seven hundred years, and again about the year 1000, and later, there were many more signs of Christ's coming than there are now—more trouble of nations, more distress, more sickness, more terror. It may be said that we cannot hope, and fear, and expect, and wait, as we will—but that we must have *reasons* for so doing; and that if we are persuaded, in our deliberate judgment, that Christ's coming is not probable, we cannot make ourselves feel as if it were probable.

Now in considering this objection, which I shall do, I may have an opportunity of stating a great principle which obtains in Christian duty, the subjection of the whole mind to the law of God.

(1) I deny, then, that our feelings and likings are only moved according to the dictates of what we commonly mean by reason; so far from it, that nothing is more common, on the other hand, than to say that reason goes one way, and our wishes go another. There is nothing impossible, then, in learning to look out for the day of Christ's coming more earnestly than according to its probability in the judgment of reason. As reason may be a right guide for our feelings and likings to go by up to a certain point, so there may be cases in which it is unable to guide us, from its weakness; and as it is not impossible for sinful and irreligious men to like what their reason tells them they should not like; therefore it is not impossible for religious men also to desire, expect, and hope, what their reason is unequal to approve and accept. What is more common than to hear it said, "I love a person more than I respect him," or, "I admire him more than I love him"? Or, again, we know how easy it is to open the mind to the influence of some feeling or emotion, and how difficult it is to avoid such influence; how difficult it is to get a thought out of the mind, which reason says ought to be kept out, and which will intrude itself again and again; how difficult to restrain anger, fear, or other passion, which yet reason tells us should be restrained. It is, then, quite possible to have feelings and thoughts present with us in a way which is disproportionate, according to the judgment of reason. Or, take another instance. We know how the mind sometimes dwells upon the chance of what is barely possible, quite unreasonably, and often wrongly and dangerously. A number of things may happen, one perhaps as likely as another; and yet, from weakness of health, or excitement, it often happens that we cannot help thinking overmuch of some one of these possible events, and getting unduly anxious lest it should happen. Thus, if some dreadful occurrence has

taken place, a fire, or a murder, or some horrible accident, persons become frightened, lest the same should happen to them, in a measure far exceeding what a mere calculation of probabilities warrants. Their imagination magnifies the danger; they cannot persuade themselves to look at things calmly, and according to their general course. They fix their thoughts upon one particular chance, in a way quite contrary to what reason suggests. Thus, so far from our feelings being moved according to the strict probabilities of things, the contrary is rather the rule. What Almighty God then requires of us is, to do that in one instance for his sake, which we do so commonly in indulgence of our own waywardness and weakness; to hope, fear, expect our Lord's coming, more than reason warrants, and in a way which his word alone warrants; that is, to trust him above our reason. You say, that it is not probable Christ will come at this time, and therefore you cannot expect it. Now, I say, you can expect it. You must feel there is a chance that he will come. Well, then, dwell on that chance; open your mind to it; treat that chance just as you so often treat the chance of fire, or peril by sea, or peril by land, or thieves. Our Lord says, that he shall come as a thief in the night. Now you know that if there has been some remarkable robbery, people are frightened far more than according to the chance of their being themselves robbed. They are haunted by the idea; it may be that the probability of their own houses being attempted is but small, yet the thing itself is an object of great apprehension to them, and they think more of the grievousness of the event apprehended, should it happen, than of the small chance of its happening. They are moved by the risk. And in like manner, as regards the coming of Christ; I do not say we must be excited, or unsettled, or engrossed with the thought, but still we must not let the long delay persuade us not to watch for it. "Though it tarry, wait for it." If he bids us, as a matter of duty, impress the prospect of his coming upon our imagination, he asks no hard thing; no hard thing, that is, to the willing mind; and what we can do we are bound to do.

(2) This is what first suggests itself, but it opens the way to further thoughts. For only reflect, what is faith itself but an acceptance of things unseen, from the love of them, *beyond* the determinations of calculation and experience? Faith outstrips argument. If there is only a fair chance that the Bible is true, that heaven is the reward of obedience, and hell of willful sin, it is worthwhile, it is safe, to sacrifice this world to the next. It were worthwhile, though Christ told us to sell all that we have and follow him, and to pass our time here in poverty and contempt, it were worthwhile on that chance to do it. This, then, is what is meant by faith going against reason, that it cares not for the measure of probabilities; it does not ask whether a thing is more or less likely; but if there is a fair and clear likelihood what God's will is, it acts upon it. If Scripture were not true, we should in the next world be left where we were; we should, in the event, be no worse off than before; but if it be true, then we shall be infinitely worse off for not believing it than if we had believed it. We all know the retort which the aged saint made in the story, when a licentious youth reminded him, how he would have wasted life if there were *no* future state of recompense: "True, my son," he answered, "but how *much* worse a waste is yours if there *is*."

Faith, then, does not regard *degrees* of evidence. You might lay it down as a rule, speaking in the way of reason, that we ought to have faith according to the evidence; that the more evidence there is, the more firm it should be; and the less evidence, the weaker will it be required of us. But this is not the case as regards religious faith—which accepts the word of God as firmly on the evidence which it is vouchsafed, as if that evidence were doubled. This, indeed, we see to be the case as regards things of earth; and surely what we do towards men, we may bear to do towards God. If anyone whom we trust and revere told us any news, which he had perfect means of knowing, we should believe him; we should not believe it more thoroughly because presently another told it to us also. And in like manner, though it is quite certain that Almighty God

192

might have given us greater evidence than we possess, that he speaks to us in the Bible; yet since he has given us enough, faith does not ask for more, but is satisfied, and acts upon what *is* enough; whereas unbelief is ever asking for signs, more and greater, before it will yield to the divine word.

Returning to my main subject, I observe, in like manner, what is true of faith is true of hope. We may be commanded, if so be, to hope against hope, or to expect Christ's coming, in a certain sense, against reason. It is not inconsistent with God's general dealings towards us that he should bid us feel and act as if that were at hand which yet, if we went by what experience tells us, we should say was not likely to be at hand. If he bids us to believe in him with our whole heart, whether the evidence of his speaking to us be greater or less, why may he not bid us wait for him perseveringly, though the signs of his coming disappoint us, and reason desponds? We cannot tell in such a matter what is more probable and what is not; we can but attempt what we are told to do. And *that* we can do: we can direct and fashion our feelings according to his word, and leave the rest to him.

(3) Here, then, I am led to make a further remark; that as it is our duty to bring some things before our minds, and contemplate them much more vividly than reason by itself would bid us, so, again, there are other things which it is a duty to put away from us, not to dwell upon, and not to realize, though they be brought before us. And yet it is evident, too, that persons might here also object, and say that it is impossible to help being moved and influenced by what we know for certain, just as they say that it is impossible to believe and expect what we know to be not certain.

For instance, we know that it is a duty not to be vain and conceited about any personal advantage we may happen to possess. Yet a man might ask, How is it possible to help it? He might say,

If persons excel in any respect, they must know it; it is quite absurd to suppose, as a rule, that they should not; but if they

193

know it, how is it possible they should not take pleasure in their own excellence, and admire themselves for it? Admiration is the natural consequence of the sight of excellence: if persons know they excel, they cannot help admiring themselves; and if they excel, generally speaking, they cannot but know it; and this, whatever it be they excel in, whether in personal appearance, or in power of speech, or in gifts of mind, or in character, or in any other way.

But now, on the other hand, I suppose that it is quite certain that Scripture tells us *not* to pride ourselves on anything we are, anything we do; that is, not to indulge those feelings which, it seems, are the natural and legitimate result of our knowing what we do know. Now what is to be said to this? How are these opposites to be reconciled?

One answer would of course be this; that religious men know how defective, after all, their best deeds are, or their best points of character; or they know how much more others do; or they know their own great deficiencies in other respects; or they know how trifling some of those points are on which they may happen to be superior to others. But this is not a sufficient answer; because the points in question *are* excellences, whether great excellences or not, or whether or not there be others greater, or however wanting the parties may be in other respects. And herein lies, I think, the temptation which all persons have to self-esteem, that in a certain sense their judgment about themselves is not wrong; not that they are not very deficient in many things, not as if they did not know this, but that they *have* certain excellences, which really *are* excellences, and they *feel* them; and the question is, how can they help feeling them?

It may be suggested, perhaps, to account for the humility of religious men, that, whatever personal gifts they may have, they are *used* to them; and this it is which keeps them from thinking much of them. There is truth in this remark, of course, but it does not explain why they *once* have not thought much of them, viz., when the sight of what they were, was not so familiar to them as it is; and if they did, we may be sure that the effects of their former self-conceit will remain upon them now, having become habitual.

Another and far better reason why religious persons are not self-conceited is that they dislike to think of whatever is good in them, and turn away from the thought of it, whether their superiority to others be in mind or body, in intellectual powers or in moral attainments. But there is, I think, another more direct reason, and more connected with my present subject.

It is this: though religious men have gifts, and though they know it, yet they do not *realize* them. It is not necessary here to explain exactly what is meant by the word "realizing"; we all understand the word enough for my present purpose, and shall all confess that, at least, there is an abundance of matters which men do *not* realize, though they ought to do so. For instance, how loudly men talk of the shortness of this life, of its vanity and unprofitableness, and of the claims which the world to come has upon us! This is what we hear said daily, yet few act upon the truths they utter; and why? Because they do not *realize* what they are so ready to proclaim. They do not see him who is invisible, and his external kingdom.

Well, then, what men omit to do when the doing is a duty, that they can surely also omit to do in cases when omission is a duty. Serious men may know indeed, if it so be, what their excellences are, whether religious, or moral, or any other, but they do not feel them in that vivid way which we call realizing. They do not open their hearts to the knowledge, so that it becomes fruitful. Barren knowledge is a wretched thing, when knowledge ought to bear fruit; but it is a good thing, when it would otherwise act merely as a temptation. When men realize a truth, it becomes an influential principle within them, and leads to a number of consequences both in opinion and in conduct. The case is the same as regards realizing our own gifts. But men of superior minds know them without realizing. They may know that they have certain excellences, if they have them, they may know that they have good points of character, or abilities, or attainments; but it is in the way of an unproductive knowledge, which leaves the mind just as it found it. And this seems to be what gives such a remarkable simplicity to the character of holy men, and amazes others so much that they think it a paradox or inconsistency, or even a mark of insincerity, that the same persons should profess to know so much about themselves, and yet so little—that they can hear so much said about themselves, that they can bear so much praise, so much popularity, so much deference, and yet without being puffed up, or arrogating aught, or despising others; that they can speak about themselves, yet in so unaffected a tone, with so much nature, with such childlike innocence, and such graceful frankness.

Another instance of this great gift of knowing without realizing is afforded us in relation to subjects to which I will but allude. Men who indulge their passions have a knowledge, different in kind from those who have abstained from such indulgence; and when they speak on subjects connected with it, realize them in a way in which others cannot realize them. The very ideas which are full of temptation to the former, the words which are painful to them to utter, all that causes them shame and confusion of face, can be said and thought of by the innocent without any distress at all. Angels can look upon sin with simple abhorrence and wonder, without humiliation or secret emotion; and a like simplicity is the reward of the chaste and holy; and that to the great amazement of the unclean, who cannot understand the state of mind of such a one, or how he can utter or endure thoughts which to themselves are full of misery and guilt. And hence sometimes you find men in these days, in which the will of the natural man is indulged to the full, taking up the writings of holy men who have lived in deserts or in cloisters, or with an angel's heart have ruled Christ's flock, and broken with holy hands the bread of life, and viewing their words in their own murky atmosphere, and imputing to them their own grossness; nay, carping at the words of Holy Scripture, which are God's, and at the words of the church, as if the sacred mystery of the Incarnation had not introduced a thousand new and heavenly associations into this world of sin.

And hence, again, you will find self-indulgent men unable to comprehend the real existence of sanctity and severity of mind in anyone. They think that all persons must be full of the same wretched thoughts and feelings which torment themselves. They think that none can avoid it, from the nature of the case; only that certain persons contrive to hide what goes on in their hearts, and, in consequence, they call them pretenders and hypocrites.

This, too, is what they also say as regards the instance which I took first—a man's knowledge of his gifts. They think that men who appear to think little of themselves are conceited within, and that what is called modesty is affectation.

I might make the same remark also as regards the absence of resentment upon injury or insult, which characterizes a really religious man. Often, indeed, such a one feels keenly what is done against him, though he represses the feeling as a matter of duty; but the higher state of mind is when he does not feel, that is, when he does not realize, that any injustice has been done him; so that if he attempts to speak of it, it will be in the same sort of strange, unreal, and (as I may say) forced and unnatural way in which pretenders to religion speak of religious joy and spiritual comfort, for he is as little at home with anger and revenge as hypocrites are with thoughts of heaven.

Again; we may so unduly realize that a life of virtue is for our interest, as to act on prudential motives, not from a sense of duty. And again; though it be our duty to inquire and search out for ourselves the truth in religious matters, yet we may so vaunt in our private judgment, and make a merit of the exercise of it, that our search becomes almost a sin.

Here then are a number of cases, all in point, to illustrate one and the same truth, that the Christian's character is formed by a rule higher than that of calculation and reason, consisting in a divine principle of life, which transcends the anticipations and criticisms of ordinary men. Judging by mere worldly reason, the Christian ought to be self-conceited, for he is gifted; he ought to understand evil, because he sees and speaks of it; he ought to feel resentment, because he is conscious of being injured; he ought to act from self-interest, because he knows that what is right is also expedient; he ought to be conscious and fond of the exercises of private judgment, because he engages in them; he ought to be doubting and hesitating in his faith, because his evidence for it might be greater than it is; he ought to have no expectation of Christ's coming, because Christ has delayed so long; but not so: his mind and heart are formed on a different mold. In these, and ten thousand other ways, he is open to the mis-apprehensions of the world, which neither has his feelings nor can enter into them. Nor can he explain and defend them on considerations which all men, good and bad, can understand. He goes by a law which others know not; not his own wisdom or judgment, but by Christ's wisdom and the judgment of the Spirit, which is imparted to him—by that inward in-communicable perception of truth and duty which is the rule of his reason, affections, wishes, tastes, and all that is in him, and which is the result of persevering obedience. This it is which gives so unearthly a character to his whole life and conversation, which is "hid with Christ in God"; he has ascended with Christ on high, and there "in heart and mind continually dwells"; and he is obliged, in consequence, to put a veil upon his face, and is mysterious in the world's judgment, and "becomes as it were a monster unto many," though he be "wiser than the aged," and have "more understanding than his teachers, because he keeps God's commandments." Thus "he that is spiritual judgeth all things, yet he himself is judged of no man"; and with him "it is a very small thing to be judged of man's judgment," for "he that judgeth him is the Lord." [1]

One additional remark is necessary in conclusion, with reference to the subject with which I began, the duty of

[1] I Cor. 2:15; 4:3, 4.

waiting for our Lord's coming. It must not be supposed, then, that this implies a neglect of our duties in this world. As it is possible to watch for Christ in spite of earthly reasonings to the contrary, so is it possible to engage in earthly duties, in spite of our watching. Christ has told us that when he comes two men shall be in the field, two women at the mill, "the one shall be taken, and the other left." You see that good and bad are engaged in the same way; nor need it hinder anyone from having his heart firmly fixed on God, that he is engaged in worldly business with those whose hearts are upon the world. Nay, we may form large plans, we may busy ourselves in new undertakings, we may begin great works which we cannot do more than begin; we may make provision for the future, and anticipate in our acts the certainty of centuries to come, yet be looking out for Christ. Thus indeed we are bound to proceed, and to leave "times and seasons in his Father's power." Whenever he comes, he will cut things short; and, for what we know, our efforts and beginnings, though they be nothing more, are just as necessary in the course of his providence as could be the most successful accomplishment. Surely, he will end the world abruptly, whenever he comes; he will break off the designs and labors of his elect, whatever they are, and give them what their dutiful anxiety aims at, though not through it. And as he will end, so did he begin the world abruptly; he began the world which we see, not from its first seeds and elements, but he created at once the herb and the fruit tree perfect "whose seed is in itself," not a gradual formation, but a complete work. And with even a greater abruptness did he display his miracles when he came and new made all things, creating bread, not corn, for the supply of the five thousand, and changing water, not into any simpler, though precious liquid, but into wine. And as he began without beginning, so will he end without an ending; or rather, all that we do—whatever we are doing —whether we have time for more or time for less—yet our work, finished or unfinished, will be acceptable, if done for him. There is no inconsistency, then, in watching yet working, for we may work without setting our hearts on our work. Our sin will be if we idolize the work of our hands; if we love it so well as not to bear to part with it. The test of our faith lies in our being able to fail without disappointment.

Let us pray God to rule our hearts in this respect as well as in others; that "when he shall appear, we may have confidence, and not be ashamed before him at his coming."

# TWELVE

# Toward Christian Maturity

## Equanimity

*"Rejoice in the Lord alway: and again I say, Rejoice."*—Phil. 4:4

IN OTHER PARTS OF Scripture the prospect of Christ's coming is made a reason for solemn fear and awe, and a call for watching and prayer, but in the verses connected with the text a distinct view of the Christian character is set before us, and distinct duties urged on us. "The Lord is at hand," and what then?—why, if so, we must "rejoice in the Lord"; we must be conspicuous for "moderation"; we must be "careful for nothing"; we must seek from God's bounty, and not from man, whatever we need; we must abound in "thanksgiving"; and we must cherish, or rather we must pray for, and we shall receive from above, "the peace of God, which passeth all understanding," to "keep our hearts and minds through Christ Jesus."

Now this is a view of the Christian character definite and complete enough to admit of commenting on—and it may be useful to show that the thought of Christ's coming not only leads to fear, but to a calm and cheerful frame of mind.

Nothing perhaps is more remarkable than that an apostle— a man of toil and blood, a man combating with powers unseen, and a spectacle for men and angels, and much more that St. Paul, a man whose natural temper was so zealous, so severe, and so vehement—I say, nothing is more striking and significant than that St. Paul should have given us this view of what a Christian should be. It would be nothing wonderful, it *is* nothing wonderful, that writers in a day like this should speak of peace, quiet, sobriety, and cheerfulness as being the tone of mind that becomes a Christian; but considering that St. Paul was by birth a Jew, and by education a Pharisee, that he wrote at a time when, if at any time, Christians were in lively and incessant agitation of mind; when persecution and rumors of persecution abounded; when all things seemed in commotion around them; when there was nothing fixed; when there were no churches to soothe them, no course of worship to sober them, no homes to refresh them; and, again, considering that the gospel is full of high and noble, and what may be called even romantic, principles and motives, and deep mysteries—and, further, considering the very topic which the apostle combines with his admonitions is that awful subject, the coming of Christ—it is well worthy of notice that, in such a time, under such a covenant, and with such a prospect, he should draw a picture of the Christian character as free from excitement and effort, as full of repose, as still and as equable, as if the great apostle wrote in some monastery of the desert or some country parsonage. Here surely is the finger of God; here is the evidence of supernatural influences, making the mind of man independent of circumstances! This is the thought that first suggests itself; and the second is this, how deep and refined is the true Christian spirit!—how difficult to enter into, how vast to embrace, how impossible to exhaust! Who would expect such composure and equanimity from the fervent Apostle to the Gentiles? We know St. Paul could do great things; could suffer and achieve, could preach and confess, could be high and could be low: but we might have thought that all this was the limit and the perfection of the Christian temper, as he viewed it; and that no room was left him for the feelings which the text and following verses lead us to ascribe to him.

And yet he who "laboured more abundantly" than all his brethren is also a pattern of simplicity, meekness, cheerfulness, thankfulness, and serenity of mind. These tempers were especially characteristic of St. Paul, and are much insisted on in his epistles. For instance—"Mind not high things, but condescend to men of low estate. Be not wise in your own conceits. . . . Provide things honest in the sight of all men. If it be possible, as much as lieth in you, live peaceably with all men." He enjoins, that "the aged men be sober, grave, temperate, sound in faith, in charity, in patience." "The aged women likewise . . . not false accusers, not given to much wine, teachers of good things; that they may teach the young women to be sober, to love their husbands, to love their children, to be discreet, chaste, keepers at home, good, obedient to their own husbands." And "young men" to be "sober minded." And it is remarkable that he ends this exhortation with urging the same reason as is given in the verse after the text: "looking for that blessed hope, and the glorious appearing of the great God and Saviour Jesus Christ." In like manner, he says, that Christ's ministers must show "uncorruptness in doctrine, gravity, sincerity, sound speech, that cannot be condemned"; that they must be "blameless, not selfwilled, not soon angry . . . lovers of good men, sober, just, holy, temperate." [1] All this is the description of what seems almost an ordinary character; I mean, it is so staid, so quiet, so unambitious, so homely. It displays so little of what is striking or extraordinary. It is so negligent of this world, so unexcited, so single-minded.

It is observable, too, that it was foretold as the peculiarity of gospel times by the prophet Isaiah: "The work of righteousness shall be peace; and the effect of righteousness' quietness and assurance for ever. And my people shall dwell in a peaceable habitation, and in sure dwellings, and in quiet resting places." [2]

Now then let us consider more particularly what is this

[1] Rom. 12:16–18; Titus 2:2–13; 1:7, 8.
[2] Isa. 32:17–18.

state of mind, and what the grounds of it. These seem to be as follows: The Lord is at hand; this is not your rest; this is not your abiding-place. Act then as persons who are in a dwelling not their own; who are not in their own home; who have not their own goods and furniture about them; who, accordingly, make shift and put up with anything that comes to hand, and do not make a point of things being the best of their kind. "But this I say, brethren, the time is short." What matters it what we eat, what we drink, how we are clothed, where we lodge, what is thought of us, what becomes of us, since we are not at home? It is felt every day, even as regards this world, that when we leave home for a while we are unsettled. This, then, is the kind of feeling which a belief in Christ's coming will create within us. It is not worthwhile establishing ourselves here; it is not worthwhile spending time and thought on such an object. We shall hardly have gotten settled when we shall have to move.

This being apparently the general drift of the passage, let us next enter into the particular portions of it.

(1) "Be careful for nothing," he says, or, as St. Peter, "casting all your care upon him," or, as he himself, "Take no thought" or care "for the morrow: for the morrow shall take thought for the things of itself." [3] This of course is the state of mind which is directly consequent on the belief, that "the Lord is at hand." Who would care for any loss or gain today, if he knew for certain that Christ would show himself tomorrow? No one. Well, then, the true Christian feels as he would feel, did he know for certain that Christ would be here tomorrow. For he knows for certain that at least Christ will come to him when he dies; and faith anticipates his death, and makes it just as if that distant day, if it *be* distant, were past and over. One time or another Christ will come, for certain: and when he once *has* come, it matters not what length of time there was before he came; however long that period may be, it has an end. Judgment is coming, whether it

[3] I Pet. 5:7; Matt. 6:34.

comes sooner or later, and the Christian realizes that it is coming; that is, time does not enter into his calculation, or interfere with his view of things. When men expect to carry out their plans and projects, then they care for them; when they know these will come to naught, they give them over, or become indifferent to them.

So, again, it is with all forebodings, anxieties, mortifications, griefs, resentments of this world. "The time is short." It has sometimes been well suggested, as a mode of calming the mind when set upon an object, or much vexed or angered at some occurrence, what will you feel about all this a year hence? It is very plain that matters which agitate us most extremely now will then interest us not at all; that objects about which we have intense hope and fear now, will then be to us nothing more than things which happen at the other end of the earth. So will it be with all human hopes, fears, pleasures, pains, jealousies, disappointments, successes, when the last day is come. They will have no life in them; they will be as the faded flowers of a banquet, which do but mock us. Or when we lie on the bed of death, what will it avail us to have been rich, or great, or fortunate, or honored, or influential? All things will then be vanity. Well, what this world will be understood by all to be then, such is it felt to be by the Christian now. He looks at things as he then will look at them, with an uninterested and dispassionate eye, and is neither pained much nor pleased much at the accidents of life, because they are accidents.

(2) Another part of the character under review is, what our translation calls moderation; "Let your moderation be known unto all men," or, as it may be more exactly rendered, your consideration, fairness, or equitableness. St. Paul makes it a part of a Christian character to have a reputation for candor, dispassionateness, tenderness towards others. The truth is, as soon and in proportion as a person believes that Christ is coming, and recognizes his own position as a stranger on earth, who has but hired a lodging in it for a season, he will

feel indifferent to the course of human affairs. He will be able to look on, instead of taking a part in them. They will be nothing to him. He will be able to criticize them, and pass judgment on them, without partiality. This is what is meant by "our moderation" being acknowledged by all men. Those who have strong interests one way or the other, cannot be dispassionate observers and candid judges. They are partisans; they defend one set of people and attack another. They are prejudiced against those who differ from them, or who thwart them. They cannot make allowances, or show sympathy for them. But the Christian has no keen expectations, no acute mortifications. He is fair, equitable, considerate towards all men, because he has no temptation to be otherwise. He has no violence, no animosity, no bigotry, no party feeling. He knows that his Lord and Savior must triumph; he knows that he will one day come from heaven, no one can say how soon. Knowing then the end to which all things tend, he cares less for the road which is to lead to it. When we read a book of fiction, we are much excited with the course of the narrative, till we know how things will turn out; but when we do, the interest ceases. So is it with the Christian. He knows Christ's battle will last till the end; that Christ's cause will triumph in the end; that his church will last till he comes. He knows what is truth and what is error, where is safety and where is danger; and all this clear knowledge enables him to make concessions, to own difficulties, to do justice to the erring, to acknowledge their good points, to be content with such countenance, greater or less, as he himself receives from others. He does not fear; fear it is that makes men bigots, tyrants, and zealots; but for the Christian, it is his privilege, as he is beyond hopes and fears, suspense and jealousy, so also to be patient, cool, discriminating, and impartial; so much so that this very fairness marks his character in the eyes of the world, is "known unto all men."

(3) Joy and gladness are also characteristics of him, according to the exhortation in the text, "Rejoice in the Lord alway," and this in spite of the fear and awe which the thought

of the Last Day ought to produce in him. It is by means of these strong contrasts that Scripture brings out to us what is the real meaning of its separate portions. If we had been told merely to fear, we should have mistaken a slavish dread, or the gloom of despair, for godly fear; and if we had been told merely to rejoice, we should perhaps have mistaken a rude freedom and familiarity for joy; but when we are told both to fear and to rejoice, we gain thus much at first sight, that our joy is not to be irreverent, nor our fear to be desponding; that though both feelings are to remain, neither is to be what it would be by itself. This is what we gain at once by such contrasts. I do not say that this makes it at all easier to combine the separate duties to which they relate; that is a further and higher work; but thus much we gain at once, a better knowledge of those separate duties themselves. And now I am speaking about the duty of rejoicing, and I say that whatever be the duty of fearing greatly and trembling greatly at the thought of the Day of Judgment, and of course it is a great duty, yet the command so to do cannot reverse the command to rejoice; it can only so far interfere with it as to explain what is meant by rejoicing. It is as clear a duty to rejoice in the prospect of Christ's coming as if we were not told to fear it. The duty of fearing does but perfect our joy; that joy alone is true Christian joy, which is informed and quickened by fear, and made thereby sober and reverent.

How joy and fear can be reconciled, words cannot show. Act and deed alone can show how. Let a man try both to fear and to rejoice, as Christ and his apostles tell him, and in time he will learn how; but when he has learned, he will be as little able to explain how it is he does both, as he was before. He will seem inconsistent, and may easily be proved to be so, to the satisfaction of irreligious men as Scripture is called inconsistent. He becomes the paradox which Scripture enjoins. This is variously fulfilled in the case of men of advanced holiness. They are accused of the most opposite faults; of being proud, and of being mean; of being over-simple, and being crafty; of having too strict, and, at the same time, too lax a conscience; of being unsocial, and yet being worldly; of being too literal in explaining Scripture, and yet of adding to Scripture, and superseding Scripture. Men of the world, or men of inferior religiousness, cannot understand them, and are fond of criticizing those who, in seeming to be inconsistent, are but like Scripture teaching.

But to return to the case of joy and fear. It may be objected that at least those who fall into sin, or who have in times past sinned grievously, cannot have this pleasant and cheerful temper which St. Paul enjoins. I grant it. But what is this but saying that St. Paul enjoins us *not* to fall into sin? When St. Paul warns us against sadness and heaviness, of course he warns us against those things which make men sad and heavy; and therefore especially against sin, which is an especial enemy of joyfulness. It is not that sorrowing for sin is wrong when we *have* sinned, but the *sinning* is wrong which causes the sorrowing. When a person has sinned, he cannot do anything better than sorrow. He ought to sorrow; and so far as he does sorrow, he is certainly *not* in the perfect Christian state; but it is his sin that has forfeited it. And yet even here sorrow is not inconsistent with rejoicing. For there are few men, who are really in earnest in their sorrow, but after a time may be conscious that they are so; and, when man knows himself to be in earnest, he knows that God looks mercifully upon him; and this gives him sufficient reason for rejoicing, even though fear remains. St. Peter could appeal to Christ, "Lord, thou knowest all things; thou knowest that I love thee." We of course cannot appeal so unreservedly—still we can timidly appeal—we can say that we humbly trust that, whatever be the measure of our past sins, and whatever of our present self-denial, yet at bottom we do wish and strive to give up the world and to follow Christ; and in proportion as this sense of sincerity is strong upon our minds, in the same degree shall we rejoice in the Lord, even while we fear.

(4) Once more, peace is part of this same temper also. "The peace of God," says the apostle, "which passeth all understanding, shall keep your hearts and minds through Christ

Jesus." There are many things in the gospel to alarm us, many to agitate us, many to transport us, but the end and issue of all these is *peace*. "Glory to God in the highest, and on earth peace." It may be asked indeed whether warfare, perplexity, and uncertainty be not the condition of the Christian here below; whether St. Paul himself does not say that he has "the care," or the anxiety, "of all the churches," and whether he does not plainly evince and avow in his Epistles to the Galatians and Corinthians much distress of mind? "Without were fightings, within were fears." [4] I grant it; he certainly shows at times much agitation of mind; but consider this. Did you ever look at an expanse of water, and observe the ripples on the surface? Do you think that disturbance penetrates below it? Nay; you have seen or heard of fearful tempests on the sea; scenes of horror and distress, which are in no respect a fit type of an apostle's tears or sighings about his flock. Yet even these violent commotions do not reach into the depths. The foundations of the ocean, the vast realms of water which girdle the earth, are as tranquil and as silent in the storm as in a calm. So is it with the souls of holy men. They have a well of peace springing up within them unfathomable; and though the accidents of the hour may make them seem agitated, yet in their hearts they are not so. Even angels joy over sinners repentant, and, as we may therefore suppose, grieve over sinners impenitent—yet who shall say that they have not perfect peace? Even Almighty God himself deigns to speak of his being grieved, and angry, and rejoicing—yet is he not the unchangeable? And in like manner, to compare human things with divine, St. Paul had perfect peace, as being stayed in soul on God, though the trials of life might vex him.

For, as I have said, the Christian has a deep, silent, hidden peace, which the world sees not—like some well in a retired and shady place, difficult of access. He is the greater part of his time by himself, and when he is in solitude, that is his real state. What he is when left to himself and to his God, that is his true life. He can bear himself; he can (as it were) joy

4 II Cor. 7:5.

in himself, for it is the grace of God within him, it is the presence of the eternal Comforter, in which he joys. He can bear, he finds it pleasant, to be with himself at all times—"never less alone than when alone." He can lay his head on his pillow at night, and own in God's sight, with overflowing heart, that he wants nothing—that he "is full and abounds"—that God has been all things to him, and that nothing is not his which God could give him. More thankfulness, more holiness, more of heaven he needs indeed, but the thought that he can have more is not a thought of trouble, but of joy. It does not interfere with his peace to know that he may grow nearer God. Such is the Christian's peace, when, with a single heart and the cross in his eye, he addresses and commends himself to him with whom the night is as clear as the day. St. Paul says that "the peace of God shall *keep* our hearts and minds." By "keep" is meant "guard," or "garrison," our hearts; so as to keep out enemies. And he says, our "hearts and minds" in contrast to what the world sees of us. Many hard things may be said of the Christian, and done against him, but he has a secret preservative or charm, and minds them not.

These are some few suggestions on that character of mind which becomes the followers of him who was once "born of a pure virgin," and who bids them as "newborn babes, desire the sincere milk of the word, that they may grow thereby." The Christian is cheerful, easy, kind, gentle, courteous, candid, unassuming; has no pretence, no affectation, no ambition, no singularity; because he has neither hope nor fear about this world. He is serious, sober, discreet, grave, moderate, mild, with so little that is unusual or striking in his bearing that he may easily be taken at first sight for an ordinary man. There are persons who think religion consists in ecstasies, or in set speeches; he is not of those. And it must be confessed, on the other hand, that there is a commonplace state of mind which does show itself calm, composed, and candid, yet is very far from the true Christian temper. In this day especially it is very easy for men to be benevolent, liberal, and dispassionate. It costs nothing to be dispassionate when you feel nothing, to be cheerful when you have nothing to fear, to be generous or liberal when what you give is not your own, and to be benevolent and considerate when you have no principles and no opinions. Men nowadays are moderate and equitable, not because the Lord is at hand, but because they do not feel that he is coming. Quietness is a grace, not in itself, only when it is grafted on the stem of faith, zeal, self-abasement, and diligence.

May it be our blessedness, as years go on, to add one grace to another, and advance upward, step by step, neither neglecting the lower after attaining the higher, nor aiming at the higher before attaining the lower. The first grace is faith, the last is love; first comes zeal, afterwards comes loving-kindness; first comes humiliation, then comes peace; first comes diligence, then comes resignation. May we learn to mature all graces in us; fearing and trembling, watching and repenting, because Christ is coming; joyful, thankful, and careless of the future, because he is come.

# THIRTEEN

# The Christian
# Character of Joy

## Peace in Believing

*"And one cried unto another, and said, Holy, holy, holy, is the Lord of hosts."*—Isa. 6:3

EVERY LORD'S DAY IS a day of rest, but this, perhaps, more than any.* It commemorates, not an act of God, however gracious and glorious, but his own unspeakable perfections and adorable mysteriousness. It is a day especially sacred to peace. Our Lord left his peace with us when he went away; "Peace I leave with you, my peace I give unto you: not as the world giveth, give I unto you";[1] and he said he would send them a Comforter, who should give them peace. Last week we commemorated that Comforter's coming; and today we commemorate in an especial way the gift he brought with him, in that great doctrine which is its emblem and its means. "These things I have spoken unto you, that in me ye might have peace. In the world ye shall have tribulation." [2] Christ here says that instead of this world's troubles, he gives his disciples peace; and, accordingly, in to-day's collect, we pray that we may be kept in the faith of the

---

* Preached on Trinity Sunday.
[1] John 14:27.
[2] John 16:33.

eternal Trinity in Unity, *and* be "defended from all adversities," for in keeping that faith we are kept from trouble.

Hence, too, in the blessing which Moses told the priests to pronounce over the children of Israel, God's name is put upon them, and that three times, in order to bless and keep them, to make his face shine on them, and to give them peace. And hence again, in our own solemn form of blessing, with which we end our public service, we impart to the people "the peace of God, which passeth all understanding," and "the blessing of the Father, the Son, and the Holy Ghost."

God is the God of peace, and in giving us peace he does but give himself, he does but manifest himself to us; for his presence is peace. Hence our Lord, in the same discourse in which he promised his disciples peace, promised also that he would come and "manifest himself unto them," that he and his father would "come unto them, and make their abode with them." [3] Peace is his everlasting state; in this world of space and time he has wrought and acted; but from everlasting it was not so. For six days he wrought, and then he rested according to that rest which was his eternal state; yet not so rested, as not in one sense to "work hitherto," in mercy and in judgment, towards that world which he had created. And more especially, when he sent his only-begotten Son into the world, and that most gracious and all-pitiful Son, our Lord, condescended to come to us, both he and his Father wrought with a mighty hand; and they vouchsafed the Holy Ghost, the Comforter, and he also wrought wonderfully, and works hitherto. Certainly the whole economy of redemption is a series of great and continued works; but still they all tend to rest and peace, as at the first. They began out of rest, and they end in rest. They end in that eternal state out of which they began. The Son was from eternity in the bosom of the Father, as his dearly-beloved and only-begotten. He loved him before the foundation of the world. He had glory with him before the world was. He was in the Father, and the Father

[3] John 14:21, 23.

in him. None knew the Son but the Father, nor the Father but the Son. "In the beginning was the Word, and the Word was with God, and the Word was God." He was "the brightness of God's glory, and the express image of his person"; and in this unspeakable unity of Father and Son, was the Spirit also, as being the Spirit of the Father, and the Spirit of the Son; the Spirit of both at once, not separate from them, yet distinct, so that they were three persons, one God, from everlasting.

Thus was it, we are told, from everlasting; before the heavens and the earth were made, before man fell or angels rebelled, before the sons of God were formed in the morning of creation; yea, before there were seraphim to veil their faces before him and cry "Holy," he existed without ministers, without attendants, without court and kingdom, without manifested glory, without anything but himself; he his own temple, his own infinite rest, his own supreme bliss, from eternity. O wonderful mystery! O the depth of his majesty! O deep things which the Spirit only knoweth! Wonderful and strange to creatures who grovel on this earth, as we, that he, the all-powerful, the all-wise, the all-good, the all-glorious, should for an eternity, for years without end, or rather, apart from time, which is but one of his creatures, that he should have dwelt without those through whom he might be powerful, in whom he might be wise, towards whom he might be good, by whom he might be glorified. O wonderful, that all his deep and infinite attributes should have been without manifestation! O wonderful thought! and withal, O thought comfortable to us worms of the earth, as often as we feel in ourselves and see in others gifts which have no exercise, and powers which are quiescent! He, the all-powerful God, rested from eternity, and did not work; and yet, why *not* rest, wonderful though it be, seeing he was so blessed in himself? Why should *he* seek external objects to know, to love, and to commune with, who was all-sufficient in himself? How could he need fellows, as though he were man, when he was not solitary, but had ever with him his only-begotten Word in whom he delighted, whom he loved ineffably, and the eternal Spirit, the very bond of love and peace, dwelling in and dwelt in by Father and Son? Rather how was it that he ever began to create, who had a Son without beginning and without imperfection, whom he could love with a perfect love? What exceeding exuberance of goodness was it that *he* should deign at length to surround himself with creation, who had need of nothing, and to change his everlasting silence for the course of providence and the conflict of good and evil! I say nothing of the apostasies against him, the rebellions and blasphemies which men and devils have committed. I say nothing of that unutterable region of woe, the prison of the impenitent, which is to last for eternity, coeval with himself henceforth, as if in rivalry of his blissful heaven. I say nothing of this, for God cannot be touched with evil; and all the sins of those reprobate souls cannot impair his everlasting felicity. But, I ask, how was it that he who needed nothing, who was all in all, who had infinite equals in the Son and the Spirit, who were one with him, how was it that he created his saints, but from simple love of them from eternity? Why should he make man in the image of God, whose image already was the Son, all-perfect, all-exact, without variableness, without defect, by a natural propriety and unity of substance? And when man fell, why did he not abandon or annihilate the whole race, and create others? Why did he go so far as to begin a fresh and more wonderful dispensation towards us, and, as he had wrought marvelously in providence, work marvelously also in grace, even sending his eternal Son to take on him our fallen nature, and to purify and renew it by his union with it, but that, infinite as was his own blessedness, and the Son's perfection, and man's unprofitableness, yet, in his loving-kindness, he determined that unprofitable man should be a partaker of the Son's perfection and his own blessedness?

And thus it was that, as he had made man in the beginning, so also he redeemed him; and the history of this redemption we have been tracing for the last six months in our sacred services. We have gone through in our memory the whole course of that dispensation of active providences which God, in order to our redemption, has superinduced upon his eternal and infinite repose. First, we commemorated the approach of Christ, in the weeks of Advent; then his birth, of the blessed Mary, after a miraculous conception, at Christmas; then his circumcision; his manifestation to the wise men; his baptism and beginning of miracles; his presentation in the temple; his fasting and temptation in the wilderness, in Lent; his agony in the garden; his betrayal; his mocking and scourging; his cross and passion; his burial; his resurrection; his forty days' converse with his disciples after it; then his ascension; and, lastly, the coming of the Holy Ghost in his stead to remain with the church unto the end—unto the end of the world; for so long is the almighty Comforter to remain with us. And thus, in commemorating the Spirit's gracious office during the past week, we were brought, in our series of representations, to the end of all things; and now what is left but to commemorate what will follow after the end? The return of the everlasting reign of God, the infinite peace and blissful perfection of the Father, the Son, and the Holy Ghost, differing indeed from what it once was by the fruits of creation and redemption, but not differing in the supreme blessedness, the ineffable mutual love, the abyss of holiness in which the three persons of the eternal Trinity dwell. He, then, is the subject of this day's celebration—the God of love, of holiness, of blessedness; in whose presence is fullness of joy and pleasures forevermore; who is what he ever was, and has brought us sinners to that which he ever was. He did not bring into being peace and love as part of his creation, but he was himself peace and love from eternity, and he blesses us by making us partakers of himself, through the Son, by the Spirit, and he so works in his temporal dispensations that he may bring us to that which is eternal.

And hence, in Scripture, the promises of eternity and security go together; for where time is not, there vicissitude also is away. "The eternal God is thy refuge," says Moses, before his death, "and underneath are the everlasting arms:

and he shall thrust out the enemy from before thee; and shall say, Destroy them. Israel then shall dwell in safety alone." And again, "Thou wilt keep him in perfect peace, whose mind is stayed on thee: because he trusteth in thee. Trust ye in the Lord for ever; for in the Lord Jehovah is everlasting strength." And again,

> Thus saith the high and lofty One that inhabiteth eternity. . . . I dwell in the high and holy place, with him also that is of a contrite and humble spirit, to revive the spirit of the humble, and to revive the heart of the contrite ones. . . . I create the fruit of the lips; Peace, peace to him that is far off, and to him that is near.

And, in like manner, our Lord and Savior is prophesied of as being "The *everlasting* Father, The Prince of *Peace*." And again, speaking more especially of what he has done for us, "The work of righteousness shall be *peace*; and the effect of righteousness quietness and *assurance for ever*." [4]

As then we have for many weeks commemorated the economy by which righteousness was restored to us, which took place in time, so from this day forth do we bring before our minds the infinite perfections of Almighty God, and our hope hereafter of seeing and enjoying them. Hitherto we have celebrated his great works; henceforth we magnify himself. Now, for twenty-five weeks we represent in figure what is to be hereafter. We enter into our rest, by entering in with him who, having wrought and suffered, has opened the kingdom of heaven to all believers. For half a year we stand still, as if occupied solely in adoring him, and, with the seraphim in the text, crying, "Holy, holy, holy," continually. All God's providences, all God's dealings with us, all his judgments, mercies, warnings, deliverances, tend to peace and repose as their ultimate issue. All our troubles and pleasures here, all our anxieties, fears, doubts, difficulties, hopes, encouragements, afflictions, losses, attainments, tend this one way. After Christmas, Easter, and Whitsuntide, comes Trinity Sunday, and the weeks that follow; and in like manner, after our souls' anxious travail; after the birth of the Spirit; after trial and temptation; after

[4] Deut. 33:27–28; Isa. 26:3–4; 57:15, 19; 9:6; 32:17.

sorrow and pain; after daily dyings to the world; after daily risings unto holiness; at length comes that "rest which remaineth unto the people of God." After the fever of life; after wearinesses and sicknesses; fightings and despondings; languor and fretfulness; struggling and failing, struggling and succeeding; after all the changes and chances of this troubled unhealthy state, at length comes death, at length the white throne of God, at length the beatific vision. After restlessness comes rest, peace, joy—our eternal portion, if we be worthy—the sight of the blessed Three, the holy One; the Three that bear witness in heaven; in light unapproachable; in glory without spot or blemish; in power without "variableness, neither shadow of turning." The Father God, the Son God, and the Holy Ghost God; the Father Lord, the Son Lord, and the Holy Ghost Lord; the Father uncreate, the Son uncreate, and the Holy Ghost uncreate; the Father incomprehensible, the Son incomprehensible, and the Holy Ghost incomprehensible. For there is one person of the Father, another of the Son, and another of the Holy Ghost; and such as the Father is, such is the Son, and such is the Holy Ghost; and yet there are not three Gods, nor three Lords, nor three incomprehensibles, nor three uncreated; but one God, one Lord, one uncreated, and one incomprehensible.

Let us, then, use with thankfulness the subject of this day's festival, and the creed of St. Athanasius, as a means of peace, till it is given us, if we attain thereto, to see the face of God in heaven. What the beatific vision will then impart, the contemplation of revealed mysteries gives us as in a figure. The doctrine of the blessed Trinity has been made the subject of especial contention among the professed followers of Christ. It has brought a sword upon earth, but it was intended to bring peace. And it does bring peace to those who humbly receive it in faith. Let us beg of God to bless it to us to its right uses, that it may not be an occasion of strife, but of worship; not of division, but of unity; not of jealousy, but of love. Let us devoutly approach him of whom it speaks, with the confession of our lips and of our hearts. Let us look forward to the time when this world will have passed away and all its delusions; and when we, when everyone born of woman, must either be in heaven or in hell. Let us desire to hide ourselves under the shadow of his wings. Let us beg him to give us an understanding heart, and that love of him which is the instinct of the new creature, and the breath of spiritual life. Let us pray him to give us the spirit of obedience, of true dutifulness; an honest spirit, earnestly set to do his will, with no secret ends, no selfish designs of our own, no preferences of the creature to the Creator, but open, clear, conscientious, and loyal. So will he vouchsafe, as time goes on, to take up his abode in us; the Spirit of truth, whom the world cannot receive, will dwell in us, and be in us, and Christ "will love us, and will manifest himself to us," and "the Father will love us, and they will come unto us, and make their abode with us." And when at length the inevitable hour comes, we shall be able meekly to surrender our souls, our sinful yet redeemed souls, in much weakness and trembling, with much self-reproach and deep confession, yet in firm faith, and in cheerful hope, and in calm love, to God the Father, God the Son, God the Holy Ghost; the blessed Three, the holy One; three persons, one God; our creator, our redeemer, our sanctifier, our judge.

*Indexes*

# GENERAL INDEX

Abbot, Walter M., 8 n. 9
Abiram, 87
Abraham, 87, 145–47, 151, 163
Ahab, 167
Allchin, A. M., 5 n., 9 n.
Ananias, 90, 129
Andrewes, Lancelot, 27
Anglican Evangelicals, 58
Aristotle, 25, 36
Arnold, Matthew, 46, 55–57
Athanasius, 3, 46, 218
Augustine, 4

Baal, 167
Balaam, 81–88, 89, 90–91, 92, 93, 99, 127
Balak, 83–84, 85, 88, 90, 91
Barberi, Dominic, 9
Barmann, Lawrence F., 7 n. 8, 47 n. 2, 48 n. 4
Barnabas, 111
Becker, Werner, 7 n. 7, 8 n. 10
Bethel, 146, 148
Bible Christianity, 5, 22
Biblical criticism, 55
Bibliolatry, 51
Blehl, Vincent F., 7 n. 8, 47 n. 2, 48 n. 5
Body of Christ, 5
Bossuet, Jacques, 27
Bouyer, Louis, 62
Bremond, Henri, 46 n. 47
Brilioth, Yngve, 12 n. 3

Broad Church, 5
Butler, B. C., 5

Canaan, 130, 148, 178
Chadwick, Owen, 3 n.
Christ, 68, 69, 198, 199, 200, 211
Christian socialists, 52 n.
Church, Richard W., 3 n., 7 n. 6, 12, 13–14, 62
Church of England, 47
Coleridge, Samuel Taylor, 3, 51
Copeland, W. J., 6, 62
Coulson, John, 5 n., 6 n. 4, 9 n.
Coupet, Armel J., 7 n. 8, 47 n. 2
Covenant, 179, 202
Cruse, Amy, 13 n. 7
Culler, A. Dwight, 51 n. 14
Cyprus, 111

Daniel, 112
Darwin, Charles, 4, 52
Das Kapital, 58
Dathan, 87
David, 144, 150
Davies, Horton, 3 n., 12 n. 3, 13 n. 7, 50, 51 n. 13, 57 n. 17
Dessain, Charles Stephen, 2 n., 7 n. 6, 48 n. 3, 61 n.
Doctrine, 134
Dublin, Ireland, 24

*Ecclesiam Suam,* 8
Egypt, 148, 178
Elisha, 90, 127
Emerson, Ralph Waldo, 46
Ephraim, 148
Erastianism, 3
Esau, 145, 146, 147
Eschatology, 59
Evangelicals, 12, 13, 14, 15, 18, 19

Fairweather, Eugene R., 3 n., 18 n.
Faith
  and confidence, 113
  and duty, 109
  and justification, 107
  and things unseen, 192, 193
  and uncertainty, 108
  without sight, 110
Francis de Sales, 30 n. 11
Fries, Heinrich, 7 n. 7, 8 n. 10
Fulfillment of the law, 75–77

Gable, Sister Mariella, 30 n. 12
God
  and duty, 88
  favor of, 82
  glory of, 167
  kingdom of, 119
  and mystery, 86
  providence of, 92
  servants of, 124
  will of, 82
Gospel preachers, 15

Heaven, 126, 213–15
Herbert, George, 3
Hollis, Christopher, 10 n. 12

Humanity
  and aspiration, 119, 120
  and death, 165–67
  and everlasting life, 169–72
  gifts of, 195–97
  and immortality, 165, 166
  and spiritual consciousness, 163–64

Inge, W. R., 51
Isaac, 148, 151, 163
Isaiah, 127, 144

Jacob, 46, 127, 141, 144–50, 151, 164
James, 106, 113, 138
Jereboam, 90
Job, 127, 149
John, 106, 113, 128, 138
John Chrysostom, 46
Joseph, 145, 148
Joshua, 127, 130
Josiah, 87, 167
Joy, 209, 210
Judah, 90

Kerygma, 60
Korah, 87

Law, 80
Leah, 148
Lent, 105, 216
Liberalism, 51, 54
Littlemore, Oxford, England, 7, 16
Love
  and law, 98
  and principles, 101, 102

and repentance, 100–1
and sacrifice, 96
and self-denial, 97
and self-discipline, 103–4
Luke, 108
Lyell, Charles, 52

McGrath, Fergal, 24 n. 1
Manasseh, 148
Marx, Karl, 4, 52
Mary, 117, 216
Maurice, F. D., 4, 52, 58
Methuselah, 164
Micah, 85
Moab, 84, 85
Moses, 127, 130, 213, 216

Newsome, David, 16 n. 10, 51
n. 12

Obedience, Christian, 70–72
Old Catholics, 4
Old Testament, 80, 81, 118
Oriel College, Oxford, England,
1, 8, 43, 46
Oxford, England, 44
Oxford Movement, 3, 4, 6, 12,
18, 56
Oxford Newman Symposium, 8
Oxford University, Oxford, Eng-
land, 1, 46, 48

Pascal, Blaise, 161
Paul, 46, 69, 77, 80, 81, 112,
118, 123, 124, 128, 130,
144, 145, 161, 178, 187,
202, 205, 209
Pelagianism, 18

Peter, 108, 113, 129, 138, 204,
208
Philistinism, 57
Pope Leo XIII, 4
Pope Paul VI, 8, 9
Pourrat, Pierre, 48
Preaching, 24–47
of Evangelicals, 14–16, 19, 20,
21
Prophets, 80
Psalms, 118

Rachel, 148
Rebekah, 148
Religion
and feeling, 194
the keeping of, 75, 76, 77
and love, 98, 99
and negative attributes, 88–89
as principle, 99
and sincerity, 137, 138
of the world, 75
Renan, Ernst, 52
Return of Christ, 189–91
Revealed religion, 3, 54
Rickards, S., 43
Righteousness, imparted, 18

St. John, Ambrose, 61
St. Mary-the-Virgin Church, Ox-
ford, England, 1, 7, 10, 25,
46, 47, 48, 62
Samuel, 92
Sapphira, 90
Saul, 92
Science and religion, 55
Second Vatican Council, 5, 8, 9
Semi-pelagianism, 60

Sermon on the Mount, 117
Simon, 129
Spark, Muriel, 48
Strauss, David F., 52

Taylor, Jeremy, 32–33
Thomas, 147
Tillotsonian school, 16 n. 10
Topical preaching, 50, 53
Tractarians, 12, 18

Trevor, Meriol, 2 n.
Trinity, the, 213, 216, 218
Tristram, Henry, 11 n.

Ultramontanes, 4

Ward, Maisie, 50 n. 11
Wesleyan Movement, 6
Willey, Basil, 47 n. 1
Williams, Isaac, 17, 18, 24

# SCRIPTURE INDEX

## OLD TESTAMENT

*Genesis*
28:20-21—146
32:9-10—149
32:10—141
35:3—149
37:35—147
42:36, 38—147
43:14—147
45:26, 27—147
47:9—149, 163
48:3, 7, 15-16, 21—149
49:29-31, 18—149

*Numbers*
22—83
22:38—80
23—83

*Deuteronomy*
26:5-10—149
33:27-28—217

*Joshua*
24:16-19—130

*II Samuel*
23:1—142

*I Chronicles*
29:9-14—143

*Job*
1:21—150

*Psalms*
78:67-71—144

*Proverbs*
16:14—84

*Ecclesiastes*
2:16—167

*Isaiah*
6:3—212
9:6—217

25:7—128
26:3-4—126, 217
26:11—93
30:20—128
32:3, 5—128
32:17—217
32:17-18—203
33:17—127
40:31—79
41:8, 14—151
43:1-3—151
53:2—152
57:15, 19—217

*Daniel*
10:12—125

*Micah*
6:8—85

*Habakkuk*
2:1-4—188


NEW TESTAMENT

*Matthew*
5:2-10—117
5:39—122
6:34—204
8:20—130
12:32—159
12:37—131
13:43—168
18:5—161
19:29-30—115
19:30—116
20:22—106, 130

20:26-28—120
25:35-40—161

*Mark*
3:21—154
10:17-21—130

*Luke*
6:24-26—117
12:33—112
14:8, 10-12—122
14:25-28—130
14:28-30, 33—109
16:9—112
21:25-26, 28—182

*John*
1:5—152
1:19—129
6:68-70—130
13:36—108
14:9—152
14:21, 23—213
14:27—212
16:33—212
21:22—108

*Acts*
9:4—161

*Romans*
6:18—67
8:19—168
9:13—144
12:16-18—203
12:19-20—123

*I Corinthians*
1:26-29—118

2:3—177
2:15—198
4:1—10
4:3, 4—198
6:12—187
13:1—95
15:8—144
15:19—107

*II Corinthians*
1:12—129
1:17-20—129
7:5—209
8:9—124
10:5—189
12:10—123

*Ephesians*
1:18—128
3:17—128
5:19-20—142

*Philippians*
4:4—201
4:4, 11, 18—142
4:6—142

*Colossians*
3:3—169
3:15, 16—142

*I Thessalonians*
1:10—174
5:18—142

*I Timothy*
1:12-14—142
6:10—124

*II Timothy*
3:16—80

*Titus*
1:7, 8—203
2:2-13—203

*I Peter*
5:7—204

*II Peter*
3:4, 8—176
3:12—174

*I John*
2:8—128
3:2-3—126
5:20—128

*Revelation*
3:14—129
3:15-16—130
19:14-15—118
22:20—173

# THE PREACHER'S PAPERBACK LIBRARY

Volumes already published:

1. *The Servant of the Word* by H. H. Farmer. 1964.

2. *The Care of the Earth and Other University Sermons* by Joseph Sittler. 1964.

3. *The Preaching of F. W. Robertson* edited with an Introduction by Gilbert E. Doan, Jr. 1964.

4. *A Brief History of Preaching* by Yngve Brilioth. 1965.

5. *The Living Word* by Gustaf Wingren. 1965.

6. *On Prayer* by Gerhard Ebeling. 1966.

7. *Renewal in the Pulpit*—Sermons by Younger Preachers edited with an Introduction by Edmund A. Steimle. 1966.

8. *The Preaching of Chrysostom: Homilies on the Sermon on the Mount* edited with an Introduction by Jaroslav Pelikan. 1967.

9. *Violent Sleep*—Notes Toward the Development of Sermons for the Modern City by Richard Luecke. 1969.

10. *The Preaching of John Henry Newman* edited with an Introduction by W. D. White. 1969.

*Type,* 10 on 11 and 9 on 9 Garamond
*Display,* Garamond